Neuro-Linguistic Programming:

Volume I

The Study of the Structure of Subjective Experience

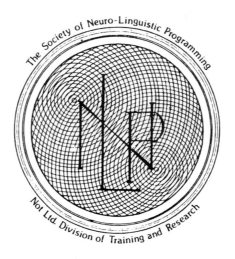

Robert Dilts
John Grinder
Richard Bandler
Judith DeLozier

Meta Publications
P.O. Box 565
Cupertino, California 95014

Library of Congress Card Number 80–50147
I.S.B.N.   0–916990–07–9

ACKNOWLEDGEMENTS:

We would like to acknowledge Doug Davis for all his help with the copyreading and editing of this book, and Terrence McClendon who participated as a co-facilitator in a number of the clinical incidents described within these pages.

Illustrations by Robert Dilts

TABLE OF CONTENTS

Contents

Contents

Contents

VII. CONCLUSION

NOTA BENE

RECOMMENDED READINGS

PREFACE

There comes a time when it is both useful, and appropriate, for the purpose of continuing to expand our understanding of the universe we live in, for entirely new fields of study to be created. Separating new from old, exceptions from rules, and useful from previously unquestionable. So learning and experiences from entirely divergent fields have the opportunity to combine knowledge and experience into configurations that allow further growth, understanding, and impact upon ourselves as a species. It is in this way that neuro-linguistic programming came into being. We wish at this point to separate our NLP from the many fields from which it draws information, from the many fields for which it has application. And in this way have greater clarity and freedom to delineate NLP's own methodologies and basic purpose.

While it may be fundamentally correct to say that all knowledge is part of one field, it is fundamentally impractical to approach learning in this way. By separating biology from chemistry they later recombined and both held shared value for each other. By separating electronics from optics, new technologies and application came into being. NLP could be described as an extension of linguistics, neurology, or psychology; separations that although may in fact be ficticious in nature are in fact expedient for human learning and the development of knowledge that is practical and inpactful on our lives. These separations are based primarily on the purpose of the study of the field itself. The purpose of NLP is as discrete from linguistics as logic is to philosophy, as discrete from psychology as neurology to medicine. Although interaction of these fields yields useful results, the lack of interaction in some areas is also useful so developments in one field can aid another. The chemist, the doctor, the psychologist, the mathematician all individually better define their separate purpose and develop their skills, so when combination and interaction occur it can yield more results, be more fruitful. An ancient Greek said it quite well in the early times of western thought:

The same, but different.

Epictetus

We would like to add, it is only the difference that makes a difference, and the same which provides the vehicle for useful interaction between fields. For instance, even though two sentences of English may use similar letters, a through z, many of these sentences will differ in meaning. Without both, language and learning would be impoverished.

So now NLP, the study of the structure of subjectivity, can take its place with other fields of study, with its own methodologies, and its own purpose, drawing information from wherever it can, offering that which is uniquely its own. So the evolution of ideas, conscious and pragmatic skill can go forward.

We ask only you, the reader, to go on. Turning this page opens the doorway to new possibilities we have found worthwhile, but years ago we would not have thought possible or real. We now know they are possible, and recognize they are only the beginnings of a continuing process. The Horizon has been identified. The adventure of exploration is for those who wish the burden and joy of confronting the awesome power of the new.

IN HOPE

NLP is the unexpected byproduct of the collaboration of John Grinder and Richard Bandler to formalize impactful patterns of communication (e.g. therapeutic, sales etc. . . .) With the addition of Robert Dilts, and Judith De Lozier, NLP took form into more than any one of us ever expected. Not just useful models and patterns formalized from various activities, but an extension of how those patterns and models came into being, thus a field both informative and practical, but most significant . . . unique in its purpose and methodology. Proving once again the old adage that the sum is greater than the whole. As the tools of NLP find their ways into other fields and the number of NLP'ers increases, we will witness in our lifetime marvels as grandiose as a man on the moon, the permanent elimination of smallpox from the planet earth, and atomic power. We may witness perspectives as broad as ecology, relativity, and civil, woman's, and human rights. The limits of human potential for progress and humanity, war and other acts of myoptic thinking are the by-product of subjective experience. Understood, and used with the elegance and pragmatism with which NLP was created we may not only discover how Freud made Einstein's theories possible, but a way to influence and predict the very elements that would make humans capable of being humane, by subjectively valuing what creations, creating can offer.

Subjectively

Robert Dilts
Richard Bandler
John Grinder
Judith De Lozier

Footnotes

1.   For the physicist, the question of whether the tree which falls in the forest, makes a sound even when there is no one to hear it, has the same force as how many angels can dance on the head of a pin.

2.   Even the format specified by journals etc. as appropriate for reporting scientific generalization demands this. The syntactic device of a passive construction is stated as the most highly valued —expressions such as:

> "the animals were sacrificed . . ."
> "the results were obtained . . ."

where the writer has deleted the subject/actor/agent.

3.   Behaviorism in psychology was the reflex of Logical Positivism which spawned a number of improbable systems in various disciplines.

Forward to Neuro-Linguistic Programming, Volume I

. . . . . . a beginning . . . . . .

Welcome! It is a pleasure to introduce you, the reader, to the field of Neuro-Linguistic Programming (NLP). Our purpose here is to place NLP in some historical context and to make some suggestions about how to use what follows.

Neuro-Linguistic Programming is the discipline whose domain is the structure of subjective experience. It makes no commitment to theory, but rather has the status of a model—a set of procedures whose usefulness not truthfulness is to be the measure of its worth. NLP presents specific tools which can be applied effectively in any human interaction. It offers specific techniques by which a practitioner may usefully organize and re-organize his or her subjective experience or the experiences of a client in order to define and subsequently secure any behavioral outcome.

Historically—Recent

NLP begins in the early 70's when we found ourselves in possession of a set of extremely powerful and effective communication models. We had originally developed these models for use in the psychotherapeutic context. It quickly became apparent that they could be easily generalized to other areas of human communication—specifically, business (sales, negotiation), law and education. With these tools we were able to secure results—5 minute guaranteed "cure" for phobias in psychotherapy; quick, graceful and satisfying resolution of conflict in dead-locked negotiations and settlements in business; success in teaching "educationally handicapped" children formerly impossible skills measured in minutes —results which bordered on magical for the professionals of these disciplines.

Having recognized and demonstrated the power of these tools to create an effective model which was not limited to the resolution of intra and inter personal conflict or problems, but a model which was evolutionary—a model which was not limited to remedial contexts but one which explicitly offered a step by step process which people could use to evolve themselves into any effective behavior of their choice.

Historically–Remote

Since its birth it has been a goal of behavioral science to achieve the same degree of elegance, reliability and precision which characterizes the physical sciences. From the vantage point offered by NLP, the inability of behavioral science to fully achieve this outcome becomes quite understandable. Historically, the physical sciences developed long before the behavioral ones. As many historians and philosophers of science have pointed out, the high regard and prestige which the physical sciences had attained seduced the founders of the behavioral sciences into adopting the methodology and form of the physical models. I select Newtonian physics as an initial reference point. The Newtonian model of physical systems was a representation of regular interactions which occur independently of the human observer. The most highly valued description or pattern or law in the Newtonian system was one where the maximum amount of context is deleted. In other words, heat, volume, density relationships of a gas in a confined space must hold independently of whether it's night or day, whether it's under water or in deep space, whether it's painted green or red, whether I want it to or not, . . .[1]

Note, by the way, that while portions of models of physical systems may be effectively represented without appeal to NLP methodology, the representations themselves are subject to NLP modeling. Perhaps a simple example will be useful to the reader. All of us are conversant with a special mini-language called arithmetic. Arithmetic is a language which expresses facts about quantity. You, as the reader know which of the following expressions are well-formed, legitimate expressions in the language of arithmetic and which are not (   ).

$$(72+3)^3 \qquad =$$
$$7- \qquad\qquad =14$$
$$=4(7-3)$$

Further, you are able to evaluate the truth of well-formed legitimate expressions

$$20+4 = 3^3-3 \qquad \text{(true)}$$
$$71-8 = 7+10+\tfrac{1}{2} \qquad \text{(false)}$$
$$4\sqrt{16} = 2 \ (2^3) \qquad \text{(true)}$$

Now, consider the following expressions:

$$17+3\sqrt{81}+2 \ (5^2) \ +6=3 \ (6^2) \ -8$$
$$33+66+1=100$$

As the reader can easily determine (at least with a calculator) both
of the expressions are well-formed, legitimate expressions in the
language of arithmetic. Further, if the reader takes the time to
compute them, it is easy to determine that they are both true—not
only true, but each of them expresses the same fact, $100=100$.
Examine them carefully; and then consider the next expression:

$$8+27+1+64=100$$

Also states $100=100$ if we first change the sequence of this expression

$$1+8+27+64=100$$

then recode it into another form (chunking) leaving the meaning
the same;

$$1^3+2^3+3^3+4^3=10^2$$

This expression is also well formed, true and expresses the same
fact as the last three. Note that

$$1+2+3+4=10$$

that is, the sum of the first four whole integers (on the left hand
of the expression) adds up to the integer on the right. A response
is immediate—I become curious as to whether I could add the next
whole integer and still preserve the truth of the statement—that is:

$$1^3 + 2^3 + 3^3 + 4^3 + 5^3 = 15^2$$

And, in fact, the relationship holds. The point is that in terms of *facts* about quantities there is no difference in these last four expressions—that is, they all are well-formed true statements which express the same fact $100 = 100$. Thus any difference in the response that I or any other person makes to them must be attributed to the sequence and *form* or *representation* of the expressions not the facts or content. But the response that we make is profoundly different. The form

$$1^3 + 2^3 + 3^3 + 4^3 = 10^2$$

immediately invites me to a generalization—it suggests to me a pattern. The representation interacts in some yet unexplained way with my internal neurological organization so as to draw from me new possibilities or outcomes in algebraic code:

$$1^3 + 2^3 + 3^3 + \ldots + n^3 = (\Sigma n)^2$$

In words: the sum of the cubes of the first n members of the set of whole integers equals the square of the sum of those numbers. Thus it seems highly likely that it is not only the observation of facts, nor only their measurement that engages human curiosity to extrapolate and explore. But the sequence and very form of data interacts with our neurology influencing it to subjectively make form of the same facts the basis of new meanings, while others lead us down old paths.

For example, one of the characteristics of a highly valued physical law in the Newtonian model is that any reference to humans is to be excluded.[2] Herein lies the flaw which has handicapped the behavioral scientist in ways it only detained the physical scientist.

In writing an introduction to the first of the books Bandler and I published, *The Structure of Magic, vol. 1,* Gregory Bateson states,

> "Above all, they (behavioral scientists generally and psychiatrists specifically—J.G.) borrowed the concepts of physics and mechanics—energy, tension and the like—to create a scientism."

In Newtonian physical, mechanical systems, it is very useful to arrive at patterns which are independent of human influence. Technology is the application of those principles by humans to secure specific outcomes at the physical level. In arriving at patterns in human communication systems, it is wholly inappropriate to attempt to exclude reference to human influence since this is an essential portion of the domain of the field of study itself.

In fact, among behavioral scientists there has been a growing uneasiness with the requirement to exclude from description the influence of the human agent (e.g. R Rosenthal experimenter effect).

Note that even in the physical sciences in more recent years the Newtonian theory of physical systems has been dislodged by a framework, whose origin is attributed primarily to Albert Einstein—a relativistic model. One of the significant differences between the Newtonian model and its successor is that the more recent model requires the inclusion of the perceptual point of the observer. As is implied in its name, the relativistic model demands an explicit representation of the perceptual position of the observer in describing certain space/time interaction.

The inclusion of the perceiver in descriptions of physical interactions represents a major increase in the descriptive power of the model. Take, for example, the Heisenberg Uncertainty Principle. Crudely put, the principle states that either the position or the state (kinetic energy) of the particle may be determined with precision but not both. The perceiver, in measuring the precise location of a particle, will disturb the state of that particle and vice versa— thus the value of both variables, location and state, can never be measured with precision.

There are three characteristics of effective patterning in NLP which sharply distinguish it from behavioral science as it is commonly practiced today. First, for a pattern or generalization regarding human communication to be acceptable or well-formed in NLP, it must include in the description the human agents who are initiating and responding to the pattern being described, their actions, their possible responses. Secondly, the description of the pattern must be represented in sensory grounded terms which are available to the user. This user-oriented constraint on NLP ensures usefulness. We have been continually struck by the tremendous gap between theory and practice in the behavioral sciences—this requirement closes that gap. Notice that since patterns must be represented in sensory grounded terms, available through practice to the user, a pattern will typically have multiple representation—each tailored for the differing sensory capabilities of individual users. I point out in passing that this requirement immediately excludes statistical statements about patterning as being well-formed in NLP as statistical statements are not user oriented. At best they indicate what the user might experience over a number of contexts but do not offer information about any specific situation. Insurance companies can predict costs, but salesmen will not know if *this* individual will trust, or dislike him or the inverse in advance, or initially face to face selling will succeed.

Thirdly, NLP includes within its descriptive vocabulary terms which are not directly observable. In the early part of this century, again profoundly influenced by the initial successes of the Newtonian model in physics, a movement called Behaviorism in psychology[3] established a well-formedness condition on descriptions of human behavior—namely, that only those events which are observable may be included in descriptions of human behavior. Individuals were represented as a black box devoid of knowable internal structure. While a case may be argued that within its historical context Behaviorism had a salutary effect, the long term outcome was stultifying. The behavioral scientist who accepted the Behaviourists dictum regarding observables found himself in the same position as someone who attempts to develop a theory of speed, frequency and trajectory of tennis balls passing over the net without allowing himself access to the tennis players themselves. Just as recent advances in physics have been intimately associated with a finer and finer analysis of what was previously considered an unanalyzable unit—witness the outstanding success in predicting function form structure in the proliferation of sub-atomic particles—so NLP proposes a vocabulary for the inside of the black box which has been demonstrated tremendously effective in business, education, law, and therapy—the vocabulary of representational systems and strategy. This vocabulary offers the NLP practitioner the most powerful set of behavioral organizing principles presently available—and, most importatntly, they work.

At present, you have before you a written representation of the model called NLP. I choose the term *model* deliberately and contrast it with the term *theory*. A model is simply a description of how something works without any commitment regarding why it might be that way. A theory is taxed with the task of finding a justification of why various models seem to fit reality. We are modelers and we ask that you evaluate this work as a model, ignoring whether it is true or false, correct or incorrect, aesthetically pleasing or not, in favor of discovering whether it works or not, whether it is useful or not.

Let me also reassure the reader that what you might experience as complex or difficult in the NLP model as you absorb the written representation is an artifact of the medium in which it is represented. In our various seminars for executives, attorneys, managers, salespersonnel, educators, therapists, and other professionals, the live presentation of NLP in a face-to-face context with immediate feedback has consistently resulted in a highly effective and enjoyable learning experience, as the reader can validate should you choose to join us.

In the introduction to the book we first published, Gregory Bateson paid us a very fine compliment:

> "... John Grinder and Richard Bandler have done something similar to what my colleagues and I attempted fifteen years ago ... to create the beginnings of an appropriate base for the describing of human interaction."

That was the beginning of our efforts to build a description of not only what needs describing in human beings, but to include the position of the describer, and more importantly for NLP, what processes select what is worthy of description and the very processes building those decriptions themselves, i.e. subjectivity. Science avoids the limitations described by the Heisenberg Uncertainty Principle. NLP exposes these scientific limitations as the very evolutionary tool to project our species into purposeful and productive unknowns.

This book is only the beginning of NLP, not the beginning itself nor the end. Discover the ecstasy of richer experience, thus the value of no end. Just more— new— old— now. The universe is as immense as your ability to perceive it. May you enjoy your journey.

John Grinder
and
Richard Bandler

Neurolinguistic Programming

I. Introduction

When a magician in top hat and cape calls for his beautiful assistant to lead an enormous elephant to center stage, we lean back in our chairs and prepare to enjoy the illusion. "Presto!" he shouts, and the giant Jumbo disappears, right on schedule. We smile to ourselves, knowing the "magic" was performed with mirrors, but feeling good just the same in deliberately allowing our perceptions to be fooled by a highly skilled entertainer. Were we to step onstage with the magician and his assistant, we would be entering another world—a world in which the mirrors themselves were visible and the elephant so near that we'd hear its breathing and feel the stage moving slightly as Jumbo shifted from foot to foot. There is something slightly disconcerting about being near the "source" of an illusion, but once we learn precisely how the "elephant disappearing act" is done, our enjoyment is enhanced rather than diminished—we learn to watch for and enjoy the skill with which the magician performs as well as retaining the option of taking pleasure in the illusion itself. We may begin to understand that the ability to make such distinctions is a very special and unique resource, one that extends far beyond the world of stages, mirrors and magicians in its significance.

Neurolinguistic programming is a model about the special world of magic and illusion of human behavior and communication—the study of the components of perception and behavior which makes our experience possible. The name *neurolinguistic programming* stands for what we maintain to be the basic process used by all human beings to encode, transfer, guide, and modify behavior.

1

For us behavior is programmed by combining and sequencing neural system representations—sights, sounds, feelings, smells and tastes—whether that behavior involves making a decision, throwing a football, smiling at a member of the opposite sex, visualizing the spelling of a word or teaching physics. A given input stimulus is processed through a sequence of internal representations, and a specific behavioral outcome is generated.

"Neuro" (derived from the Greek *neuron* for nerve) stands for the fundamental tenet that all behavior is the result of neurological processes. "Linguistic" (derived from the Latin *lingua* for language) indicates that neural processes are represented, ordered and sequenced into models and strategies through language and communication systems. "Programming" refers to the process of organizing the components of a system (sensory representations in this case) to achieve specific outcomes.

No matter what background or occupation you have, the reader has probably at some time or other had the experience of interacting with someone on the stage on which you perform, in a way that was particularly effective and allowed you to get some specific outcome that was of importance for you, the other person and/or a number of other people. This may have been the communication or learning of some important information, making a sale, solving a problem, or so on. Afterwards, though delighted with yourself, you may have had no real idea of what it was that characterized and distinguished that occasion, and the effectiveness, speed and elegance of your communication, from a normal situation.

Or perhaps you have met a person or had the experience of spending time with an individual who is eminently successful in the particular field they have chosen to accept and you have wondered what characterized the differences in their behavior from yours or from that of other individuals. You may have asked yourself what is it that allows them to do what may seem incredible or magical to others.

Or perhaps you yourself have a particular talent or ability that you would like to offer or teach to others, but have no real idea of what it is that enables you to perform your task with such elegance and sophistication.

This book is about how to unpack and repackage behavior, like that in the examples above, into efficient and communicable sequences that will be available to every member of the species. It will provide the reader with a set of tools that will enable him or her to analyze and incorporate or modify any sequence of behavior that they may observe in another human being.

1. Modeling

Down through the ages human beings have evolved many systems or models for understanding and dealing with the universe we live in. These models for organizing and coding the interactions of people in their environment have been handed such names as culture, religion, art, psychology, philosophy, politics, industry and science. Each model typically overlaps with other models and may include smaller models nested inside itself, just as science includes physics, biology, oceanography, chemistry, etc. and overlaps with industry in the area of research. Each model differs from the others in terms of that portion of human experience it represents and emphasizes and in terms of the way it organizes and uses its selected set of representations. All are similar in their ultimate concern with the outcomes of human behavior.

The purpose of each model is to identify patterns in the interaction between human behavior and the environment, so that the behavior of individual human beings can be systematized within the selected context to achieve desired and adaptive outcomes more efficiently, effectively and consistently. For example, scientists are trained to operate within a specific model to help them organize their behavioral priorities in gathering and interpreting data. They are taught to recognize and work toward specific desired outcomes—as are businessmen, artists, politicians and medical doctors.

1.1 The Map Is Not the Territory

As participant organisms within the universe,[1] we, the model-makers who devise, perpetuate and extend our cultural models, *do not operate directly on the world.* Rather, we operate through coded interpretations of the environment as received and experienced in our sensory representational systems—through sight, sound, smell, taste and feeling. Information about our external universe (as well as our internal states) is received, organized, consolidated and transmitted through an internal system of neural pathways that culminate in the brain—our central processing biocomputer. This information is then transformed through internal processing strategies that each individual has learned. The result is what we call "behavior." In NLP *behavior is defined as all sensory representations experienced and expressed internally and/or externally for which evidence is available from a subject and/or from a human observer of that subject.* That is, the act of skiing down a beautiful snow-covered mountainside and the act of imagining oneself doing so are equally to be considered behaviors in the context of neurolinguistic programming.

Both macrobehavior and microbehavior are, of course, programmed through our neurological systems. Macrobehavior is overt and easily observable, as in driving a car, speaking, fighting, eating, getting sick or riding a bicycle. Microbehavior involves subtler though equally important phenomena such as heart rate, voice tempo, skin color changes, pupil dilation and such events as seeing in the mind's eye or having an internal dialogue.

Obviously, not all culturally transmitted models for behavior have been incorporated into all members of the human species, but most of us have many of them available in our representational systems.[2] The development, then, of these models—and the behavior generated through them—form a significant statement about the neurological systems of those individuals who have adopted them as organizational strategies for their behavior. That is, the variety and range of human behavior, viewed in the context of the models that generate those behaviors, tells us much about human neurological organization. The state of these models today—the most current point in their development—represents the evolution of ideas, the surviving wisdom of our predecessors. Ultimately, after the uproar of economic, religious and ideological disputes has subsided, models are kept or discarded on the basis of their adaptiveness or usefulness as guides for the behavior of members of the species. The acceptance or rejection, the elaboration and expansion of these models reflects the evolution of human thought and behavior.[3]

1.2 A New Model

Neurolinguistic programming is a natural extension of this evolutionary process—a new model. It is important to realize that models such as those described in Section 1 are not simply "out there" somewhere, external to us as individuals. Rather, politics, religion, psychology and the other models are ways of looking at, talking about and feeling about the same experiential domain: human behavior. NLP differs from other models of behavior in that it is specifically a model of our behavior as model-makers. It is what we call a *meta-model,* a model of the modeling process itself.

Implicit in NLP as a meta-model is its broad range of practical applications. From individual interactions to group, corporate and system dynamics of any kind, the behavioral parameters can be identified, organized and programmed to obtain specific objectives. When the confusions and complexities of life experience are examined, sorted and untangled, what remains is a set of behavioral elements and rules that aren't so difficult to understand after all. In this book we will describe techniques and applications derived from NLP and designed for use in behavioral interactions in any area of human endeavor.

1.3 The Structure of Models

The construction of all models requires the identification and representation of 1) a set of structural elements and 2) a syntax. The *structural elements* are the "building blocks" of a model. The *syntax* is the set of rules or directives that describe how the building blocks may be put together.

In linguistic models, for example, the structural elements are typically words: written and/or spoken vocabularies. The syntax is the set of grammatical rules that dictate how the various words may be fitted together. The English language has a relatively small vocabulary (about 36,000 words), yet throughout the history of English speaking people, millions of different sentences have been uttered and millions of different ideas have been put into words. This is possible because the words may be assembled in different orders, sequences and forms which provide particular contexts in which words can evoke unique meaning and significance. All the books ever written in the English language are composed of the same words used over and over in different orders; the words, in turn, are assembled from the same twenty-six letters of the alphabet.

To be a fluent speaker of the language, one does not have to memorize all possible word combinations accepted as being well-formed sentences. That would be impossible. Yet somehow, we know that certain sequences of words constitute understandable sentences while others do not. For example, consider the previous sentence with the words reversed:

> Not do others while sentences understandable constitute
> words of sequences certain that know we somehow yet.

Although each word may be easily understood, this sequence doesn't impress us as a meaningful sentence. Since the words are precisely the same set presented previously in a different order, we may conclude that the condition of well-formedness must be attributed to the order or sequence in which we see or hear the words. Given a finite vocabulary and a small set of generating principles, a syntax, it is possible to create an infinite number of well-formed sentences by changing the order of the words in an appropriate manner. To learn a language, it is necessary only to learn its vocabulary and syntax.[4]

In particle physics, electrons, protons, neutrons and other subatomic entities make up the set of structural elements; the syntax is the set of rules of possible interactions among various combinations of particles. In a similar manner, models such as banking, government, art, agriculture and film production are constructed of a set of structural elements and a syntax.

Neurolinguistic programming shows us that the complexities of human behavior, like the infinite number of possible well-formed sentences in a language, can be reduced to a finite number of structural elements and a syntax. In the context of the NLP model we maintain that all behavior—from learning, remembering and motivation to making a choice, communication and change—is the result of systematically ordered sequences of sensory representations. Many of the problems and phenomena that have baffled behavioral scientists in the past can be understood, predicted and changed by using the NLP model. To accomplish this, we join the magician on his stage, so to speak, and begin to poke around the mirrors and other apparatus of the thaumaturgical art to gain a new perspective on what happens before, during and after the waving of that magic wand which generates such a fascinating array of experiences for us all.

Because certain aspects of the structural elements and syntax of every model are experienced (or defined) as being within or beyond human control, every model contains within itself another behavioral model that identifies the possibilities and limitations of human behavior with respect to desired goals or outcomes.

Borrowing a flow chart from decision theory, we can represent this model visually as:

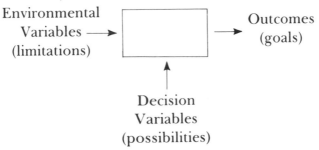

Environmental
Variables ⟶
(limitations)

Outcomes
(goals)

Decision
Variables
(possibilities)

We will assume that the people concerned with the model represented by this diagram agree that *environmental variables* include all dimensions of experience *beyond* their control and that *decision variables* include all dimensions of experience *within* their control. For example, an executive planning committee would agree that they could decide when and where to build a new manufacturing plant toward achieving the outcome of increased production and sales; they would also agree that production and sales would be affected by inflation, government monetary policy, competition and consumer demand, which lie outside their control.

Again, the magician knows that under the watchful eyes of an attentive audience, on a stage of limited size, he can't possibly "make" an elephant weighing several tons disappear—unless he utilizes those same constraints (environmental variables) effectively in achieving his outcome—the disappearing act. Outcomes depend on contributions from both environmental variables and decision variables.

In fact, one of the major historical trends in the evolution of models of behavior is the transformation or utilization of experiences once regarded as environmental variables into decision variables. This trend is particularly evident in recent technological advances in the computer sciences and in manned space travel—

more effective models operating to expand the potentials of human behavior.

Just as the computer and information processing industries have advanced tremendously in the past twenty five years due to the new technology provided by the semiconductor (the processing capacity of what once used to require a machine that filled a large room is now available from a chip no bigger than the head of a pin), so too we intend that the behavioral professions and sciences will advance in the coming decades as the result of the new technology provided by neurolinguistic programming.

1.4 Western Scientific Models

In many ancient traditional cultures, much of the activity of the people was experienced as being determined by forces beyond their control, forces often assumed as originating outside the realm of experience available to the human senses. Decisions such as when to plant, how to cope with disease and when to change living sites were regarded as a function of these forces—the gods, the planets or other entities whose processes were either capricious or at least beyond human comprehension.

Western scientific models, in contrast, are grounded in the realm of sensory experience. By claiming sense phenomena as their structural elements or building blocks, scientific models derive the generalizations they offer as guiding principles for human behavior from a domain of experience that is available, potentially at least, to all members of the human species. Observations and/or experiments are conducted to determine whether aspects of patterning (often required to be measurable or quantifiable) can be discovered. The attitude implicit in the scientific model is that any portion of our experience can be understood and eventually controlled if we are willing to study the processes which underlie that experience. Technology, the systematic application of scientific principles to obtain useful outcomes, evolves as we discover how our behavior affects a particular set of structural elements in the context of each new scientific discovery. Useful applications may be many steps removed or only indirectly related to the immediate frame of reference of a new discovery, but practical uses or outcomes often become evident if the search is undertaken.

As a result of this process, more and more dimensions of experience from the class of environmental variables have been shifted to the class of decision variables. Not long ago in our historical past, waterfalls—though considered awe-inspiring and beautiful—were thought to be a hindrance to the spread and development of industry and commerce because they prevented rivers from being utilized for transportation and communication. Today we have learned to use them as sources of hydroelectric power which, in turn, has paved the way to greatly increased choices with respect to transportation and communication. Again, we once viewed the appearance of mold on bread as a sign that the bread was useless. We learned, however, to use the mold itself by deriving penicillin from it—one of the most brilliant and useful medical discoveries in history. The principle of inoculation in preventive medicine involves the transformation of bacteria and viruses associated with the onset of particular diseases into weakened forms whose introduction into the human body stimulates our immunological systems to protect us from those same diseases.

Such examples could easily be multiplied, and they all share a common pattern: phenomena which at one point in history were considered a nuisance, an obstacle or even a danger have been studied and understood sufficiently to allow us to utilize them in ways that benefit us. We have expanded or changed our models to transform problematic phenomena thought to be outside our control into valuable contributions to human well-being, within our control. Each of the examples in the previous paragraph, taken in its historical context, involved the shift of a portion of our experience from the class of environmental variables into the class of decision variables by reframing or restructuring the way a problematic phenomenon fit into our models. It is the continuation of this process, the shifting of environmental variables into decision variables by sorting and punctuating the way the variables fit into context, that is the goal of neurolinguistic programming. In our modern technologically oriented culture we have developed a large number of machines and devices which we use in our everyday activities. Nearly without exception these machines embody one or more of the forces of gravity, electricity or magnetism as an integral part of their functioning. Yet an adequate theory of these primary forces remains an elusive goal for the scientist. Fortunately effective models which secure the outcomes for which they are designed do not require complete and satisfactory theories. The reader will search in vain for any theory of human perception, communication and experience within these covers. Our goals here are much more modest—a model of a portion of these complex human activities which works.

Throughout the development of western scientific models there has been a major limitation imposed on the possible outcomes of human behavior, a limitation buried deeply in the empirical heart of scientific methodology itself. If we imagine ourselves stepping into the scientist's shoes, slipping into a crisp white lab coat and looking through the scientist's eyes, we may picture a universe of phenomena neatly interconnected by formulas, laws, theories and hypotheses—all "out there," either already discovered and explained or waiting to be discovered and explained. What's missing? To find out we remove the lab coat, step out of the scientist's shoes, take three steps back and look again. The scientist is missing. The model-maker, observer, measurer, mathematician, inventor of laws, theories and hypotheses—gone. According to its own empirical constraint, the syntax of science simultaneously defines an external model of "reality" and banishes the scientist from that model. By definition, the locus of behavioral control is "out there" in the model, not in us.

This pattern is particularly evident in the model of modern medicine. This model postulates that internal disorders such as tumors, infections, diseases and other pathological conditions inside the individual are caused primarily by environmental variables (such as germs, viruses, smog, heat, cold, ultraviolet light, etc.) and necessarily require external remedial treatment to restore the human body to health. Rather than utilize ways in which the biologicial system could be altered, regulated or adapted by the individual himself to change the pathological condition. Simplified, the remedial treatments of choice reduce to adding or subtracting something from the biological system —i.e., chemotherapy, radiation therapy, surgery or some combination of these. In this model even behavioral disorders such as schizophrenia are thought to originate from causes outside the behavior of the individual and to require external remedial treatment.

On the other hand, phenomena like the placebo effect, statistically important in all clinical drug research, are generally ignored because they can't be adequately explained in the context of the current medical model. When a patient responds to a placebo, a "fake" pill or injection of chemically inactive ingredients, by recovering from an ailment, he or she is considered an oddity who has been fooled by the fake medicine. Such cases are generally filed and forgotten, rather than being taken seriously as pointing in the direction of an alternative model of medicine. If the behavior of those who respond well to placebos can be modeled, their strategies for self-healing might be taught to others, an option for recovery that wouldn't require the ingestion of chemically active drugs with their typically undesirable side-effects. In the current medical model, the patient places the locus of behavioral control in the physician; the physician places it in the model. The placebo effect suggests that "getting sick" and "getting well" are, in fact, behaviors and, further, that the locus of behavioral control is in the individual—that sickness can be a decision variable for the individual.

This pattern of placing behavioral control outside ourselves has undoubtedly evolved from the fact that scientists have always looked outside themselves for variables and for sources of instrumental control that more easily lend themselves to measurement and reproducible results. The original model of behavioral science, like that of modern medicine, adopted the pattern of locating behavioral control outside the individual. Because the internal sensory-motor processes of the organism aren't measurable by the instruments available to the behavioral scientist, they are not considered to be part of the domain of the model.

1.5 Extending the Modern Scientific Model

As we pointed out earlier in this chapter, neurolinguistic programming constitutes the next natural extension in the evolutionary development of cultural models. By understanding that human beings do not operate directly on the world they are experiencing but through sensory transforms of that world, we also understand that "truth" is a metaphor rather than a yardstick calibrated to some absolute standard of external reality. Cultural models, including that of science, do not express "truth," but prescribe domains of experience within which behavior is organized into certain patterns. To the extent that the structural elements, syntax and limits of each model are arbitrarily selected and defined, we might suggest that models, in general, are metaphors for the convenient assumption that experience and reality are the same. Similarly, NLP is not the "truth" either, but another metaphor—a user oriented metaphor designed to generate behavioral options quickly and effectively.

NLP extends the limits of the modern scientific model by placing the locus of behavioral control in the individual. Einstein's relativity theory indicates that time, mass and spatial dimensions change relative to the observer's frame of reference at speeds approaching the speed of light. Although Einstein's theory represents an extension of the limits of preceding scientific models by its inclusion of the observer's perspective, behavioral control in his theory is a function of the relation between the velocity of the system and that of the speed of light, both of which are assumed to be external to the observer. NLP takes one further step and proposes to examine the correlations between what we experience as the external environment and our internal representations of that experience. To accomplish this, NLP draws from many recent advances in the neurosciences, psychophysiology, linguistics, cybernetics, communication theory and the information sciences.

To understand how our neurological processes are related to behavioral models, it is useful to represent mathematical equations from the scientific model as metaphors for those processes. Each mathematical equation defines a pattern in which a sequence of operations performed on specific variables results in a given outcome. For example, Newton's equation $F=ma$ defines force as a function of (and equivalent to) the product of mass and acceleration. Each appropriate set of numerical values plugged into m and a, when multiplied together, expresses a specific outcome—force. The form of the equation remains the same, no matter what quantitative values are substituted for m and a, just as the form of a neurological pattern or sequence of operations remains the same, no matter what content is processed through it. It isn't important whether $F=ma$ describes a real physical law; what's important about this formula is its demonstration of the human capacity to develop neural patterns that allow us to organize our representations of physical phenomena to obtain desired outcomes. Just as we have invented complex neural patterns that allow us to tie our shoelaces, play golf or read a book, we can develop neural patterns that fulfill other objectives.

All behavioral models—from complex governmental and business operations involving thousands of people to individual activities like eating an apple and jogging—exist and function through laws, rules and assumptions incorporated into individuals in the form of neural patterns. If the neural pattern is absent, the behavior is absent; if the behavior is ineffective or inappropriate, the neural pattern is not adequately organized to elicit an effective or appropriate behavior. The overt and implied laws, rules and assumptions of any model function as codes or metaphors for different patterns of neurological organization aimed at producing a particular set of behavioral outcomes.

Since NLP is concerned with form, not content, strategies for effective and appropriate behaviors may be drawn from any model and applied to any other model of our choice. For example, the creative strategy of an artist may be appropriately transferred to an uninspired aerodynamic engineer faced with a challenging design problem. Or, the operational motivation strategy of a highly efficient business organization may be adapted to a sluggish government department. Because NLP is ultimately concerned with representations of experience at the neurological level, it is unnecessary to refer to the names or contents of the models from which particular forms, structural interrelationships and outcomes have been derived, except for illustration purposes. It is not important to us whether an individual claims the source of an inspiration to be God, a delicious chocolate mousse or the beauty of a mountain lake—if the same neural strategy sequence in each case produces identical behavioral outcomes.

Just as behavioral strategies may be transferred from one person to another, the same person may apply a successful strategy from one aspect of his or her experience (skill at bridge playing, for example) to another aspect (difficulty in decision-making, for example). Typically, each person has a rich endowment of experiential assets to draw from and may choose to adapt strategies from strong areas of experience to weak or impoverished areas by using methods we will describe in forthcoming chapters.

Neurolinguistic programming is a model designed to increase the possible outcomes of behavior—that is, a model for transforming more environmental variables to the class of decision variables.

The process of modifying behavior, whether applied to an individual, group or organization in order to achieve new outcomes can be described in its most general form as a *three-point process:*

(1) Representation of the present state
(2) Representation of the outcome or target state
(3) Representation of resources

Resources are accessed and applied to the problematic or present state of affairs to help the individual, group or organization move to the outcome or desired state:

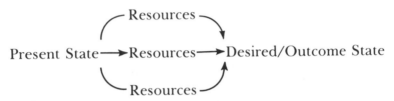

The remainder of this book will essentially deal with the nature of each of these three steps. It will involve, more specifically, such issues as:

a) the nature of maladapted behavior—what constitutes a problematic response;

b) the nature of growth, choice and generative behavior;

c) how to identify, in sensory specific terms, a specific outcome, set or class of outcomes;

d) how to identify and represent, in the appropriate sensory modalities, the elements (resources, external and behavioral) involved in achieving that outcome;

e) the representation of the forms and rules of interaction between these elements that identify, generate and predict the desired outcomes; and

f) how to identify and represent the present state of progress or development so that it may be used to provide the individual, family or organization with feedback on where they are with respect to their outcomes.

Our claim is that if any individual or group displays any sequence of behavior which others find useful, we—employing the tools and principles of NLP—can chunk and punctuate that sequence into units that can be practiced and readily learned by any other member of the species.

NLP is a new way of thinking—a new model—which involves the use of changing patterns dependent on contextual conditions and upon feedback within and between behaviors observable in your ongoing experience. While both formal and systematic, the NLP process is held rigorously accountable to the evidence of sensory experience—yours and that of others who use the process. As a model of the modeling process, it is constantly changing and growing on the basis of feedback from its own discoveries. (For a further elaboration of this discussion, see our forthcoming book *Modeling.*)

1.6 Modeling Elegance

In the modeling and reproduction of strategies for eliciting outcomes, we are also extending another evolutionary trend in the development of behavioral models with NLP. This is the trend toward increasingly elegant models. The term "elegance" here refers to the number of rules and distinctions a particular model requires to be able to account for all of the outcomes for which it has been designed. The most elegant model would be the one which employs the fewest number of distinctions and which is still able to secure a domain of outcomes equal to or greater than that of more complex models. For people and organizations, this means a significant saving of time and energy in the development and implementation of behavioral outcomes necessary to achieve their goals.

The transition of models toward increased elegance occurs in two ways:

(1) The elements identified as having casual importance become more basic to the particular interactions involved in achieving outcomes. In NLP, for instance, we begin by showing how the five classes of sensory experience (seeing, hearing, feeling, smelling and tasting) are the basis for the strategies people have for generating and guiding behavior, rather than more complex and abstract concepts such as "ego," "mind," "human nature," mechanisms," "morals," "reason," etc., employed by other behavioral models.

(2) The orientation of the model turns much more toward

form than content. By "form" we mean the principles or rules of interaction between structural elements that generate the possible states or interactions of the system. The basic equations or physical "laws" developed by Newton, for instance, are simple and elegant statements of the relationships between physical elements (at a certain level of experience) that can be used to describe, predict and prescribe the changing events that make up the content of a large portion of our physical universe. These same formal rules hold for the motions and interactions of many different objects: springs, billiard balls, pendulums, cars, projectiles and so on.

The reduction of the syntax of a model to that set of rules necessary and sufficient to describe interactions among its structural elements increases rather than diminishes the power and effectiveness of the model. For example, chemists don't need to test all possible chemical combinations to discover which outcomes will be successful. A knowledge of the basic properties of atomic elements and molecular structures allows them to predict, in many cases, which chemical interactions will work and which will not. The elegance of the model of modern chemistry enhances efficiency and streamlines the operational strategies for predicting and generating outcomes.

Modeling elegance serves a similar function in NLP, cutting through the complexities of human behavior to reveal the underlying rules that govern behavioral interactions. NLP is concerned with the generative principles of behavior rather than the content, which in its infinite variety may become infinitely complicated and confusing. Because it concentrates on form, NLP is freed from attachment to a particular behavioral content. In this perspective the evolution of behavior offers us an alternative to "specialization," which is often just familiarity with content.

By knowing the basic elements and generative rules of a particular model of behavior, whether that of science, technology, business, law, therapy, medicine, politics or education, it isn't necessary to spend years studying the particulars of behavior within each model in order to master it. Indeed, progress in the efficiency and potential of education has always occurred as more elegant models have developed.

1.7 Representational Systems: The Building Blocks of Behavior

The basic elements from which the patterns of human behavior are formed are the perceptual systems through which the members of the species operate on their environment: *vision* (sight), *audition* (hearing), *kinesthesis* (body sensations) and *olfaction/gustation* (smell/taste). The neurolinguistic programming model presupposes that all of the distinctions we as human beings are able to make concerning our environment (internal and external) and our behavior can be usefully represented in terms of these systems. These perceptual classes constitute the structural parameters of human knowledge.

We postulate that all of our ongoing experience can usefully be coded as consisting of some combination of these sensory classes. In our previous work (see *Patterns II*) we have chosen to represent and abbreviate the expression of our ongoing sensory experience as a *4-tuple*. The 4-tuple is shown visually as:

$$< A^{e,i}, V^{e,i}, K^{e,i}, O^{e,i} >$$

Here, the capital letters are abbreviations for the major sensory classes or representational systems that we use to make our models of the world:

> A = Auditory/Hearing
> V = Visual/Sight
> K = Kinesthetic/Body Sensations
> O = Olfactory/Gustatory—Smell/Taste

The superscripts "e" and "i" indicate whether the representations are coming from sources external, "e", to us, as when we are looking at, listening to, feeling, smelling or tasting something that is outside of us, or whether they are internally generated, "i", as when we are remembering or imagining some image, sound, feeling, smell or taste. We can also show the 4-tuple iconically as:

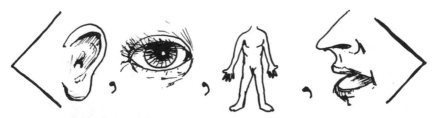

The following excerpt from *Patterns II* will further assist the reader in understanding the 4-tuple:

"Assuming that you are a reader who at this point in time is sitting comfortably in a quiet place and that you are reading alone, the 4-tuple can be used to represent your present experience of the world as follows:

$$\left\langle \begin{array}{llll}
\text{the printed words of} & \text{the feeling of} & \emptyset & \text{the smell of} \\
\text{the book, the} & \text{the chair, the} & & \text{the room, the} \\
\text{lighting pattern of} & \text{temperature of} & & \text{freshness of} \\
\text{the room} \ldots & \text{the room} \ldots & & \text{the air} \ldots \text{i}
\end{array} \right\rangle$$

The specific 4-tuple which represents the reader's experience where i is the referential index of the reader and the blankspace $\emptyset$ indicates no experience in that mode.

"In words, the reader's present experience of the world is represented by a description of the visual input from the words, his present kinesthetic sensations and the olfactory sensation available. Since, by our assumption, the reader is in a place where he is presently receiving no auditory input from the external world, the value of the variable A_t (the auditory tonal portion of his experience) is $\emptyset$. The values of the V, K and O variables are specified by a description of the input from the world that is impinging on the reader at this point in time. Notice that in specifying the 4-tuple for the reader's present experience, we restricted ourselves to representing experience originating in the world external to the reader. The 4-tuple can also be used to represent the reader's total experience—that is, his present ongoing experience independently of whether it originates in the world external to the reader or not. We have found it useful in our work to identify the origin of the portion of the experience described in the 4-tuple—that is to distinguish between which portion of the experience represented by the 4-tuple originates in the world external to the person whose experience is represented by the 4-tuple and which portion is generated by the person's own internal processes. One easy way of representing this distinction is by simply attaching a superscript to each component of the 4-tuple—either an i (internally generated) or an e (externally generated). Thus assuming that the reader is reading with internal dialogue at this point in time and using the superscripts which distinguish the internally generated from externally originated components of the 4-tuple, the reader's 4-tuple would look like:

the printed words [e],	the feeling of [e],	the tempo and tonal [i],	the smell of [e],
of the book,	the chair, the	qualities of	the room, the
the lighting pattern	temperature of	the auditory	freshness of
in the room . . .	the room . . .	internal dialogue . . .	the air . . .

"As with all the distinctions in the model, this superscript distinction between internally and externally generated experience will be employed only when it is useful for the task for which it is to be used."

In NLP, sensory systems have much more functional significance than is attributed to them by classical models in which the senses are regarded as passive input mechanisms. The sensory information or distinctions received through each of these systems initiate and/or modulate, via neural interconnections, an individual's behavioral processes and output. Each perceptual class forms a sensory-motor complex that becomes "response-able" for certain classes of behavior. These sensory-motor complexes are called *representational systems* in NLP.[5]

Each representational system forms a three part network: 1) input, 2) representation/processing and 3) output. The first stage, *input*, involves gathering information and getting feedback from the environment (both internal and external). *Representation/processing* includes the mapping of the environment and the establishment of behavioral strategies such as learning, decision-making, information storage, etc. *Output* is the casual transform of the representational mapping process.

"Behavior" in neurolinguistic programming refers to activity within any representational system complex at any of these stages. The acts of seeing, listening or feeling are behavior. So is "thinking," which, if broken down to its constituent parts, would include sensory specific processes like *seeing* in the mind's eye, *listening* to internal dialogue, having *feelings* about something and so on. All output, of course, is behavior—ranging from micro-behavioral outputs such as lateral eye movements, tonal shifts in the voice and breathing rates to macro-behavioral outputs such as arguing, disease and kicking a football.

Our representational systems form the structural elements of our own behavioral models. The behavioral "vocabulary" of human beings consists of all the experiential content generated, either internally or from external sources, through the sensory channels during our lives. The maps or models that we use to guide our behavior are developed from the ordering of this experience into patterned sequences or "behavioral phrases," so to speak. The formal patterns of these sequences of representations are called *strategies* in neurolinguistic programming.

The way we sequence representations through our strategies will dictate the significance that a particular representation will have in our behavior, just as the sequencing of words in a sentence will determine the meaning of particular words. A specific representation in itself is relatively meaningless. What is important is how that representation functions in the context of a strategy in an individual's behavior.

Imagine a young man wearing a white smock, sitting in a comfortable position, sunlight streaming through a high window to his right and behind him. To his left is a red book with silver lettering on its cover. As we look closer, we see him staring at a large white sheet of paper, the pupils of his eyes dilated, his facial muscles slack and unmoving, his shoulder muscles slightly tense while the rest of his body is at rest. His breathing is shallow, high in his chest and regular. Who is this person?

From the description he could be a physicist, visualizing a series of complex mathematical expressions which describe the physical phenomena he wishes to understand. Equally consistent with the above, the young man could be an artist, creating vivid visual fantasies in preparation for executing an oil painting. Or, the man could be a schizophrenic, consumed in a world of inner imagery so completely that he has lost his connection with the outside world.

What links these three men is that each is employing the same representational system—attending to internal visual images. What distinguishes them from one another is how each utilizes his rich inner experience of imagery. The physicist may in a moment look up to a fellow scientist and translate his images into words, communicating through his colleague's auditory system some new pattern he's discovered through his visualizations. The artist may in a moment seize the white sheet of paper and begin to rough in shapes and colors with a brush—many of them drawn directly from his inner imagery—translating inner experience into external experience. The schizophrenic may continue his internal visual reverie with such complete absorption that the images he creates within will distract him from responding to sensory information arriving from the outside world.

The physicist and the artist differ from the schizophrenic in terms of the function of their visualizations in the context of the sequence of representational system activities that affect the outcome of their behavior: in how their visualizations are utilized. The physicist and the artist can choose to attend visually to the world outside or to their own inner visual experience. The process of creating inner visual experience is the same, neurologically, for all three men. A visual representation in itself—like the waterfall or the mold on the bread previously discussed—may serve as a limitation or a resource to human potential depending on how it fits into context and how it is used. The physicist and the artist control the process; the process controls the schizophrenic. For the physicist and the artist, the natural phenomenon of visualization belongs to the class of decision variables; for the schizophrenic it belongs to the class of environmental variables.

Each of you reading this sentence has a strategy for taking the peculiar patterns of black ink on this white page and making meaning out of them for yourself. These sequences of letters, like the other visualization phenomena just described, are meaningless outside of the sensory experiences from your own personal history that you apply to them. Words, both written and spoken, are simply codes that trigger primary sensory representations in us. A word that we have never seen or heard before will have no meaning to us because we have no sensory experience to apply to it. (For a further discussion of language as secondary experience see *Patterns II.*)

As you read these words you may, for example, be hearing your own voice inside your head saying the words as your eye reports the visual patterns formed by letters in this sentence. Perhaps you are remembering words that someone else has spoken to you before that sounded similar to those printed here. Perhaps these visual patterns have accessed some feelings of delight or recognition within you. You may have noticed, when you first read the description of the young man in the white smock, that you made images of what you were reading—you were using the same representational strategy for making meaning that the young man in our description was using.

The ability to transform printed symbols into internal images, into auditory representations, into feelings, tastes or smells, allows us to use strategies for making meaning that are available to each of us as human beings. Certain strategies are highly effective for creating meaning in certain contexts while others are more effective for other tasks. The strategy of taking external visual symbols and translating them into internal auditory dialogue would not be appropriate if you were listening to a record, doing therapy or playing football.

This book presents what we call meta-strategies: strategies about strategies. More specifically, this book describes how to elicit, identify, utilize, design and install strategies that allow us to operate within and upon our environment. NLP is an explicit meta-strategy designed for you—to shift dimensions of your experience from the class of environmental variables to the class of decision variables and, when appropriate, to assist others to do so. NLP is an explicit meta-strategy by means of which you may gain control over portions of your experience which you desire to control, an explicit meta-strategy for you to use to create choices that you presently don't have and to assist others in securing the choices they need or want.

The principles of NLP are equally applicable in assisting business executives to reorganize their priorities and generate new options; in helping scientists and engineers get the most from their research and upgrade their teaching ability; in showing educators new and remarkably effective educational system design principles; in extending to lawyers and judges features of communication that greatly facilitate settlements; in aiding therapists to more effectively and quickly aid their clients. NLP is for people interested in getting things done and enjoying themselves in the process.

An important aspect of NLP is its versatility. Its methods of pattern identification and sequencing may be generalized from individual human beings to larger order systems, from contexts involving remedial change (problem solving) to those involving evolutionary change (extending the domain of decision variables beyond the present state for an individual or system now functioning effectively). NLP may be applied as profitably to the internal organization of a bureaucratic hierarchy as to the representational systems of an individual. In all cases the formal sequencing and scheduling of activity between the structural components of a system will determine the possible outcomes of that system and the effectiveness of that system in securing those outcomes.

In an organization, its departments or employees take the place of representational systems within a single human being. Each is responsible for a certain set of inputs, processing and outputs that contribute to one or more other sets of inputs, processing and outputs of the other members of the system and of that system as a whole. By understanding the functional characteristics of the components (employees, departments, sections, divisions, etc.) of an organization and the desired outcomes of that organization, the neurolinguistic programmer can assist in sequencing or resequencing the interactions between components to achieve the desired outcome in the most elegant and effective manner.

1.8 Synesthesia

The existence of the ordered sequences of representation that we call strategies presupposes interconnected networks of activity at the neurological level. Crossover connections between representational system complexes, such that the activity in one representational system initiates activity in another system called *synesthesia* in NLP.

Hearing a harsh tone of voice and feeling uncomfortable is an example of auditory-kinesthetic synesthesia. Seeing blood and feeling nauseous would be a visual-kinesthetic synesthesia. Feeling angry and blaming someone verbally inside your head would be a kinesthetic-auditory synesthesia. Hearing music and imagining a beautiful scene would constitute an auditory-visual synesthesia.

Synesthesia patterns constitute a large portion of the human meaning making process. Correlations between representational system activities are at the root of such complex processes as knowledge, choice and communication. The skills and abilities that humans develop in all areas, fields and disciplines are the direct result of the establishment of crossover connections between neural representational complexes. The major differences among individuals possessing different skills, talents and abilities are derived from the synesthesia correlations within their particular domains of experience.

By making these correlative patterns explicit, neurolinguistic

programming provides a working model, an applied technology
for the strategic utilization of correlative patterns to secure any
behavioral outcome. By identifying synesthetic sequences that lead
to specific outcomes and by making them available to those who
desire to achieve those outcomes we can, in essence, replicate any
behavior—whether that of a businessman, scientist, healer, athlete, musician or anyone that does something well. With the tools
provided by NLP, we believe anyone can be transformed into a
modern "renaissance" person.

Footnotes

1. The term *participant organisms* is intended to indicate one of the primary distinctions between NLP and traditional behavioral science. In traditional science, generalizations which omit reference to the observer (objective description) are highly valued. In NLP a generalization or pattern must include the user/observer position and action.

2. Strictly speaking, there are two possibilities—the models are stored:
   (a) Extra-somatically—written form, pictures, engravings. . . .
   (b) Somatically—as discussed in the text. Some fascinating implications of the method of storage are drawn in Delozier (1978).

3. The term *evolution* is not intended here to indicate a linear progression such that each succeeding model encapsulates the contents of the previous one. We intend *evolution* in the sense developed by Kuhn (1970)—each succeeding model represents the orientation and values of the culture in which it is embedded.

4. In the actual experience of learning a language, its syntax is understood to include more than simply formal grammatical rules, particularly in spoken language where rhythm, tone, inflection, rate of delivery, volume shifts, etc. contribute to the meaning-making process. Slang, vernacular, regional dialects and the specialized languages of various professions and trades constitute special mini-languages within the domain of the primary language.

5. The concept of representational systems and various methods of utilization have been discussed at length in other of our works. Specifically, *The Structure of Magic* Volume II, *Patterns of the Hypnotic Techniques of Milton H. Erickson M.D.* Volumes I & II, and *Changing with Families* Volume I.

II: Strategies

All of our overt behavior is controlled by internal processing strategies. Each of you has a particular set of strategies for motivating yourself out of bed in the morning, for delegating job responsibilities to employees, for learning and teaching, for conducting business negotiations, and so on. Yet our cultural models do not explicitly teach us the specifics of the strategies that are required to achieve the behavioral goals expressed or implied by each model. Until the advent of neurolinguistic programming this has been left almost exclusively to personal trial and error.

We may succeed magnificently with particular strategies (making money, for example), yet fail completely with others (personal relationships, for example). What, precisely, is it about strategies that generates successful outcomes in some instances and disastrous outcomes in other instances? By applying the techniques and procedures developed and described in NLP, individuals in many walks of life and professionals in many fields have learned to modify existing strategies or to create new ones for themselves and their associates to achieve exactly the outcomes they desire. The magic of success is a matter of employing the most effective strategies. Most strategies can be easily learned or modified to accomplish goals of our own choosing.

2. TOTEs and Strategies

The basic format we will use to describe a specific sequence of behavior is the TOTE (Test-Operate-Test-Exit), a model proposed by George Miller, Eugene Galanter and Karl Pribram in their book *Plans and the Structure of Behavior* (1960). A TOTE is essentially a sequence of activities in our sensory representational systems that has become consolidated into a functional unit of behavior such that it is typically executed below the threshold of consciousness (see *Patterns II*). As an example, a handshake for adults in western cultures is a single unit of behavior that often has the status of a TOTE.

The behavioral sequence that makes up a TOTE can range from the simple to the complex. For the beginning musician, the playing of a single note may be the largest chunk of behavior that he or she can handle. As the musician's skill increases, however, the performance of an entire scale or melody may be comfortably undertaken as a single unit of behavior—a complex sequence of activities that has become incorporated as a TOTE.

In our experience, the advantages of TOTE over other models for analyzing behavioral units are its elegance (it requires the fewest distinctions) and its incorporation of the important properties of *feedback* and *outcome.* Developed by Miller, Galanter and Pribram as an extension of the "reflex arc" (the stimulus-response concept) in behaviorist theory, the TOTE model retains the basic simplicity of its predecessor but far surpasses it in usefulness as a neurological model of the formal internal processing sequence triggered by a stimulus. That is, it extends the "reflex arc" model to include a feedback operation as an intermediate activity between the stimulus and the response. As Miller, Galanter and Pribram explain:

> "The test represents the conditions that have to be met *before* the response will occur." (p. 24)

If the conditions of the *test* phase (a comparison of present state and desired state) are met, the action initiated by the stimulus *exits* to the next step in the chain of behavior. If not, there is a feedback phase in which the system *operates* to change some aspect of the stimulus or of the organism's internal state in an attempt to satisfy the test once again. The test-operate feedback loop may recycle many times before the test is passed and the action exists.* Miller, Galanter and Pribram write:

---

*The TOTE will also exit if, after many trials, its operation phase fails to have any significant effect on the outcome of the test, although not to the same behavior as it would have if it had passed the test.

". . . the response of the effector (the output neuron) depends
on the outcome of the test and is most conveniently conceived of
as an effort to modify the outcome of the test. The action is initiated by an "incongruity" between the state of the organism and
the state that is being tested for, and the action persists until the
incongruity is removed. The general pattern of the reflex action,
therefore, is to test the input energies against some criteria established in the organism, to respond if the result of the test is
to show an incongruity, and to continue to respond until the incongruity vanishes, at which time the reflex is terminated. Thus
there is "feedback" from the result of the action to the testing phase, and we are confronted by a recursive loop." (pp. 25–
26)

The TOTE process is represented visually by Miller, Galanter
and Pribram as:

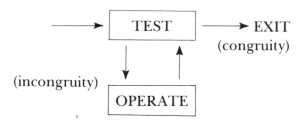

A simple example of a TOTE's test phase would be that of a
threshold test. In this example the stimulus must be above or
below a certain quantitative threshold value to satisfy the test for
congruity before the TOTE will exit to the next step in the chain
of behavior. If it is not, the organism will operate to increase or
decrease either the stimulus or its own threshold level in order to
pass the test. When you adjust the volume dial on your radio or
stereo, you are performing a TOTE of this type. As you turn the
knob, you continually test the sound volume by listening to it. If
the volume is too low, you operate by turning the knob clock-
wise. If you overshoot and the volume becomes too loud, you
operate by turning the knob counterclockwise to reduce the intensity of the sound. When you have adjusted the amplifier to the
appropriate volume, you exit from the "volume-adjusting"

TOTE and settle into your comfortable armchair to continue reading.

We can illustrate this example of the TOTE process in the following way:

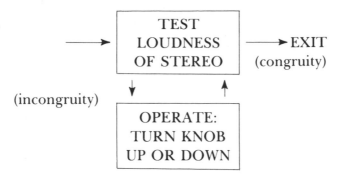

The three-step process we described earlier as the most general description of NLP, of applying resources to a present state of behavior in order to achieve a new outcome state, may also be represented as another example of the TOTE process:

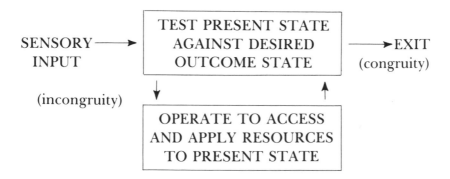

In this generalized illustration, the NLP practitioner repeatedly tests the present state of an individual, group or organization against a specific desired outcome state, continuing to access and apply resources to the system until the two states become congruent. The present state and the outcome state will be defined in terms of the distinctions available to the client (individual, group or organization) in each of the two states. The resources available to the client will be made up of the strategies in the client's repertoire and those in the programmer's repertoire, including the programmer's meta strategies for modifying or replacing the client's strategies when necessary to achieve congruity in the two states. The operations involved in indentifying, accessing and applying resource strategies will be presented in the following chapters on Elicitation, Utilization, Design and Installation.

2.1 Nested TOTEs

An important aspect of the TOTE model is that the *operate* phase of one TOTE may include *other* TOTEs—with their own tests and operations—nested inside it. TOTEs may exhibit a hierarchic structure, then, with respect to one another. A simple example of this "nesting" arrangement, offered by Miller, Galanter and Pribram, is that of hammering a nail.

A carpenter, for instance, may start with a very abstract form of TOTE that we'll call "making a table." The operate phase for this TOTE requires a number of subroutines or subTOTEs including "attach legs to table surface." This TOTE, in turn, is composed of other subTOTEs such as "hammer nail through table surface into leg." The test for this TOTE is that the nail head must be flush with the table surface before the carpenter can exit to another step. If this test is not satisfied, the carpenter will go through a somewhat noisy operate phase called "hammering," which involves two subTOTEs, "lifting hammer" and "striking nail." The specific TOTE sequence of hammering a nail is described as follows by Miller and his co-authors:

> "If this description of hammering is correct, we should expect the sequence of events to run off in this order: Test nail. (Head sticks up). Test hammer. (Hammer is up). Strike nail. Test hammer. (Hammer is down). Test nail. (Head sticks up). Test hammer. And so on, until the test of the nail reveals that its head is flush with the surface of the work, at which point control can be transfered elsewhere. Thus the compound of TOTE units unravels itself simply enough into a coordinated sequence of tests and actions, although the underlying structure that organizes and coordinates the behavior is hierarchical and not sequential."

The compound of "nested" TOTEs described in the above excerpt can be represented visually in the following diagram:

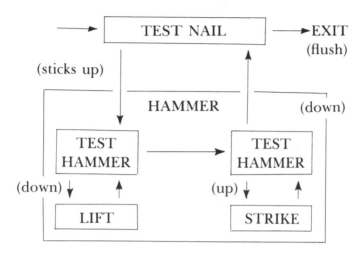

2.2 Refining the TOTE Model With Representational Systems.

The neurolinguistic programming model refines the TOTE concept by specifying the components of TOTES in terms of representational systems and strategies. NLP asserts that for behavioral processes (including cognitive activities) the test conditions and the operations of the TOTE can usefully be described as taking place through our representational systems. We are able to identify and assign with precision some representational system, or combination of representational systems, for each step in the TOTE sequence.

In the above example of hammering a nail, for example, the test of whether or not the nail is flush may be made by comparing the incoming visual experience of the position of the nail with some stored internal visual representation of what the nail looks like when it is flush. To make our TOTE analysis simpler we will borrow from the 4-tuple and abbreviate visual experience which comes from external sources as V^e. Internally generated visual representations will be abbreviated as V^i. The formal aspects of the testing of the nail in the hammering example, if it is done by looking at the nail, involves the comparison of external and internal visual representations—or V^e/V^i.

This same comparison could also be made through tactile kinesthetic experience—the feelings in the carpenter's hand and arm will be different when s/he hits a nail that is flush than they will when s/he hits a nail that is still sticking up. The comparison here will take place between external kinesthetic sensations and internally generated kinesthetic experience—or K^e/K^i. The same type of comparison may also be made auditorily in that the sound of the blow of the hammer against the nail will be different when the nail is flush and when it is not. The formal aspects of this particular comparison would involve auditory external (A^e) vs. auditory internal (A^i); that is, A^e/A^i.

An experienced journeyman carpenter can probably make the test easily and comfortably through any of these three representational systems; the inexperienced carpenter may not be able to do so. The ability to substitute different representational systems during a particular task may serve as a reliable measure of competence, experience and flexibility for those involved in many different occupations.

The operations of the carpenter, in this case, will be represented through the external kinesthetic system since they involve only the lifting and striking actions of the carpenter's arm. (We class *motor* responses as kinesthetic external (K^e) because it is through the tactile and proprioceptive systems that such movement will be represented to the individual.)

The experience of "congruence" (the exit point in the TOTE) and of "incongruence" (the operate point in the TOTE) as the result of a test will also be represented through one of the representational systems. When the carpenter tests the nail, for example, and notices that it is not flush, the incongruence between the incoming experience of the nail and the stored representation of what the nail should be like (that causes the carpenter to operate) may be represented through an image, sound or feeling. He may get a certain feeling in the stomach area that initiates the "hammering" subroutine. He may actually hear a voice in his head that says, "No, needs more hammering," or he might see an internal image of his hammer hitting the nail again.[1]

Notice that a test need not take place only between externally and internally generated representations. A test may also take place between two internally stored or generated representations. The two compared representations, however, will often remain in the same representational system. A visual representation will most accurately be tested against another visual representation; auditory with auditory; and kinesthetic with kinesthetic. (It can be postulated that the simultaneous pairing of two different representations within the same representational system is one of the functions of the two cerebral hemispheres in human beings.[2])

Not all tests, however, involve the comparison or matching of two representations; some may be tests of the *intensity* of particular representations. That is, some feeling, sound or image may be required to reach a certain threshold value (due to the operation procedure) before the TOTE will exit. In this kind of comparison a representation from one system is often "tested" against a representation from a different system—for example, when something *looks* good but just doesn't *feel* right. This kind of test often takes place in decision and motivation strategies. Depending upon the nature of the behavior involved, the "incongruence" resulting from this kind of test is often experienced as stress or internal conflict. The conflict is resolved when one of the representations becomes strong enough that it assumes prime control by initiating the next step in the chain of response, or when the individual, through his or her operations, changes, balances or compromises the representations so that they become congruent with one another.

Other examples of this multi-representational testing would be instances where a particular behavior *feels* good but something *tells* you that you shouldn't be doing it; or when an option *sounds* like a good idea but you can *see* there may be negative consequences. Operations for assisting people in dealing with the "incongruence" caused by these sorts of conflicts have been presented in our other works *(Patterns II* and *Structure of Magic II).*

2.3 Applying the Representational Analysis of TOTEs.

By making the representational form of test and operate procedures explicit, the NLP model makes the analysis and transfer of any behavior much more accessible and systematic. By identifying the representational type and the function of each step out of a behavioral continuum of steps, NLP describes how to unpack essentially any behavioral sequence so that it may be easily taught, communicated or modified. NLP also provides important and useful insights into such complex behavioral structures as "personality."

The concept of "representational system primacy" (or "most highly valued representational system") was introduced in *Structure of Magic II* and *Patterns I*. It asserts that many individuals tend to value and use one representational system over others to perform their tests and operations. A visually oriented person would consistently choose to look at the hammer and nail to test for congruence. A more kinesthetically oriented individual would consistently do it by "feel." This kind of preference is often generalized to many different types of tasks, even to those for which the preferred representational system is inappropriate or inadaquate.

TOTE and representational systems analysis are also very useful, as we pointed out earlier, in working with group or organizational dynamics. For example, consider two individuals involved in making a decision. They could be business executives, administrators, a therapist and a client, a husband and wife or any two people involved in a decision-making process. One of the individuals tests the material to be decided upon visually—his criterion involves *seeing* the results of the decision clearly—perhaps plotted on a graph, perhaps through internally constructed images, etc. The other tests on the basis of how she *feels* or how she thinks the outcome of the decision would feel to those affected by it.

The process of making the decision on the larger scale will require a comparison of the visual criteria of the one individual and the kinesthetic criteria of the other—images with feelings. The two people involved as a team in the decision-making process then operate through discussion, negotiation, perhaps even fighting or arguing, until any discrepancies in their combined representations are resolved or changed. Depending on the nature of their operation procedures, the different representational processes of the two individuals could either serve as a positive resource to them, and to the system or organization of which they are a part, or as a hindrance or detriment. We began our presentation of effective group operations in *Changing With Families* (with Virginia Satir), for family systems specifically. Throughout this book we will provide other strategies and operations that we consider to be effective for working with other groups and organizations as well as for families.

2.31 Matching Representational Systems to Task.

As we pointed out earlier, some representational systems are more suited to the test and operation procedures of specific tasks than others, for achieving effective outcomes. The representational systems analysis of TOTEs provides an extremely useful way of sorting effective behavioral strategies for particular tasks. This offers a reliable and powerful means for increasing individual or group effectiveness in any occupation or endeavor.

Let's start out with a simple example from elementary education, of two different spelling strategies: the visual approach and the phonetic strategy. We have observed that a "visual" speller, when presented with a word (an external auditory stimulus—A^e), will go through a synesthetic operation in which s/he constructs a visual image of the letters of the word from the sound. This constructed visual image (V_c^i—the "c" stands for "constructed") is then tested against a remembered visual image of the word written out somewhere that the individual has seen it before (a remembered visual image is notated V_r^i). The congruence or incongruence of the two images is represented as internal kinesthetic feelings (K^i). If the constructed image does not "look right" the speller gets a negative feeling and operates to construct another image. If the two images are congruent the student gets a positive feeling and exits to a TOTE in which the image is vocalized.

The operate phase of this particular TOTE will probably consist of some synesthetic sequence in which the speller repeats the word to be spelled, or some problematic syllable, internally or aloud, and another image is constructed. This loop continues until an image is generated which, when tested (V_c^i / V_r^i), initiates a positive feeling (K_+^i).

The "visual" spelling TOTE is shown in Figure A:

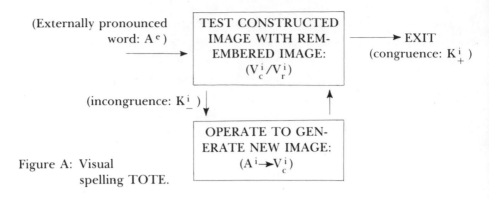

Figure A: Visual
        spelling TOTE.

Figure B shows the TOTE of a phonetic speller:

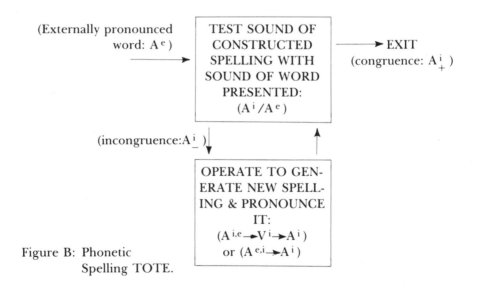

Figure B: Phonetic
        Spelling TOTE.

The phonetic speller tests the spelling s/he has constructed by
finding out if it "sounds right." This requires comparing the sound
of the word s/he has generated with the sound of the word originally presented. The operation phase of the phonetic speller involves "sounding out" the word by breaking it down verbally into
syllables, and sounding out individual letters from there. The

breaking down process may be done either aloud or internally. Once each of the letters has been sounded out, the individual then repronounces them in sequence, and tests the pronunciation against that of the word originally presented. We have abbreviated the process of sounding out as $A^{i,e} \longrightarrow A^i$. The "i,e" superscript to the auditory component tells us that the original word may be broken down internally or aloud. Sometimes the phonetic speller will even have an operation phase in which the student makes a visual image of the letters in each syllable or phoneme. To test the spelling, however, the individual pronounces the image (aloud or internally) and compares it with the pronunciation of the presented word. We have abbreviated this operation as $A^{i,e} \longrightarrow V^i_c \longrightarrow A^i$: break word down into syllables or phonemes—construct image of letters in syllables—pronounce spelling.

Although the incongruence between mismatched pronunciations could be represented kinesthetically, as with the visual speller, we have chosen to show that it could be represented auditorily in this TOTE. Here, the speller may actually hear words such as "That's it" (A^i_+) in his/her head if the pronunciations match, or "No, try again" (A^i_-) if they do not. The student may alternatively hear a separate harmonious (A^i_+), or discordant (A^i_-) sound as a representation of congruence or incongruence.

It has been our experience that, since the visual coding of the English language frequently does not follow phonetic rules, individuals with a visual strategy are consistently much better spellers. "Their", "there", and "they're", for example, may all be pronounced the same although visually they are different. For the phonetic speller, "ghoti" may be the appropriate spelling for the word "fish"—that is, "gh" as in lau*gh*; "o" as in w*o*men; and "ti" as in mo*ti*on! The sounding out or phonics strategy may be very good for oral reading presentations where what is important is that the words are pronounced clearly; but for the specific task of spelling, it is inappropriate. The name of the system itself—"phonics" —cannot be spelled accurately with a phonetic strategy.

In most educational institutions, children are not yet taught the formal aspects of task-specific learning when they are learning to spell—they are simply given gross feedback for whether they have spelled "correctly" or "incorrectly." The children are left on their own to come up with a strategy (of which those previously described are only two of a large number of possible permutations) which may or may not be the most effective for the task of spelling.[3] They are not taught strategies, but rather simply content.

What we hope to accomplish by making such formal strategies explicit through the neurolinguistic programming model is to increase the effectiveness of education in all disciplines. Many types of outcomes, to be achieved effectively and efficiently, involve the utilization of specific representational systems in specific sequences. Others are more flexible with respect to which representational systems occupy which nodes in the TOTE sequence. By using the elicitation and design techniques of NLP these distinctions may be made explicitly available.

The goal of TOTE and representational systems analysis is twofold:

a. To find the most appropriate representational systems for the TOTE steps that lead to a particular outcome (such as using the visual representational system for spelling).
b. To be able to use all representational systems as resources for learning and performing. This means that in cases where more than one representational system may be used for a particular step in a task (such as testing the nail in the hammering example), that one may choose to substitute another representational strategy should it be appropriate or necessary for the context. This serves to greatly expand one's flexibility and repertoire of choices requisite variety.

2.4 Modifying TOTE Notation for Strategies.

The TOTE is the basic unit used to identify a particular sequence of behavior. A *strategy* is the basic unit of analysis of a particular TOTE, or set of TOTEs. Strategy analysis breaks a TOTE down into its representational components and describes the order of the particular representational activity that leads to the specific behavioral outcome.

We have found TOTE diagrams to be somewhat laborious and impractical as a notational format for strategies. Moreover, it is often inefficient and sometimes arbitrary to try to identify the specific function, within the framework provided by the TOTE, of each step in a sequence of behavior. As we mentioned earlier the test phase of one TOTE may be part of the operation phase of another TOTE. Making this functional distinction is sometimes just a matter of how you punctuate the sequence; that is, it depends on where you choose to start analyzing the sequence, and which representations you decide to put where in the TOTE framework. Spending too much time on such issues when you are communicating with an individual or group can be counterproductive.

In neurolinguistic programming we have chosen to streamline this TOTE framework into a linear string of representations that we call a "strategy." The two most important aspects of a strategy are:

a. The representational system in which information is coded.
b. The sequential relationship between representations.

With the strategy, of course, we will presuppose the underlying TOTE framework: every strategy will be assumed to perform some tests on the input experience of the individual and to contain an operate point and an exit point. Some strategies, though, will be complex and lengthy, incorporating many strings of TOTEs. The functional significance of each individual step (that is, whether it is a representation involved in a test, operation, indicating an incongruence, both a test and an operation, etc.) will not always be specifically identified unless, of course, it is important for securing the outcome. And even though we will be primarily using linear notation for strategies, we will feel free to employ the TOTE diagram when it is useful to illustrate important aspects of some behavioral sequence.

Thus, we could notate the diagram of the visual spelling TOTE shown in figure A as:

$$A^{e,i} \rightarrow V^i_c / V^i_r \rightarrow K^i \rightarrow EXIT$$
$$\underbrace{\phantom{A^{e,i} \rightarrow V^i_c / V^i_r}}_{(-)} \quad (+)$$

This shows that the individual inputs auditorily, by listening to the word presented (the "e,i" superscript indicates that this input may come from either external or internal sources—this may also be indicated by putting no superscript above the A, showing that it is not specified whether the auditory stimulus comes from internal or external sources). The individual next constructs a visual image from the auditory input (V_c^i) and tests it against some remembered image (V_c^i/V_r^i). If the internal feeling (K^i) the individual derives from the test is negative ($-$) the individual loops back to the beginning of the strategy and processes the word again; if the internal feeling is positive ($+$) the individual exits.

Depending on what one intends with the strategy, notation can be streamlined even more, simply showing the basic representational progression:

$$A \rightarrow V^i \rightarrow K^i \rightarrow EXIT$$

This indicates that, for spelling, the individual begins auditorily (whether the stimulus comes from external or internal sources is unspecified), derives an internal image from the sound, and from the image derives a feeling which will either send the strategy back through the loop or allow it to exit.

Both diagrams above carry most of the information shown in the TOTE diagram. Each demonstrates strategy analysis at a different level of detail. It will be up to the programmer to choose which level of detail will be the most appropriate for achieving the outcomes desired within the particular context with which s/he is dealing. In general, the programmer will choose the most elegant level of detail—that is, the one that employs the fewest number of distinctions and is still capable of eliciting all the outcomes desired in that situation. This will, of course, be dependent on the types of outcomes involved. We will expand on the issues and aspects of strategy notation further in the Elicitation Section of this book.

2.5 The Implications of Strategies.

One way to talk about strategies is to suggest that they are, in many ways, like using a telephone. Representational systems (both of internal and external orientation) are like the digits on the telephone keyboard. The way we sequence and order the activity of these representational systems leads us to different outcomes, just as the use of different combinations of numbers on the phone will get us different localities and people.

A telephone number, like a strategy, is a means to access resources. One must, of course, select the appropriate number to reach the appropriate resource. If we want to call an ambulance, find out about repairing a car, order musical equipment or make reservations for dinner, we must know which numbers to use. Changing or mixing up one digit leads to an entirely different outcome. Some places have more than one telephone number, and it will be possible to dial several different sequences to reach them. Others will have one number and one number only.

To contact the appropriate party long distance, it is necessary to prefix the number we are attempting to reach with an area code sequence of digits. So it is with strategies—every step in the strategy, and the eventual outcome, is dependent on the steps that have come before. In certain contexts individuals and groups may need to prefix their operations or strategies with other actions or representations as a necessary preparation toward securing the outcome they desire or need. If they do not test for certain important conditions in the beginning of the strategy before they have initiated some later operation they may run up against interference or blocks to achieving their outcome that could have been more easily dealt with earlier in the sequence. Some people and organizations get stuck in strategies similar to that of an individual who keeps punching only the last four digits of a seven-digit phone number and wonders why he keeps ending up with only the dial tone. Others may needlessly and inefficiently overprepare like the individual who uses the area code for telephone numbers in his own locality.

People may also fall into situations in which they forget about an important or appropriate strategy, or the representational sequence of a strategy, as one may forget a phone number or mix it up with numbers that they use frequently. Applying often used or highly valued strategies in contexts in which they are inappropriate is one of the most common difficulties people experience with strategies. Applying a habitual strategy in an inappropriate context would be like moving from California to Alabama then dialing your old California fire department number when you have a fire at your new home because it's the only number you know.

The well known Peter Principle in the business world, that people become promoted past their level of competence, is an example of what happens when a person is inflexible with his strategies. The strategies that will make a person successful at a lower level in a corporate hierarchy may be inappropriate for the tasks that confront that person when he is promoted. A good strategy for managing people in a face-to-face situation may be a poor strategy for designing fiscal policy. If the individual who is being promoted does not have the variability to adapt his or her strategies to the new tasks created by the change in their job they will become incompetent.

A good example of a representational mismatch in a strategy as the result of applying a highly valued or habitual strategy in an inappropriate context is that of a woman, with whom one of the authors was working, who had trouble with mathematics because as a child she had learned arithmetic by coding numbers kinesthetically instead of visually. Each digit from zero to nine she represented to herself as a particular feeling that matched the way she felt about herself and other people in her environment at that time. For example, "four" had the feelings of a potential prodigy that was always being suppressed for some reason; "eight" was a particularly passive number and "seven" felt very energetic to her. "Nine" was a strong feeling that matched how she felt about her mother at the time—very powerful and protective.

As she performed various arithmetic operations, these feelings would combine with one another additively or multiply to form other feelings of differing degrees of complexity and intensity. As a result, she had always found mathematics fascinating but was unable to become adept at it. For instance, she encountered difficulty in adding certain numbers together because the feelings were not compatible, and she would have to count by ones on her fingers to get the answer.

When she began to mature, her relationships and feelings changed, and her sense of particular numbers changed with them. In later years she couldn't understand why working with numbers often made her feel greatly perplexed. This strategy seriously interfered with her professional life until she began working with one of the authors to develop a new strategy for arithmetic that substituted internal visualization of the digits.

This example has its parallels in many kinds of learning situations, including how we develop personal relationships with friends, family members, business and professional associates and so on. Troublesome behaviors like phobic responses, losing one's temper, jumping to conclusions and many of those behaviors we call "bad habits" are examples of how we may generalize strategies that are or were appropriate and adaptive in certain past or present contexts into situations in which they become inappropriate. Quite often people don't incorporate into these contextually problematic strategies an adequate test to indicate when it is appropriate to operate with the strategy in question. Rather, such persons typically find themselves suddenly involved in their responses, too late to change their behavior. These individuals need more appropriate and adaquate operations in their repertoire of choices to be able to deal resourcefully with life situations.

A good example of how a representational system which serves as an appropriate testing mechanism in some situations may become mismatched for a particular task is found in the behavior of ants. The most highly developed representational system of ants, as with most insects, is the olfactory sense—the information in this sense tends to preempt the ant's other sensory input. Dead ants, for instance will be groomed and treated by other workers as if they were still alive for a day or two until chemical decomposition products accumulate and stimulate the workers to drag the corpse to the refuse pile outside the nest. The crumpled posture and complete immobility of the dead ant will by themselves produce no response in the other ants. When other innanimate objects or even living worker ants are daubed with chemicals from decomposed ants they are immediately carted off to the dead pile as well, despite the struggling of the living ants. Live workers will climb down from the refuse pile and return to the nest only to be dragged back to the pile over and over again until the scent of death is finally worn off.

Incredible as the above example may seem to some of you readers, we have found counterparts almost as striking in human behavior when people refuse to change highly valued but inappropriate test criteria.

One of the authors once worked with a woman who was consistently verbally and physically abused by her husband. She had intended to leave the relationship after each incident (which were getting more and more violent) but her husband would always buy her something or do something to make up with her so she wouldn't go. After a few days or weeks, however, her husband would again become violent and the pattern would repeat itself much to the dismay of the unhappy and confused woman. After listening to the woman's description of her problem the author told her a story that he had been told as a child. The story was about a man who worked in a saw mill. The man was in one part of the mill stacking some freshly cut boards when he suddenly heard a terrible cry coming from the other room. He immediatly rushed in the other room to investigate and came across one of his co-workers standing by an enormous circular saw. The co-worker was clutching his hand and in great pain, and had obviously just severed a finger from his left hand. The man who had just entered the room ran up to him exclaiming, "Oh my God, what happened?" To which the other responded, "Well I was just reaching for that board like this and . . . . . OUCH . . . THERE GOES ANOTHER ONE!"

The woman left the author's office somewhat dazed by the story but called the author back about a month later with the news of the great changes she had made in her life. She had been abused by her husband again but this time she had moved out, gotten herself a job, thwarted his attempts to lure her back and was living happily in another town. She finished her triumphant account with the comment, "I didn't want to cut off another finger."

2.6 The Mechanics of Strategies

We have mentioned a number of times that during the securing of a particular outcome, whether it be developing a particular skill, making or keeping oneself healthy, learning a new task, communicating with a particular individual, etc., it is necessary at certain points in time to tune into the information in one particular representational system to a greater degree than information in the others. The order in which we do this and the way in which the information we tune into initiates or modulates information in our other representational systems is also of extreme importance. An individual learning to compose music, for example, will probably pay more attention to the auditory class of sensory experience than would an individual learning chemistry or juggling. In fact, an individual who composes music effectively will probably sequence his/her representational systems differently than an individual who effectively performs music. The two are essentially different tasks and involve different strategies.

Those attempting to apply the same perceptual-motor tests and operations for learning something like mathematics (which tends to be a primarily visual skill) to tasks like learning football or gymnastics (which require much greater attention to tactile and proprioceptive sensations) will experience difficulty.

When we talk about "paying attention to," "tuning in to," "relying on" or "valuing" a particular representational system, we do not, of course, mean to imply that the others stop working at that time. We are simply implying that the behavioral significance or signal value of the activity of the selected representational system increases with respect to the others. The 4-tuple stipulates that all of our senses are processing some reprsentation, both from internal and external sources, at any point in time. Obviously, your visual cortex does not stop functioning while you are listening intently to music or to an internal dialogue. Rather, at each step in any strategy the activity in one representational system will have a higher intensity or signal value than the others and will assume what we might call "prime control" for that particular duration of time.

In reproducing the behavioral sequence required to achieve some outcome that we are motivated to secure, whether it is an ability we have admired in someone else or a resource that we now have infrequent or irregular access to, we may need to employ varying degrees of representational activity in the system we are accessing. Some strategies involve the achievement of a very sharp signal for a particular representation; others may require rapid and complex transitions and representations. Sometimes people experience difficulty accessing a representational system with the appropriate strength, clarity and resonance. Others may tune in to a representational system too strongly.

In *Patterns II* we introduced a concept we call the "R-operator," which operates on 4-tuples at various points in time to single out one representational system as more significant in consciousness than the others. The "mechanism" of the R-operator is a combination of what we call "accessing cues" and previously established synesthesia patterns.

Accessing, or tuning in to a particular representational system, is in some ways like tuning a radio. All of the various radio stations are always transmitting through their own signal frequencies, but by adjusting the internal works of our receiver, we can tune in to one signal or frequency in such a way that we pick up little or no interference from the others.

Accessing cues are behaviors that we develop to tune our bodies and affect our neurology in such a way that we can access one representational system more strongly than the others. Just as we prepare to execute any overt behavior independently from the other choices available to us, like jumping, laughing, running or talking, by flexing our muscles and changing our breathing rates and eye scanning patterns in the specific ways that single out that behavior from all others, we operate similarly with cognitive behavior and complex internal processing. Each of us must systematically cycle through specific and recurrent behavioral cues to perform our strategies.

Right now, stop and image as vividly as possible the color and pattern on your bedspread. . . .

If this isn't in your direct line of vision, you had to just now tune your bodily and neural systems to access an internal visual image of your bedspread over the other incoming sensations in your visual, auditory, kinesthetic and olfactory systems. If it is in your direct line of vision you would still have had to tune your body and neurology to accept and focus on the external visual experience of color and pattern over your other sensory experiences. If you made an internal picture in your mind's eye, you may have noticed that to do so clearly you defocused your eyes momentarily as you stared at this page in the book, so that the words and other external visual input became blurred. Perhaps you looked away from the book to break visual contact, shifting your eyes up and to the left (or perhaps it was up and to the right, if you are left handed). You may have even closed your eyes. Did you notice any alteration in your breathing pattern? Perhaps it shifted higher up in your chest and became more shallow or stopped altogether for a moment. You might also have experienced a slight tension in your shoulder muscles, and perhaps became aware that your shoulders hunched slightly forward. To look clearly at your bedspread externally would require observable behavioral adjustments as well. You would have to orient your head in the appropriate direction and tighten or slacken certain muscles around your eyes to allow you to focus closely on the object.

Now take some time and get in touch with the last time you felt soaking wet. . . .

To access this modality-specific experience you again had to tune your body and neurology, however slightly, to make that particular representation stand out. Some of you will have noticed that to do this you had to go through a memory strategy—perhaps you started by asking yourself internally, "Now when *was* the last time I felt really wet?" and proceeded to create a series of internal images or looked around externally to see possible places in your external environment where you might have gotten wet, before you were able to achieve the outcome of accessing the feeling. Perhaps you began right off with visual images. You might have been able to access this feeling immediately, but noticed that for the task of seeing your bedspread you had to first feel yourself standing in the room before you could see the color clearly.

Irrespective of your initial experience, however, many of you probably noticed that when the feelings finally came up strongly, your breathing became deeper and shifted down into your stomach area. Your shoulders were probably more relaxed, perhaps drooping slightly, and your eyes had defocused and moved down and to the right (to the left if you are lefthanded).

Now think of the voice of a close friend or associate so that you can richly and resonantly hear the pitch, tonal qualities and tempo of their voice when s/he speaks. . . .

To completely achieve this outcome you probably noticed that again you had to make several physical adjustments. Perhaps your breathing shifted to your diaphram and you became aware that your head was cocked slightly to one side and your eyes had shifted laterally and to the left or down and to the left (again this might depend on handedness). You may have leaned back in your chair, throwing your shoulders back slightly, maybe folding your arms.

We have observed that behavioral cues, such as those listed here, consistently accompany the representational steps we go through for our strategies. Some cues seem to be quite specific to the accessing of a particular representational system and are probably genetically programmed since they are found to be consistent cross-culturally. Other cues are developed as personal triggers by each individual.

As you completed the simple tasks listed here, you may have been aware that you had an easier time accessing certain representational systems, in terms of speed and clarity. Similarly, many people are more adept at making specific synesthetic transitions from one representational system to another. This results largely from the accessing cues you have set up for yourself. If you experienced difficulties in accessing the experiences called for in this exercise, try the task again, using the behavioral processes we described following each task. You may find that using them will assist you in getting better results.[4]

One important aspect of accessing cues is that by carefully observing them you can gather a great deal of information about the steps to an individual's strategy. This aspect will be treated in detail in the next section of this book.

2.7 Defining the Strategy.

A strategy, then, is a series of overlapping 4-tuples in which, at each step, each 4-tuple is acted upon by the R-operator through accessing cues and synesthesia patterns, giving one representational system more behavioral significance than the others. The results of this process determine which 4-tuple will be triggered or anchored next, the sequence of 4-tuples and, ultimately, what behavioral outcome will result. We can show this in the following way:

```
A                             A
V     A         A             V
K→ V→ A→ V→ A→ K
O     K     V     K     V     O
      O     K     O     K
            O           O
```

How finely we tune or calibrate our neural and physiological systems to accept the information from a particular representational system, as we go through the steps of a strategy, will determine the amount of overlap or interference we get from our other representational systems.[5]

Sometimes, of course, it is useful and important to overlap the information from our different representational systems, as in multi-representational testing. Many people overlap accessing cues to contribute to the synesthetic combination of two representational systems, or to assist the process of changing synesthetically from one representational system to another. At other times, however, this kind of overlap will cause interference with, or the overriding of, important information from one particular representational system.

2.8 Strategies and "Consciousness."

It is probably obvious to most of you readers that all of the steps in a particular strategy need not be conscious in order for them to be operative. In fact, generally just the opposite is true: the more habitual and less conscious a behavior becomes, the more we can be guaranteed that we have completely incorporated it.

In neurolinguistic programming, consciousness is simply considered to be the result of the relative intensities of the activity within our representational systems. It is an indication of how much a particular representational system is being used rather than an entity in itself (as many others conceive it). In NLP consciousness is treated as an emergent property of neural system activity, not an initiator of that activity. To say that our consciousness or awareness controlled or affected our behavior would be like saying that the properties of "wetness" or "iciness" controlled or affected the structural combinations of the H_2O molecules from which these properties are derived. Consciousness is rather a side effect, an indicator of a portion of what is going on during representational processing.

We have pointed out that the behavioral significance of a particular representation will be determined by the intensity of the representation with respect to the intensity of all other ongoing representations. Our claim is that a representation becomes conscious only when it reaches a certain level of intensity. This, however, says relatively little about its behavioral significance. Consider the following graph:[6]

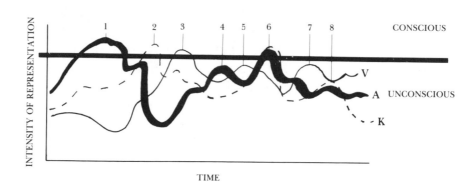

This is a graph of hypothetical fluctuations in intensity of the three basic representational systems over time. These fluctuations are contributed to by accessing cues & synesthetic neural interconnections. The center line indicates the threshold of consciousness. Representations only become conscious when their intensity rises above that value. The graph indicates that at point 1 the auditory representational system has the highest relative signal value and is conscious. At point 2, the visual representational system has the highest relative intensity and is conscious. At point 3, the kinesthetic representational system has the highest intensity and is conscious. At point 4, the auditory representational system again has

the highest relative intensity, and thus the most behavioral significance, but it has not reached the level of consciousness. Similarly,
at point 5, the kinesthetic system takes prime control at that particular time but is below the conscious level. At point 6 both the
visual and auditory representational systems are in consciousness,
but since the visual system has a slightly higher signal, it will be
most highly valued for that step. At point 7, the visual system again
assumes prime control but this time is out of consciousness. At
point 8 the visual and kinesthetic representational systems overlap
out of consciousness, perhaps performing some multi-representational test.

The graph essentially plots a portion of a strategy, which we
have chosen to divide or punctuate into eight steps:

$$A \longrightarrow V \longrightarrow K \longrightarrow A \longrightarrow K \longrightarrow V \longrightarrow V \longrightarrow V/K \longrightarrow \ldots$$
Point #: 1   2   3   4   5   6   7   8

Four of the steps, however, are below conscious awareness; 4,
5, 7, & 8. Yet this does not detract from the behavioral significance
of these steps.

It is important to point out here that behavioral significance is
determined by relative intensity of the representations and the
interaction of the system as a whole. A subliminal representation
of low intensity at one point in time will still contribute to the
overall conditions of the system and may cause changes in the
system making it or some other representational system rise to the
highest relative intensity at the next point in time. If the signal
values are close enough, it is possible for a multiple response to
occur. This would happen in the case of the individual who says
"Yes", but whose head is at the same time unconsciously shaking
"No." It is also possible for two strategies to take place simultaneously, causing split responses and behavioral incongruencies if
neither strategy is strong enough. This is where the importance of
calibration enters in.

It is also possible, since behavioral significance is a function of
relative values of intensity, that the activity of one representational
system, even though it reaches consciousness, may be relatively
insignificant. This is illustrated in the following graph:

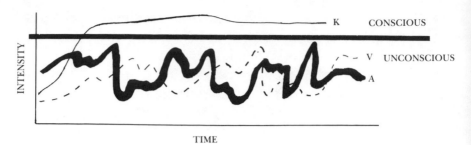

This graph shows that, even though the kinesthetic representational system has reached an intensity level high enough to enter consciousness, it has stabilized, changing very little with respect to other representational systems. Because the visual and auditory representational system signals show larger variations in amplitude with repect to one another and with respect to the kinesthetic system in this case, it is their activity which will have the most relative behavioral effect.

A person in this kind of state would be very conscious of his/her feelings. Most of their important internal processes, however, would take place below the level of awareness.

Strategies and representations which typically occur below an individual's level of awareness make up what is often called or referred to as the "unconscious mind."

In *Patterns II* we discussed some of the relationships between consciousness and learning:

> "Each of us as a human being is constantly subjected to enormous amounts of information. A portion of this stimulation is the result of the contact we have with the parts of the world which we are able to sense with our sensory channels. The amount of information available from our ongoing experience greatly exceeds our ability to sense our experience *consciously*. In fact much of the process of learning and growing is our ability to sense regularity or pattern in our experience and to develop programs within ourselves to cope effectively with the world at the *unconscious* level of behavior. For example, your ability to read and understand this very sentence is a program which at one point in your life you were unable to per-

form. You went through the task of learning to recognize first the letters, then the words and finally the phrases and sentences of English. Associated with each of these steps were the specific eye scanning patterns which were appropriate. Learning to associate a certain visual input with a set of meanings which they represent was a relatively long and arduous task. Your skill in reading rapidly and meaningfully depends in large part on your ability to operate those lower level patterns of eye scanning and letter recognition *unconsciously*. The vast bulk of our everyday lives is occupied with the execution of tremendously complex patterns of unconscious behavior. The ability we have to enjoy our experience and engage in the activities which each of us find interesting and pleasing would in large part be lost if we did not have the ability to program ourselves to carry out certain complex patterns of behavior for execution at the unconscious level of behavior. Imagine how cluttered our experience would be, for example, if it were necessary for us to consciously maintain the rate and depth of our breathing, the tonus of our muscles, the level of our blood sugar . . .

"The process of creating programs which are useful to us—the learning process—is an ongoing process of change. We refer to this process as *modeling*. Modeling occurs both at the conscious and the unconscious levels of behavior. The process of learning to understand and speak our native language is an example of the process of unconscious modeling. The process of learning to read and to spell is, for most people, an example of conscious modeling. Notice, however, even in the case of conscious modeling, much of what is learned is the sequencing and organization of lower level patterns of behavior already available at the unconscious level of behavior. For example, children learning to spell are not explicitly taught to form mental images of the words they are learning—that is, to employ their visualization strategies—yet, children who succeed in becoming excellent spellers employ this skill unconsciously.

"A young athlete learning to run the 100 meter dash is learning how to sequence and utilize patterns of muscle movements already available at the unconscious level of behavior. His ability to run the 100 meter dash at maximum speed will depend in large part on his ability to make unconscious the patterns of sequencing of those patterns of unconscious behavior already available.

". . . consciousness is a limited phenomenon. Specifically, as humans we are limited to representing to ourselves in consciousness a small finite number of chunks of information. In his now classic paper called *The Magic Number 7 plus or minus 2*, George A. Miller (1956)

carefully presents the outline of the limits of consciousness. Essentially, his research leads him to the conclusion that we are capable
of entertaining in consciousness 7 plus or minus 2 chunks of information. One of the most interesting implications of Miller's paper
is that the size of the chunk is variable. In other words, the limitation
of 7 plus 2 applies not to the number of bits of information, but
rather to the number of chunks. Thus, by carefully selecting the code
by which we organize our conscious experience, we have a great deal
of latitude in increasing the amount of bits of information we can
represent to ourselves consciously. Miller is artfully vague in his
discussion of what a chunk is. If we identify the term *chunk* with the
notion of a pattern of behavior which has not yet achieved the status
of an unconscious TOTE, then the interaction between the function
of consciousness in the learning process and chunking becomes
useful. As we learn to identify and respond systematically to patterning in our experience, we are able to make unconscious portions of
our experience which we previously had to cope with at the level of
consciousness. A *chunk* in consciousness is a patterning or regularity
in our experience which we have not yet succeeded in making unconscious. Thus, at the beginning of the learning of a particular task,
the size of the chunk will be rather small—encompassing a relatively
short patterning or regularity in our experience. As this size chunk
achieves the status of a TOTE—thus becoming unconscious—our
consciousness is free to attend to larger level patterns which are
composed of the sequencing and organizing of the TOTE's which
they are composed of, or to attend to patterning in other representational systems or areas of experience.

Consider an example from your own experience. For those of you
who at one time learned to ride a bicycle, remember how complex
it was at first. Your first time up was overwhelming. You had to think
about balancing, pushing pedals up and down, steering and watching where to steer. This was certainly more than you could handle,
so perhaps your father or a friend held the rear of the bicycle so you
only had worry consciously about steering and pedaling. And if you
were one of the fortunate ones who already had an unconscious
program for pedaling from riding a tricycle, then the task was reduced to learning to coordinate steering and pedaling. Once these
skills had been drilled into your behavior they happened automatically, then perhaps when you weren't even looking your father let
go and just ran behind and off you were, learning to coordinate the
pedaling and steering with balancing. After a time you had so programmed yourself to operate the bicycle that all aspects of the task
dropped outside of consciousness, leaving you free to enjoy the

scenery or talk with a riding companion. No matter how long it has been since you have ridden a bike, the program will be there and if you climb on a bicycle the program will activate and you will be able to ride once again without ever thinking even for a moment about all the steps in this complex process. They are all chunked and sequenced at the unconscious level leaving you free to enjoy your ride. If they were conscious you would have to think about pedaling, steering, balancing every movement and your consciousness would be so cluttered you would either fall or run into something. The learning of patterns of behavior such as bicycle riding as unconscious programs is both useful and necessary to allow us as humans to do the varied and complex things we do every day."

Some people have tests in their strategies which require them to insure that every representation in the steps of their strategy reaches the signal value necessary for consciousness. Requiring such high signals may be adaptive in some cases, but too often tends to slow the process down because the individual has to keep operating to increase the signal value.

Other people, however, distract themselves consciously to insure that the strategy will take place at the unconscious level. Consider, for instance, the following strategy of a skilled mathematician. This man regularly displayed an unusual skill in adding tremendous columns of numbers rapidly and without error. When asked how he was able to perform such feats the mathematician replied that *he* didn't have to do anything. He maintained that all he did was to make an internal image of a blackboard, and after a series of numbers was presented to him, he merely watched the blackboard in his mind's eye until a hand came into the picture and wrote down the answer. He would then simply read the answer on the blackboard.

All of this is not to say that the internal activity indicated by the property of consciousness is not important in the learning process. A high signal value in a particular representational system is in most cases very important for the initial establishment of that step in the strategy. Once the pattern is established, however, it helps to streamline the strategy if the signal habituates. Once one has learned to ride a bicycle, for example, it is a hindrance rather than a help to continue consciously attending to balance, steering, pedaling, etc.

2.9 Unpacking Unconscious Strategies.

In a TOTE that has already habituated, like the mathematician's strategy mentioned above, the fact that the signal level of the various steps is below consciousness makes it difficult for the individual to consciously communicate these steps to someone else who wishes to acquire the skill. It also becomes hard to change the various steps of a particular unconscious strategy, should it become maladaptive at some point, because the details of the steps are not explicitly known. One of the most important tasks that a neurolinguistic programmer faces is how to make unconscious strategies explicit when the individual who displays them is unable to consciously report the steps to another. This is where close observation of the accessing cues used by an individual to tune in to specific representational systems will become extremely useful. The next section of this book will be devoted to presenting explicit means with which to unpack unconscious strategies.

This skill of making unconscious strategies explicit gives the programmer access to the most effective and appropriate strategies for the specific outcomes that an individual or organization desires.

2.10 The Formal Power of Strategies.

Strategies are purely formal structures completely independent of content. The strategy identifies only the class of experience in which the representation takes place and the sequential relationship each representation has to others in the same strategy. In most cases the content of particular representations within the strategy will only determine the specifics of the outcome; it is the form of the strategy that will determine which outcome is achieved and how efficiently and effectively that outcome is obtained.

People often confuse "experience" with competence—that is, it is thought that the more time someone spends practicing or doing a particular task determines how well the person is able to perform the task. If we consider the two spelling strategies discussed in the previous chapter, however, it becomes evident that the strategy used plays a much more important role than the amount of time invested. We have come across thousands of Americans who have been spelling words almost daily for thirty years and more who, because they spell auditorily by sounding words out, consistently make the same recurrent errors in their spelling, and who spell much worse than a child with a visual strategy who has been spelling for less than five years.

Because strategies are purely formal an individual may use the same decision making strategy that she uses to select an entre from a menu to decide what kind of house to buy, how to discipline her child and who to vote for in the next election. That is, she may employ the same sequence of representational systems for test and operate procedures to make any kind of decision; only the content changes.

The same will be true of strategies for learning and motivation. A banker may employ the same motivation strategy he uses to get out of bed in the morning to become motivated to buy a particular kind of car, invest a sum of money, change his lifestyle or get out of the hospital. Once the programmer elicits the individual's motivation strategy for one particular situation, s/he may run any content experience through this strategy and end up with the appropriate outcome, that the individual will be motivated for the particular content experience specified.

The neurolinguistic programmer may utilize any strategy in this way to help the client access resources for the specific outcome that s/he desires. The strategies we have found to be the most useful and generative in our work are those for *learning, motivation, creativity, belief* (also called the *convincer* strategy), *decision making* and *remembering*. We have found that this small battery of strategies includes most of the basic operations for accessing resources needed to achieve an outcome, no matter what the particular content of the situation is.

Each of these strategies will also be important to anyone wishing to organize a group or organization of individuals to work as an efficient, harmonious and functional system. Every political, industrial, legal, economic or domestic system is composed of a number of individuals. The development, operation, efficiency and usefulness of the system will depend on how each individual's strategies for decision making, motivation, belief, etc., interrelate with those of other individuals in the system to contribute to the outcomes and goals of the system as a whole. Having the tools with which to guide and assist individuals to learn, make decisions, motivate themselves, create and so on, one can greatly increase the potentials of any system and of one's own potentials within that system.

The tools and methods for utilizing strategies effectively will be presented as we move through the remaining sections of this book.

FOOTNOTES TO CHAPTER II

1. The representational system that most often performs the function of representing the incongruence between two other representations during a test is sometimes distinguished as the "reference system" or "check system" in NLP.

2. We have observed that incongruencies experienced as a result of this kind of testing are often felt in the midline areas of the individual's stomach and chest. If indeed these tests do take place between the two cerebral hemispheres, it would make intuitive sense that any incongruencies would be experienced in the midline area, the area which contains the maximum overlap of nerve endings coming from the separate hemispheres.

3. In other words the children are given a task—"Learn these ten words for the spelling test on Friday"—without being taught specific techniques to accomplish that task. Regardless of this, the "corrected" tests are returned on Monday with the usual attendant rewards and punishments for success and failure.

4. The process of tuning one's body to help access or adjust a particular representational system to the appropriate degree is called "calibration" in NLP.

5. We are here ignoring the input channel/representational system distinction. This distinction is non-trivial—consider the power of synesthesia patterns between input and representational systems (e.g., see/feel and hear/feel, such as those discussed in *The Structure of Magic,* Vol. II, parts II and III).

6. Obviously, each representational system has its own threshold independently of the others. For illustration purposes we have combined and represented them as a single threshold.

III. Elicitation

At a dinner party, the question, "How do you make such a delicious chicken cacciatore?" will elicit from the culinary artist of the house a precise sequence of steps—a specific strategy—for securing the outcome of a "delicious chicken cacciatore." If you miss part of the strategy (leave out a spice) or reverse two of its steps, it is most unlikely that you will later be able to achieve that particular gustatory outcome. Leaving out what generates the "m-m-m-mmm" response can result in an "ugh" response, a culinary disaster. On the other hand, once you've mastered the basic recipe, creative variations can produce delightfully rewarding outcomes.

Without question skill in the elicitation process provides access to a wealth of powerful and effective behavioral options that might otherwise remain as mysterious and elusive as the sensory-specific $<V^i, A^i, K^i, O^i>$ behind the Mona Lisa's smile (judging from her accessing cues it's probably primarily A^i).

3. The Elicitation Process

By the word *elicitation* we mean the procedure the neurolinguistic programmer uses to gather the necessary information to make explicit the ordered sequence of representational system activity that constitutes a particular strategy. The first step in the process is, of course, to elicit, as a single behavioral unit, the strategy you would like to model, utilize and/or modify. There are two primary ways to elicit a strategy. First, and perhaps most commonly, it can be done verbally, through questioning. Secondly, a person may be asked to carry out a task which requires that s/he use the strategy in question. The second method has the advantages of less interference from introspection, memory and congruency check cues. To extract, unpack, break down and chunk the strategy into its individual steps two major tools of analysis are necessary:

1) A vocabulary—an explicit set of representational distinctions and a notational system with which to describe any particular sequence of human behavior (like that provided by the 4-tuple).
2) A set of sensory-grounded indicators or behavioral signals within the ongoing behavior of any individual through which these representational distinctions may be identified.[1]

3.1 Eliciting the Strategy

Many strategies will spontaneously and naturally appear during the course of a conversation or interaction; that is, *people do what they are talking about.* As a person talks to you about a problem, the outcome s/he desires, or any other aspect of experience, s/he will explicitly demonstrate, verbally and nonverbally, the strategies ordinarily used to access and make sense of that experience. By being attentive and observant the programmer can reduce much of his or her work and effort in the elicitation process. As people talk about past decisions, they re-run through their strategy steps for making those decisions, like the "instant replays" frequently shown on television sports programs. When an individual talks to you about a stressful experience s/he will cycle through the sequence of representations that lead to the stressful response. A person talking about his or her difficulty in learning will demonstrate to you the very sequence of representations that is giving them the problem.

Typically, however, the particular strategy that you wish to modify or to utilize as a resource is not immediately available to the individual. In such cases the programmer will need to draw upon his or her own resources to elicit the individual's strategy. There are a number of effective ways of doing this.

a. One way to elicit a strategy is to physically place the person in the situation in which the strategy naturally occurs—to work "on location" or "at the scene of the crime," so to speak. The context in which the strategy was developed contains many natural anchors or triggers for that strategy. This kind of elicitation would include options like putting the psychiatric patient back with his family, the pianist at her piano, the mechanic in his shop, the artist in her studio, and so on. You can also gather much useful information with this method about the context, the environment in which the strategy occurs—you will be seeing, hearing and feeling the strategy in action. In some cases, however, this procedure may be inconvenient, costly or impossible to carry out.

b. Presenting, imitating or reproducing a portion of the context in which the strategy takes place will help elicit it. You might choose to mimic the tonality and gestures of the employer, for example, that your client is having difficulty communicating with, or of the sister with whom the client enjoys communicating (depending on the purpose for which you are eliciting the strategy). In *The Structure of Magic* II we presented an example in which a young mother came to us for help with a severe and uncontrollable habit of child beating. One of the authors elicited her strategy for child beating by mimicking that portion of her child's behavior which triggered the strategy. Once made explicit, the strategy was modified and the woman's problem was solved. Playacting and role playing are other effective means of eliciting strategies using this general approach.

c. By having an individual exaggerate some small portion of the strategy available to them, you will assist that person in accessing the rest of the strategy through the process of transderivational search. We have discussed the transderivational search in detail in *Patterns* I and II. It is essentially the process of going back across representations from someone's personal history, representations that contributed to the development of some pattern in the person's ongoing behavior. It may usefully be thought of as an age regression to some experience or series of experiences in our personal history that we wish to recover and apply to our ongoing experience to help us modify, cope with or make sense of it. Using our 4-tuple description of experience, we can illustrate the process in the following way:

$$\langle A_n, V_n, K_1, O_n \rangle \quad \text{Ongoing experience}$$

$$\langle A_3, V_3, K_1, O_3 \rangle \quad \text{Age 15}$$

$$\langle A_2, V_2, K_1, O_2 \rangle \quad \text{Age 8}$$

$$\langle A_1, V_1, K_1, O_1 \rangle \quad \text{Age 3 Initial experience establishing pattern of behavior.}$$

Here, each 4-tuple is a full representation of some related experience from the client's personal history. In each case something in the context has accessed the same kinesthetic component (K_1) that was originally experienced in the 4-tuple established when the client was three years old. This kinesthetic component serves as the thread which ties all of the experiences together. As the individual exaggerates the kinesthetic component, increasing its relative intensity value, he or she will begin to trigger or anchor up the other components of the 4-tuple representations from the past, increasing their signals in the ongoing situation. For example, a client who was bothered by constant feelings of intense jealousy was assisted through the authors' use of transderivational search to go back in time and to recover full 4-tuple experiences in which he had had that same "jealous feeling." The search stopped when the client was able to describe an incident that happened when he was three years old, an incident in which he recalled screaming and crying because he did not want his mother and father to leave him with a baby sitter. With the initial triggering experience (K_1) elicited, his strategy for becoming "jealous" was modified and he experienced no further problems. Any of the representational systems can provide the thread that links a number of 4-tuples together.

Similarly, exaggerating one step in a strategy will serve to access into the present time/space other representations that are linked to it synesthetically. In the example presented in the previous paragraph, the kinesthetic component (K_1) was a key step in the client's jealousy strategy, and by asking him to exaggerate it, the authors initiated a transderivational search to experiences in his personal history where the strategy was employed before. As these experiences surfaced more and more, the other steps in the strategy began to surface and to become incorporated into his ongoing experience.

The process of transderivational search is, of course, constantly operating in the ongoing experience of all people. We continually apply representations from our personal history to help us make sense of and deal with our present time/space experience. It is one of the basic methods for learning and understanding common to all members of the human species.

d. Perhaps the most frequently used approach in eliciting a person's strategy for a particular behavior is to ask him or her direct questions about that behavior. The questions we ask will trigger representations and strategies from the individual's personal history.

For instance, if you want to elicit a person's motivation strategy, ask, "Has there ever been a time when you were really motivated to do something?" or "When was the last time you were really motivated?" Similarly, if you wish to elicit someone's creative strategy, simply ask, "What is it like when you are exceptionally creative?" or "Have you ever been in a situation where you were very creative?" As people answer these questions they will access, through transderivational search, the steps of the strategy in question.

Thus, to access someone's strategy for the behavioral outcome "X", you would simply ask questions such as:

"Can you tell me about a time when you were able to X?"

"What is it like to X?"

"Can you X?"

"How do you X?"

"Have you ever X?"

"When were you best able to X?"

"How would you know if you could X?"

"What do you need to do to X?"

"What happens as you X?"

"When was the last time you X?"

If you want to elicit a strategy to serve as a resource to help someone develop more choices about a particular behavioral difficulty, you may also want to ask questions like, "Has there ever been a time when you didn't X?" Then, find out what was different about their strategies and experience at that time as compared to the person's ongoing experience. Referring to the three-point process we presented earlier

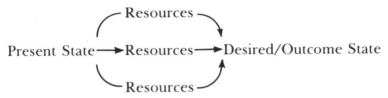

will provide a strong format within which to structure a specific procedure for elicitation in each individual case. If, for example, someone tells you, "I just can't seem to do my work right, or get it in on time. . . ." (present state), you can elicit a strategy to be used as a resource by asking, "Has there ever been a time when you were able to complete your work satisfactorily and comfortably by the appropriate deadline?" As the individual accesses and re- counts this experience, s/he will also access and demonstrate a strategy useful in obtaining the outcome desired at this point in time.

Meta Strategy 1

If someone wants to embark on a new behavioral voyage, a voyage for which no reference strategies are available from their personal history, you can still access resources for them to make the launching process easier and more efficient by asking such questions as, "Have you ever encountered an unfamiliar situation and surprised yourself with how easily you were able to learn what you needed to know to operate effectively in those circum- stances?" Again, as the individual remembers and recounts the reference experience s/he will go back through the strategy that led to that outcome.

Because strategies themselves are purely formal, they will be equally applicable no matter what the content of the ongoing situa- tion is. Creativity, motivation, remembering, decision and belief strategies can be plugged in as resources for any given context. An individual will be able to utilize a creativity strategy, for instance, no matter what situation is encountered.

Meta Strategy 2

Another resource strategy that we typically elicit is what we call "uptime." Uptime is when all of our external channels are fully open and operational, allowing us to respond easily and immediately to any appropriate external cues. To elicit this resource the programmer might ask something like, "Has there ever been a time when you had all of your full resources and potential as a person, were vibrant and alert, and able to respond appropriately to anything in your ongoing environment?"

This capacity for *immediately* eliciting resources to help people overcome difficulties or problems, or to help them change, grow and expand their potentials, is integral to NLP. Our presupposition is that *everyone already has all the resources and abilities they need to accomplish any task or to handle any situation* (by virtue of the fact that we all have access to all of our representational systems—barring severe organic damage). It is simply a matter of eliciting the sequences and reference experiences appropriate to each task or situation. If we could model and incorporate Einstein's strategies, we would in essence be able to do the same things he could do.

The process of eliciting resources in terms of reference experiences and strategies is equally applicable in working with families, groups and organizations. If a couple, for instance, is experiencing difficulties in communication and decision making and is fighting and arguing you can access resources for them by asking if there was ever a time when they were able to communicate comfortably and effectively, and arrive at a decision that was agreeable to both of them. They will begin eliciting reference experiences and strategies for themselves as a couple, and for each of them individually, in which they are able to achieve the outcome that they now desire.

For organizations and political groups caught up in bickering, in-fighting and disagreements, the same procedure will work with equal force. When the right questions are asked, people will describe and demonstrate the very resources they need to achieve the outcome they desire. These patterns apply as powerfully in complex scenarios involving negotiation, arbitration, cross-examination and team building as they do in educational and therapeutic contexts. If a group of people wants to work together efficiently and effectively, ask them—first individually and then as a group—

"Have you accomplished that outcome in the past? What would it be like if you accomplished it now? How would you know if you accomplished it now?" They will give you the strategies you need to help them achieve this outcome. If an individual is uncomfortable working with or in front of a particular group of people, ask the person, "Has there ever been a time when you were able to work with or in front of a group and were still able to be comfortable?" If the individual has no reference experience, ask them, "What would it be like if you could do it?" or "What would have to happen in order for you to be comfortable in that situation?" They will tell you the resources they need.

3.2 Unpacking the Strategy.

Once you have elicited the strategy that you wish to model, modify or utilize, you will need to unpack it and chunk it into the appropriate sequence of steps required to achieve the outcome.

As we previously mentioned, clients will go through the steps of the strategy as they access the experience in question. Internal processes often work very rapidly, however, especially those which have achieved the status of an unconscious TOTE. The client may go through a very complex sequence of representational systems in a matter of seconds. In order to be able to identify each step explicitly you will have to be able to do one of two things: (1) Increase your abilities to observe rapid and minute behavioral changes, or (2) Slow the process down so that it is easier to follow.

We strongly urge you to choose the first of these two options. Increasing your observational skills will make your work and your life much more rewarding and effective. In fact this is absolutely required for you to become a proficient neurolinguistic programmer. *There is no substitute for clean active sensory channels.*

As you begin to practice these skills, however, you will need to slow the individual's processes down at first, in order to be able to detect and retain the information that you will need. This can be done simply by asking questions like, "What happened first that allowed you to be creative in that situation?" or "What do you do first when you motivate yourself?" or "What's the first step you take when you make a decision?" The purpose of these questions is, of course, to establish the beginning of the strategy. As a general rule, you will want to find the intitial external stimulus that triggers the strategy (which from then on may involve both internal and external components of experience). So if an individual says something like, "Well I just begin to feel motivated," you will want to ask questions such as, "What happens just before that?"

From there the procedure for slowing down and unpacking the strategy into its component sequential steps is a matter of asking, "What happened next?" or "And then what do you do?"

What will be of the utmost importance in getting useful answers to these questions is that the description the individual offers you of his/her experience specifies one particular sensory channel so that you may determine the representational system for that step in the strategy.

3.21 Unpacking Through Predicates.

We said earlier in this section that there is a revealing tendency for people to do what they are talking about. One of the most effective tools for unpacking strategies is a result of the fact that the inverse of this claim is also true—that is, *people talk about what they are doing.* Through their language, people will literally tell you which representational system they are employing to make sense of and organize their ongoing experience. The words you use to communicate your experience, specifically the class of words known as *predicates* (ie., adjectives, verbs, adverbs and other descriptive language), will be an accurate transform of the way that you represent your experience.

One interesting choice as a communicator is to take people's language literally. When someone says, "I *see* what you are saying," you may legitimately respond, "How interesting! What color is it?" We accept that when a lawyer says that you should *look* at every issue from a number of *perspectives,* she is telling you to use your visual representational system. When a politician tells you that he *feels* frustrated, we accept that his kinesthetic representational system has the highest signal at that point in time. When business executives say they have *heard* about NLP, we accept that they acquired that information through their auditory representational systems. When an auto mechanic says, "That experience left a bad *taste* in my mouth," we accept that the experience has in some way become associated with a gustatory representation. Even in idiomatic language like, "I *smell* a rat," we accept that the individual has employed at some point, probably through synesthesia, their olfactory system, or, in other idioms, whatever sense has been referred to.

Some other examples of sensory specific predicates are:

a. *Visual*—I can *see* the pattern now; I just can't *picture* myself doing that; That *looks* like a good idea; I need a *clearer image* of the problem; I just go *blank;* That casts some *light* on the subject; *Looking* back on it now I can begin to *see* the *light;* An *enlightening* and *colorful* example.
b. *Auditory*—That *sounds* about right; I can *hear* your unwillingness; Does that *ring a bell;* Everything suddenly *clicked;* There's a lot of *static* inside my head; I can really *tune* in to them; *Ask* yourself if it's right and *listen* carefully for the answer; There is this idea that's been *rattling* around in my head; That has a negative *tone* to it; Something *tells* me the time is now.
c. *Kinesthetic*—I *feel* like I'm still *reaching* for an answer but I just can't seem to get a *handle* on it; It's a *heavy* problem; Things got pretty *intense;* I need to get in *touch* with my blocks; He's got a *solid* understanding of what's involved; She is so *cold* and *insensitive;* I have a *feeling* something is about to happen; *Walk* me through it.

We have presented these predicates only in terms of the three major representational classes. It will be up to you to determine from the context whether the individual is referring to internally generated experiences within the particular representational system, or whether that experience is being drawn (or was drawn at the time it occurred in the strategy) from external sources. It should be fairly obvious that when someone says "I can't *picture* that," or "I'm going *blank,* " that they will be referring to internal activity; and that when people say "Did you *see* that?", or *"Look* what you've done", they are directing visual attention externally. Similarly the difference should be fairly distinct between "That really strikes a *chord,* " (auditory, internal) and "I could *hear* the anger in his voice"; (auditory, external) and between "I *felt* bad about what happened" (kinesthetic, internal), and "Your muscles *feel* very tense" (kinesthetic, external). Others will be somewhat more unspecified like "I just couldn't *see* it," "It *sounds* pretty good," and "I kept *feeling* around for it."

We choose not to go into detail for the olfactory and gustatory senses because, in this culture at least, they are not used prominently for organizational strategies, although they are excellent triggers for past 4-tuples. A certain smell or taste can rapidly catapult you into a transderivational search. This is common for such experiences as the smell of the doctor's office, the smell of a former lover's perfume or cologne, the taste of castor oil, the smell of your father's aftershave, etc.[2]

Even though it seems that, to most people in this culture, being lead around by the nose stinks as an organizational strategy, we hope that you don't allow your ability to hear these predicates sour. Hopefully we have given you a sufficient taste of how to identify them that you can follow the scent and sniff them out for yourself.

Predicates, then, may be used to identify the steps in an individual's strategy. For example, a woman who had never heard of the notion of predicates and their connection to representational systems was being introduced to the significance of eye position in NLP. In the course of conversation the woman spontaneously responded, "You know, I really *feel* (K^i) that I can *see* (V^i) what you are *saying* (A^e) better when I don't *look* (V^e) at you as I *listen* (A^e) to you." Even though she had no conscious awareness of the significance of her words, the woman gave the author an explicit description of her strategy for making sense out of the ongoing interchange. As she listened to the external auditory output of the author (A^e) she would make internal images from the words the author was saying (V^i). She would then test the images (most likely against remembered images from her personal history), check the results through her feelings (K^i), and decide whether to operate (probably by asking the author more questions (A^e) about what he was talking about, based on her internal images) or exit, accepting the verbalizations the author was offering to her. If she watched the author, however, looking external to herself (V^e), the incoming visual sensations would interfere with her internal construction and testing process. *Externally and internally initiated experiences within the same representational system tend to interfere with one another because they share the same neural pathways in the brain;* a high external signal tends to mask internal visual experience and vice versa. This inverse function between internally and externally generated experience exists within all of the representational systems.

Because she had a kinesthetic check, then, this woman became aware of the interference between her internal and external representations through her feelings. Using the 4-tuple notation we would show this strategy in its most elegant form as:

$$A^e \longrightarrow V^i \longrightarrow K^i \longrightarrow EXIT$$

As you listen to predicates, pay attention to those which may be unspecific with respect to representational systems. Words like "light" may be interpreted kinesthetically or visually. Adverbs like "clear" may also apply to more than one representational system —you may hear something clearly as well as see something clearly. Many words like this will be specified, of course, through context, or through accessing cues (which we will detail later).

Words like "understand," "identify," "sense," "know," "think," "become aware of," "notice," etc., are also unspecified with respect to representational systems. Each of these processes may occur through any of the representational systems. A good rule of thumb to employ when confronted with words that you are not sure of, a rule that applies to all elicitation procedures, is: *when in doubt, ask.* And keep asking (operating) until you get a description that is sensory specific.

For example, suppose you have asked somebody how they begin their creative strategy and they answer, "Well, I just start getting into it." This verbalization is not specific with respect to the representational system they are using, so you will want to ask, "How specifically do you 'get into it'?" In response to this question the person replies, "I start thinking about all of the things I could do with it." Again their response is unspecified with respect to their sensory process, so you ask, "How specifically do you start 'thinking' about all of the things you could do?" The person answers this question with, "I just look at it and start to see all of these ways of using it." With this answer the individual has identified the first two steps in the strategy: "looking at it" (visual, external—V^e) and "see all these ways of using it" (visual, internal—V^i). Note that the internal visual representations follow the external input, so that there will be no interference.

The individual might also answer the question with, "I get this feeling that I'm going to really do something good." Here the individual is specifying internal kinesthetic sensations, but does not tell you what they are triggered by. In this case, then, you would want to ask, "What happens right before you get those feelings?"

You might also get an answer like, "I start going, 'Yeh, this is going to be fun! I can do this and that . . .', and so on." Here, the person is actually quoting internal dialogue, specifying auditory, internal (A^i). Again, however, if you want to specify the external stimulus which cues this internal dialogue, you will want to ask, "And what happens just before you begin to say this to yourself?" The answer may range from "I put a record on that really gets me into a creative mood" (A^e) to "I go jogging" (K^e) to "I look at the clock and see that I have a lot of time." (V^e).

You may also consistently end up with an answer, of course, like "I don't know." This indicates that the step is out of consciousness for the individual. As they answer, however, you may notice that they look up and to the left. It is here that close attention to each individual's non-verbal accessing cues will be of extreme importance. These will be presented later in this section.

The best way we know to assist you in becoming proficient at accessing the kind of sensory specific information you will require for eliciting strategies is to practice the *meta-model* that we presented explicitly in *The Structure of Magic I.* The meta-model provides powerful verbal tools with which you can decode and break down practically any verbalization into the primary sensory experience from which it was derived. We strongly suggest you look over *The Structure of Magic I* if you wish to increase your verbal skills and intuitions for any purpose. This same tool has powerful applications in decision making and management situations for securing high quality information.

Also, listen for predicate combinations which indicate synesthesia patterns. If someone says, "That *looks uncomfortable*," the term "uncomfortable" does not constitute a visual description. A visual description has to take place in terms of colors, shapes, depth, position and brightness. This utterence is rather a description of a visual-kinesthetic synesthesia—an interpretation resulting from the feelings the individual derives from looking at the phenomenon she is remarking about, probably based on past experience. Other examples of this kind of language would be:

"It *sounds* like a *colorful* place" (auditory-visual).

"Don't *look* at me with that *tone of voice*" (visual-auditory).

"It *sounded frightening*" (auditory-kinesthetic).

The Structure of Magic II contains many useful examples and exercises that will amplify your abilities to hear interpretive language and break it down into sensory specific descriptions.

3.22 Expanding 4-tuple Notation—Part 1.

Thus far we have presented, through the 4-tuple, two major distinctions with which to classify and notate the steps in the strategy that you are extracting and unpacking:

1. Representational systems—auditory (A), visual (V), kinesthetic (K), and olfactory/gustatory (O)—and

2. Whether the representational system is oriented toward internally generated experience (indicated through a superscript "i") or toward experience which is coming from sources external to the individual (indicated by a superscript "e").

There are, of course, many possible distinctions that could be made about a particular step in a strategy as you analyze it in finer detail, such as color, location, pitch, clarity, etc., each of which may be useful at some time to achieve a specific outcome. As you choose the level of detail at which you will classify the representations in the strategy you are extracting, you'll want to opt for the description which is *most elegant*—that is, the one which employs the fewest distinctions but is still able to secure the outcome for which it was designed.

We have found the two distincions presented so far to be the most essential for any adequate description of an experience. At times it may be important to add other modifiers into your notational description of a strategy, indicating which steps are involved in testing and operations, and checking the content experience being run through the strategy. We did this when we were identifying the difference between the constructed visual image (V_c^i) and the remembered visual image (V_r^i) in describing the test that took place in the visual spelling strategy. Memory (recall) and construction (imagination and fantasy) are formal distinctions that can be made for the internally generated experience in any of the representational systems, and seem to be a result of the functional differences ascribed to the two cerebral hemispheres in human beings.

Much research in recent years has been done on the functional differences in the neurological processing between the *dominant hemisphere* (the left cerebral hemisphere in most right-handed people) and the *non-dominant hemisphere* (the right cerebral hemisphere in right-handed people). The dominant hemisphere, it is claimed, tends to carry out linear, sequential, cause-effect type processing and, as a result, is responsible for the manipulation and construction of our internally generated experience. The non-dominant hemisphere, it is claimed, tends to carry out the more presentational, spatial, integrative, gestalten types of processing, and is thus responsible for much of the reaccessing and recalling of past sensory representations.[3]

Because of "handedness" (the fact that we tend to use one side of our body more than the other for many tasks), the dominant hemisphere will in many cases have a higher signal level than the activity taking place concurrently in the non-dominant hemisphere. As a result people are often more conscious of the activity taking place in their dominant hemisphere and less aware of non-dominant functions. We have found that making the distinction between dominant and non-dominant hemisphere functions (specifically those involving consciousness, memory and construction) is sometimes important for our work, particularly that involving altered states of consciousness (this is presented in detail in *Patterns I & II*). We will therefore often include some of these distinctions in our notation for strategies.

We have already used the "r" (remembered) and "c" (constructed) notation for these distinctions in this book. Using the "r" and "c" as a subscript to V^i, A^i, K^i or O^i, is redundant in the sense that we know that if someone is constructing or remembering an image they will be necessarily employing an internal orientation for that representational system. To make our notation more elegant, then, when it is necessary to indicate a remembered versus a constructed distinction, we will notate the "c" or "r" as a superscript in place of the "i". A constructed sound then will be noted as A^c; a remembered feeling will be noted as K^r; and so forth.

Another distinction related to hemispheric functioning that we consider useful is the difference between *digital* (verbal) representations in the auditory representational system, and those involving *tonal and tempo* (non-verbal) qualities. Our language (auditory, digital) representations tend to be primarily organized by neurological systems localized in our dominant hemisphere (the left hemisphere for right-handed people). Although remembered verbal experiences, such as tapeloops and clichés, become incorporated by the non-dominant hemisphere, this hemisphere seems to be somewhat specialized for organizing the tonal, melodic and rhythmic portions of our auditory experience. The information carried by each of these different processes will often have a very different functional significance. The digital portions of our communications belong to a class of experience that we refer to as "secondary experience." Secondary experience is composed of the representations that we use to *code* our primary experience—*secondary* experience (such as words and symbols) are only meaningful in terms of the *primary* sensory representations that they anchor for us. This is why we will often show the digital[4] component of an experience to be outside of the 4-tuple:

$$A_d^{e,i(r,c)} \left\langle A_t^{e,i(r,c)}, V^{e,i(r,c)}, K^{e,i(r,c)}, O^{e,i(r,c)} \right\rangle$$

Here we have distinguished between the tonal and digital portion of our auditory representational system by subscripting with a "d" for digital or verbal, and a "t" for tonal and tempo qualities. (See *Patterns II* pp.17–19 for a more explicit discussion of this distinction).

We have also indicated in this diagram the remembered and constructed distinctions as being possible subcategories of the internally generated experience.

Another possible distinction you may wish to make is that between the *tactile* (somatosensory) and *visceral* (emotional and proprioceptive) portions of kinesthetic experience.[5] Sometimes emotional or visceral representations will have a different functional significance for the behavioral task than those which involve purely external tactile sensations (pain, pressure and temperature). In general, however, we choose, for notational purposes, to class visceral sensations as kinesthetic internal experience (in the same category as remembered and constructed kinesthetic sensations).

As we said before, choose to make the distinctions you determine to be necessary to achieve the outcome you are working towards. It is sometimes important to break down the auditory digital aspects of someone's strategy into the corresponding meta-model category. For instance, we have observed that in many people the appearance of *modal operators of necessity* (words like "should," "must," "have to," "is necessary," "need to," etc.) in the verbal portions of their motivation or decision strategies often trigger the kinesthetic sensations of anxiety or stress. If they change these words to *modal operators of possibility* (words like "can," "is possible," "will," etc.) they are still able to achieve the outcome of the strategy but experience much less stress and discomfort.

You can also feel free to customize your notational system to fit your own needs, and to include distinctions that you think are important for the strategies that you find yourself working with. The distinctions we have offered here simply constitute what we believe to be the most minimal and elegant set of distinctions with which to analyze and notate strategy steps.[6]

3.23 Unpacking Strategies Through Accessing Cues.

We have previously mentioned that the verbal portion of our communication constitutes only one aspect of the entire process of communication. In fact, in our way of thinking, it often constitutes the least important part of the communication. A tremendous amount of information is communicated through the non-verbal (tonal, gestural and tactile) aspect of our communication, that typically takes place beneath the conscious awareness of most people. Further, most people are unconscious of the vast majority of representations that pass through their neurological systems as they cycle through their strategies. It is very difficult for many people to tune into their actual sensory experience, or to communicate it verbally.

By paying close attention to accessing cues and the non-verbal portions of people's behavior, you can pick up a vast wealth of information that most often passes by people's conscious attention and defies their abilities to verbalize. The behavioral accessing cues that an individual employs to tune his or her neurology to single out one particular representational system through which to accept and process some input at a particular point in time, will provide you with an excellent index with which to identify the representational system being employed for a particular strategy step. These cues will directly indicate the representational system they are being used to access. This becomes very useful when the rapid and complex representational sequences that make up some strategies are not available through the verbal report of the individual who has displayed the strategy.

In this book we will be detailing only a few of an endless range of possible indicators and accessing mechanisms, all of which are available to your ongoing sensory experience. By paying attention to the systematic and recurrent behaviors that people go through as they communicate and act, we have discovered a number of non-verbal cues which may be used to index the sensory specific processes people run through during behavioral activity. These include eye position, tonal and tempo qualities of the voice, breathing rate and position, skin color changes, body temperature, heart rate, posture and muscle tonus, even EEG activity.[7] The two basic principles that underly our method of classification are:

a. Any occurrence in one part of a system (such as the neurological and biological system that makes up a human being) will necessarily affect all of the other parts of that system in some way. When the patterns of interaction between the parts of the system are identified, the effects of the different parts of the system on one another can be predicted and utilized.
b. In humans, all behavior (macro- and micro-) is a transform of internal neurological processes, and therefore carries information about those processes. All behavior, then, is in some way communication about the neurological organization of the individual—*a person can't not communicate.*

The goal of this process of information gathering is the goal of all of behavioral science, to decode the overt transforms of neurological strategies, which are generally not available to the consciousness of those in whom they operate, in order to gain understanding of how the representational components are organized with respect to one another.

The process of discovering regularities between an individual's observable behavior and their internal processes is an example of the process we have employed to generate all of our models of behavior—*patterning*. Gregory Bateson has elegantly formalized some of the properties of this process in his work:

> "If from some perception X, it is possible to make better than random guesses about some Y, there is 'redundancy' between X and Y, 'X is a coded message about Y', or 'Y is a transform of X', or 'X is a transform of Y' . . ." ("Reality and Redundancy"—1975)
>
> ". . . when an observer perceives only certain parts of a sequence or configuration of phenomena, he is in many cases able to guess, with better than random success, at the parts which he cannot immediately perceive (guessing that a tree will have roots, for example)." (*Steps to an Ecology of Mind*— 1973)

Note that this definition says nothing of statistical verification. Statistics may support or reveal patterns but they do not establish them; nor do they determine whether a pattern will be useful or not. Statistical averaging may sometimes be used to help find a pattern, but the statistics themselves are not the pattern, as they are often assumed to be. Indeed, the behavior we are studying becomes established, not on the basis of statistical averages, but on patterns. The child learning to speak does not assimilate the language by taking statistical averages of the meanings of words s/he is learning to use, but rather on the basis of the patterns offered by relatives, friends and others as the child grows up. The overwhelming majority of children become competent native speakers of the language they learn in this way.

The patterns and generalizations we offer concerning accessing cues can be and have been supported by experimental research, but we have chosen simply to present these generalizations and patterns as we have observed them in the more useful context of our professional experience. We will present no numbers, tables or graphs.

The ultimate success of a neurolinguistic programmer will depend on the ability to observe, identify and utilize the multitude of transforms and patterns that will be constantly offered to you in your ongoing sensory experience by the members of our species; not on the ability to measure and average types of behavior or to remember numbers and tables. We offer the generalizations in this book as a way to assist you to begin the process of expanding your own perceptual abilities, not as "laws". We suggest that you develop a strategy with which to observe these patterns in your ongoing interactions and verify them for yourself until you have incorporated the strategy so thoroughly that you can let it drop out of consciousness. In our experience, the patterns we offer have held for every individual we have observed and questioned.

3.231 Eye Movements as Accessing Cues.

We have noticed that the eye movements people make as they are thinking and processing information provide a remarkably accurate index for sensory specific neurological activity. We introduced these patterns in *Patterns II:*

"When each of us selects the words we use to communicate to one another verbally, we typically select those words at the unconscious level of functioning. These words, then, indicate which portions of the world of internally and externally available experience we have access to at that moment in time. More specifically, the set of words known as predicates (verbs, adjectives and adverbs) are particularly indicative. Secondly, each of us has developed particular body movements which indicate to the astute observer which representational system we are using. Especially rich in significance are the eye scanning patterns which we have developed. Thus, for the student of hypnosis, predicates in the verbal system and eye scanning patterns in the non verbal system offer quick and powerful ways of determining which of the potential meaning making resources—the representational systems—the client is using at a moment in time, and therefore how to respond creatively to the client. Consider, for example, how many times you have asked someone a question and they have paused, said "Hmmmmm, let's see" and accompanying this verbalization they move their eyes up and to the left. Movement of the eyes up and to the left stimulates (in right handed people) eidetic images located in the non dominant hemisphere. The neurological pathways that come from the left side of both eyes (left visual fields) are represented in the right cerebral hemisphere (non dominant). The eye scanning movement up and to the left is a common way people use to stimulate that hemisphere as a method for accessing visual memory. Eye movements up and to the right conversely stimulate the left cerebral hemisphere and constructed images—that is, visual representations of things that the person has never seen before (see *Patterns,* volume I, page 182).

"Developing your skill in detecting the client's most highly valued representational system will give you access to an extremely power-ful utilization tool for effective hypnotic communication. There are two principal ways which we have found effective in teaching people in our training seminars to refine their ability to detect representa-tional systems:

(1) attending to accessing cues which may be detected visually. Specifically (for the right-handed person):

accessing cue	representational system indicated	
eyes up and to the left . . .	eidetic imagery	(V)
eyes up and to the right . . .	constructed imagery	(V)
eyes defocused in position . . .	imagery	(V)
eyes down and to the left . . .	internal dialogue	(A)
telephone positions . . .	internal dialogue	(A)
eyes left or right, same level of gaze . . .	internal auditory	(A)
eyes down and to the right . . .	body sensations	(K)
hand[s] touching on midline . . .	body sensations	(K)

(2) attending to the choice of predicates selected (typically, un-consciously) by the client to describe his experience (see *Patterns,* volume I, pages 68–76, 82–86 and *The Structure of Magic,* volume II, part I). When describing experiences, each of us selects words to describe the portions of experience we attend most closely to. Thus, as communicators, when we train ourselves to detect which repre-sentational system is presupposed by the words selected by our clients to describe their experience, we have information which we can utilize effectively in our communication with them.

"These are, of course, only two way of learning to detect repre-sentational systems—there are many others. We have found, for example, that breathing patterns are an excellent indicator of which representational system a person is using at a point in time to orga-

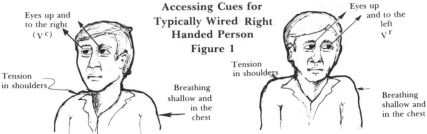

Accessing Cues for Typically Wired Right Handed Person
Figure 1

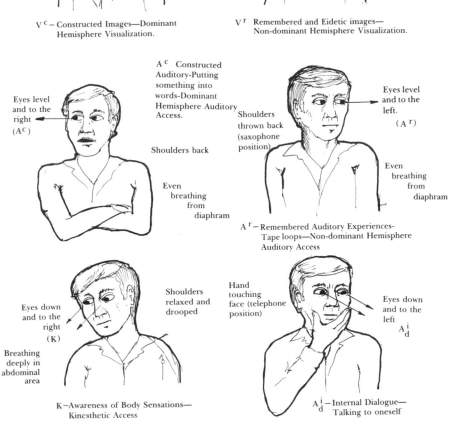

Eyes up and to the right (V^c)

Tension in shoulders

Breathing shallow and in the chest

V^c – Constructed Images—Dominant Hemisphere Visualization.

Eyes up and to the left V^r)

Tension in shoulders

Breathing shallow and in the chest

V^r Remembered and Eidetic images— Non-dominant Hemisphere Visualization.

A^c Constructed Auditory-Putting something into words-Dominant Hemisphere Auditory Access.

Eyes level and to the right (A^c)

Shoulders back

Even breathing from diaphram

Shoulders thrown back (saxophone position)

Eyes level and to the left. (A^r)

Even breathing from diaphram

A^r – Remembered Auditory Experiences- Tape loops—Non-dominant Hemisphere Auditory Access

Eyes down and to the right (K)

Breathing deeply in abdominal area

Shoulders relaxed and drooped

K –Awareness of Body Sensations— Kinesthetic Access

Hand touching face (telephone position)

Eyes down and to the left A$_d^i$

A$_d^i$ – Internal Dialogue— Talking to oneself

nize and represent their experience to themselves. During visualization, for example, the person's breathing tends to become shallow
and high in the chest. Other equally useful indicators in our experience are the shifts in the tonal qualities of the person's voice, the
tempo of speech, the color of the person's skin . . . We have presented two specific ways of detecting representational systems in
sufficient detail to allow the reader to train him or herself to detect
the representational system being used by a client at a point in time.
Once you have comfortably mastered these two techniques—refined
your ability to make these sensory distinctions—we suggest that you
explore for yourselves other indicators which allow you to gain the
same information. Such exercises in making sensory distinctions will
not only increase your ability to be effective and graceful in your
hypnotic communication but will increase and refine your ability to
have the sensory experience which is, in our experience, the very
foundation of effective communication and hypnosis."

Figure 1 depicts the eye movement index described in this excerpt in more detail, adding the tonal/digital and remembered/
constructed distinctions and the eye positions which access them.

3.232 Gestural Accessing Cues.

We also presented, in this excerpt, another form of accessing
cue/indicators involving gestural complexes—"telephone positions" for internal dialogue, and hands touching the midline of the
body for kinesthetic sensations. Telephone positions are those in
which the person leans his head on his hand or fist so that his head
tilts to one side (typically to the left) as if he were talking on a
telephone. Stroking your chin with one of your hands or touching
the area around your mouth nose and jaw is another common
indicator and accessor of internal dialogue.

People will often (consciously or unconsciously) *point to or touch with
their hands the sense organs for the particular channel of representation that
they are using* as a means to access or indicate that channel. Someone might say, "I really began to realize the importance of what
was going on," and be pointing to his or her ear—indicating auditory. More obvious is the person who says something like, "I give
myself a lot of static about that," as they make circling motions
around one of their ears with a finger.

Another example would be the person who says, "I noticed your disappointment," as she points toward her eyes, or the individual who says, "Now let me see," and begins to rub his eyes and the bridge of his nose.

Similarly, you may notice that when a person says, "That movie was really intense," she may place her hands over her chest and heart area, or when someone says "That was really delightful" he may rub or fold his hands over his stomach.

These gestures will, of course, also occur without the accompanying verbalizations.

3.233 Breathing Changes.

Breathing is one of the most profound and direct ways we have of changing or tuning our chemical and biological state to affect our neurology. Breathing at different rates, and filling or expanding different areas in our lung cavity will involve most of our body —accessing different muscle groups and changing the chemical composition of our blood (which provides the medium in which our brain operates). We have found that breathing changes constitute a powerful indicator and accessing mechanism for sensory specific states.

a. *Breathing high and shallow* in the chest (or the momentary cessation of breathing) accompanies and accesses *visual* attention.
b. *Deep, full breathing low in the stomach* area indicates *kinesthetic* accessing.
c. *Even breathing in the diaphram or with the whole chest,* often accompanied by a somewhat *prolonged exhale* (as if speaking without moving one's mouth to make the words), will accompany *internal dialogue.*

These breathing patterns access attention within representational systems either externally or internally.

3.234 Posture and Muscle Tonus Changes.

Concurrently with these different types of breathing and to help tune in a particular representational system, we adjust the mus-

culature and skeletal position of our bodies as well.[8] We have
noticed the following correlations between postural variations and
representational system accessing:

a. *Muscle tension in the shoulders, neck* and often the *abdomen; shoulders
   hunched* and *neck extended* characterize the body accessing posture for *visual* attentiveness.
b. (1) *General muscle relaxation,* with the *head sitting solidly on the
   shoulders, which tend to droop,* is characteristic of most *internal
   kinesthetic* accessing, unless the feelings are fairly intense; the
   accessing will then be accompanied/initiated by *exaggerated abdominal breathing* and *expressive or even violent gestures.*
   (2) *External (tactile and motor) kinesthetic accessing* will share the
   breathing and head position of internal kinesthetic cuing, but
   the *body will be more in motion* and the *shoulders will be held more
   broadly* (as is common to athletes).
c. *Auditory* accessing is characterized by relatively *even muscle tension*
   and *minor rhythmic movements.* The *shoulders tend to be thrown back,*
   although somewhat *slouched,* into what we call the *"saxophone"
   position* (because the individual holds his body as if s/he were
   playing a saxophone). The individual will also often have his
   head tilted to one side.

3.235 Tonal and Tempo Changes.

The breathing, postural and muscle tonus changes that an individual goes through will affect other behavioral outputs that can
also serve as effective indicators of representational system activity. Changes in voice tempo and tonality will be caused by the
changes in breathing and muscle tension in the face and neck area.
The amount of air, and the rapidity with which it is pushed over
one's vocal chords, will cause noticeable changes in voice quality.

a. *Quick bursts of words* in a *high pitched, nasal* and/or *strained tonality*
   with a typically *fast tempo* of speech accompanies *visual* processing.
b. *Slow voice tempo* with *long pauses* and in a characteristically *low,
   deep* and often *breathy tonality* indicates *kinesthetic* accessing.
c. A *clear, midrange tonality* in an *even* and sometimes *rhythmic tempo*

and typically *well enunciated words* will accompany activity in the *auditory* representational system.

Some other indicator/accessing cues for the auditory system are *tapping, snapping the fingers* and making *clicking, humming* or *whistling* noises with one's mouth.
Organizing things on one's fingers tends to accompany internal dialogue and other auditory digital accessing.

3.24 Employing the Elicitation Procedures

These distinctions as we have suggested, are but a few of the wealth of possible patterns available to you with which you can break down complex sequences of behavior. For the purposes of this book, however, we will for the most part limit our analysis to those cues involving eye movements and verbal predicates, and we will employ the other distinctions listed here only where they are important or obvious. We have found that the distinctions provided by the eye movement patterns and verbal predicates constitute the minimum number of distinctions necessary to unpack practically any strategy.

We are now ready to begin to apply all of the various components of the elicitation procedure together. Through a few examples we will demonstrate how the process as a whole takes place.

EXAMPLE A

Consider the following sequence of behavior presented by an administrative director of an organization in making a decision. She has just read a written report that had been submitted to her and must generate an outcome decision on the basis of the information contained in the report. This person could just as easily be a judge, diplomat, executive or anyone in a decision making capacity.

"As I look this over . . ." (eyes scan paper, then she pauses and takes a deep breath as her eyes shift down and to the right momentarily and then move over to the left) ". . . I get the feeling that something may have been left out . . ." (reaches up and strokes her chin) ". . . and I have to ask myself, how might this affect the results of this decision where it is so important that we have a clear understanding?" (Eyes move up and to the right where they make a number of slight lateral shifts and then move down and to the right before returning to make eye contact with the person standing before her.) "I really don't know what to say about it."

ANALYSIS

She begins with the external visual stimulus from the written report (V^e) which she has probably read in detail sometime earlier.

The visual stimulus accesses internal kinesthetic sensations (K^i) about what was printed.

These feelings then initiate an internal auditory digital response (A_d^i).

She then constructs a series of internal visual images in response to the internal verbalization (V_1^c V_2^c ... V_n^c).

The constructed images access internal feelings (K^i).

Were the decision to be made, or still in progress, the administrative director would be able to make some verbalization (A_d) in response to the feelings to either exit or continue the decision process. Her comment here, however, indicates the *absence* of experience within that representational system. (Lack of information is information.)

PREDICATES

"look over"

"I get the feeling"

"ask myself"

"clear understanding"

"don't know what to say about it."

ACCESSING CUES

Eyes scan external object.

Deep breath, eyes move down and right.

Eyes down and left, hand strokes chin.

Slight shifts of the eyes while in up and right position.

Eyes down and right.

Assume this administrative director is talking to you. Perhaps you have submitted the report she is reviewing and have some concern about the outcome of the decision. Perhaps you are a consultant assisting the person in making this important decision. In any case, you wish to access resources to help this administrator deal with her indecisiveness. In our way of thinking, arguing with or confronting the person over the content of the proposal will typically be of little value in helping her get the decision made. It is the way the individual *processes* the content (her strategy) that is important in cases like this. She has already given you all of the information you need to unpack the strategy that is leading to the indecision:

We could notate this strategy in the following way:

$$V^e \rightarrow K^i \rightarrow A_d^i \rightarrow \left\{ \begin{array}{c} V^c_1 \\ \vdots \\ V^c_2 \\ \vdots \\ V^c_n \end{array} \right\} \rightarrow K^i \rightarrow (?)A_d$$

You will notice that we have bracketed the series of constructed visual images, one beneath the other, to indicate that they occurred in the same step. We have put the (?) in front of the A_d step to indicate that even though it is the appropriate next step in the strategy, the activity within it has not reached a sufficient magnitude for the strategy to continue.

You could also punctuate the strategy into the following functional steps.

(1) The external visual experience of the written material anchors, synesthetically, the kinesthetic representation of an incongruence the administrator has derived from previous testing of the material in the report.

(2) The content of the feelings were such that they initiated an operation involving internal dialogue (asking herself a question) and generating images on the basis of the verbalization.

(3) The constructed images were then tested against one another or against remembered images (this isn't specified directly by the administrator's behavior, nor is it particularly important for the analysis of the strategy), and an incongruence again appears, in the form of feelings, that blocks the strategy from existing.

(4) Some constraint, however, prevents the individual from operating again—the first step in her operation procedure, auditory

digital activity, doesn't have enough signal strength to initiate any new images ("I don't know what to say about it.") The constraints could be caused by the feelings of incongruence overriding the administrator's internal dialogue, or by interference from other representational systems bringing up time constraints, or by the need to gather more information before a successful operation may be made, or even because the present operational strategy could be ineffectual.

From the short statement made by the administrator we can determine the essential elements of her decision making strategy. These can be represented in their most elegant form as:

$$\text{Decision Strategy:} \qquad A_d \longrightarrow V^i \longrightarrow K^i \underset{(-)}{\overset{(+)}{\longrightarrow}} \text{Exit}$$

This shows that she typically starts with auditory digital activity, derives internal visual images from that activity, tests the images, the results of which are represented kinesthetically, and on the basis of these feelings will either exit or cycle back through the strategy. We will return to this example after a brief but important excursion into notational punctuation.

3.241 Expanding 4-Tuple Notation - Part II

At this juncture we would like to add a final set of modifiers to the behavioral calculus that we have presented so far. These modifiers have to do with the relationships *between* the representational components of the strategy. These modifiers distinguish whether a step in a strategy is a *congruent response, polarity response,* or a *meta response* to the step before it.

a. We will define a *congruent* response as essentially a *continuation* of the representation before it but *in a different modality*. A "modality" difference, here, will be constituted by a change in any of the 4-tuple modifiers we have presented so far. A switch from a visual external to a visual internal representation would constitute a modality change. So would a switch from constructed auditory experience to remembered auditory experience, or from a digital auditory representation to a tonal representation.

For example, if an individual is deciding whether or not to take a swim, he may go through a strategy in which he looks up and to the left and sees how it looked through his own eyes the last time he was swimming, in his mind's eye. A *congruent* response to this image in the kinesthetic system would be experiencing the body sensations of physically being in the water. A congruent response, in turn, to these body sensations in the auditory tonal representational modality would be hearing the sounds of the water lapping the edges of the pool and covering his ears as he ducks below the water surface.

We will notate a congruent response by simply using an arrow "—→", to point from the initiating step to the one that is a congruent response to it. In the case of our example:

$$V^r \longrightarrow K^i \longrightarrow A^i_t$$

b. A *polarity* response will be defined as a representation which is essentially a *reversal in content* of the step preceding it. For instance, if the individual in the above example had made the internal image of swimming described above and, rather than experience the body sensations of being in the water, had felt frightened or nauseous, this would constitute a *polarity* response kinesthetically.

Note that hearing the sounds of the water of the pool following this kinesthetic experience would constitute a polarity response to the feelings. Hearing a worried tone of voice in internal dialogue would constitute a congruent response to the kinesthetic sensations.

We notate a polarity response as an arrow with a "p" beneath it between the two steps in question. Thus we would show the frightened feelings in response to the image, in this example, as:

$$V^r \underset{p}{\longrightarrow} K^i$$

c. A *meta* response is defined as a response *about* the step before it, rather than a continuation or reversal of the representation. These responses are more abstracted and disassociated from the representation preceding them. Getting feelings *about* the image (feeling that something may have been left out of the picture, for instance) that the individual had made of what it would look like to be swimming, rather than in direct response to the content of that image, would constitute a meta response in our example. Saying to himself, "I wonder if feeling this way means that I actually *don't* want to go swimming?" would be an internal auditory-digital meta response to these meta feelings.

We will notate the meta response modifier as an arrow between the steps with "m" beneath it, "$\underset{m}{\longrightarrow}$". We would show the three steps described in the paragraph above, then, as:

$$V^r \underset{m}{\longrightarrow} K^i \underset{m}{\longrightarrow} A^i_d$$

Remember that these distinctions are purely a matter of punctuation—of how a particular strategy step is related to the steps around it. A representation which constitutes a meta response to one step may constitute a congruent response or a polarity response to some other step (and vice versa) even though it is the exact same representation. These modifiers are not the result of physiological differences in neural structures or processes, as are the other modifiers we have presented. That is, there is no separate portion of our neurology set aside for congruent, polarity or meta responses. The significance of these distinctions is purely in relation to the steps that provide the context in which the representation occurs; they provide information about the relative contents of the representations in the strategy.

As with all of the modifiers presented, we strongly suggest that you only employ these distinctions when they are important or useful to achieving the outcome you are attempting to secure.

These distinctions are the least rigorously defined and identifiable of those we have presented in this book. They can, however, be extremely useful to you at times in identifying patterns of behavior. For instance, you may notice that someone will consistently have a kinesthetic polarity response to verbal directions ($A^e_{d,t}$)

from external sources, but a congruent response if she gives herself the directions with her own internal dialogue in her own tone of voice ($A^i_{d,t}$), even if it is exactly the same words she heard externally. Some people will have great difficulty in making decisions because their strategy involves a long string of meta responses, each about the step that has come before it, so they never get around to directly confronting the issues involved because they are caught up in their own processes. Conversely, other people who only respond with congruent responses may experience themselves as having no choices, because they can never think *about* what they are doing until after they have already gone through the behavior.

3.242 Applying the New Modifiers.

Returning to EXAMPLE A of the decision making strategy we analyzed earlier in this section, we will apply these modifiers to make a more explicit analysis of the administrator's strategy as a means to assist us in accessing more resources for her and for ourselves. We can now add the following distinctions to our analysis:

(1) The feelings that the individual has derived from her testing of the report material are a *meta* response—"I get the feeling that something may have been left out." These feelings are obviously not a congruent continuation of the content presented in the report, nor are they a negation or reversal of the content. A congruent response might be, "This proposal catches my feelings exactly." A polarity response might state, "My feeling is that we have to take an entirely different approach."

(2) The administrator begins her operation with a *meta* auditory digital response about the feelings: "I have to ask myself, how might this affect the results of this decision?" A congruent response would be something like, ". . . and I say to myself, 'yes, something really is missing'." A polarity response would have gone something like, ". . . but a part of me says, 'it's really as complete as it can be'."

(3) At this point in the elicitation process it is uncertain whether the images the administrator constructs from this verbalization are meta, polarity or congruent responses, although we can postulate

from the context in which they appear that they are probably *congruent* responses to the verbal question, "How might this affect the results of this decision?"

(4) The relationship of the feelings is also not specified verbally. However, it is likely that they are feelings *about* the images being made—a *meta* response.

(5) The final auditory digital step is a *meta* response as well. She is *saying* that she doesn't know what to say—clearly a response *about* the step.

The fully notated strategy, then, adding in the new modifiers, looks like:

$$V^e \xrightarrow{m} K^i \xrightarrow{m} A^i_d \xrightarrow{?} V^c \xrightarrow[?]{m} K^i \xrightarrow{m} A_d$$

We have put question marks under the constructed visual and the second kinesthetic steps to show that they aren't yet verified. In general, when the nature of the response is not specified, we simply show an arrow by itself "$\longrightarrow$".

To complete the elicitation process in this example, to help the person access the appropriate resources needed to make the decision, you have a number of choices available:

a. You could gather more information, specifying the relationship between (1) the constructed visual images and the preceding auditory digital response by asking questions like, "Just *how* do you *picture* the effects that the information you *feel* is missing might have on the results?" (2) the kinesthetic response and the constructed images, by asking questions like, *"What kind of feelings* do you get as you *look* at the possible effects of the missing information?"

b. You could help the individual to supply the missing auditory digital activity ("I don't know what to say") by responding, "I'd *say* (A_d) it might be a good idea to *look* at (V) some alternatives and *feel* them out (K^i)." Notice that in making a verbalization such as this you also match the decision strategy of the administrator, packaging your response to be maximally congruent with the decision strategy of the person you are assisting. (We will discuss this process in detail in the next section of this book.)

c. You can circumvent the individual's present strategy that has left her indecisive and access some possible resource strategies such as:

(1) Change the strategy she is using now, which involves testing the material to find what might be wrong or what is missing, to a strategy that operates to generate and test possible ways of solving the dilemma. The new strategy could be elicited by asking questions like *"How would you know* if this proposal were sufficiently complete and appropriate to provide a clear understanding and to get the results that are important for this decision?" Or *"What specifically do (you, I, we) need to do* in order to get the information needed to make this proposal complete and appropriate?"

(2) Elicit a reference experience from the past through transderivational search in which the individual has already employed a strategy that assisted them in breaking through to make a decision in a situation similar to the one now being faced: *"Has there ever been a time when* you were faced with a difficult decision such as this before, when after getting stuck you were able to come up with just the right answer—one that allowed you to make the most appropriate decision, getting results that were completely satisfactory to everyone involved?"

Through each of these two possible options you will elicit another sequence of representations, or strategy, that the administrator may employ as a resource to help her achieve the outcome desired. As the individual presents you, through her behavior, with the sequential steps, you would again identify the representational form of the strategy. (Techniques for the resourceful utilization of these strategies will be presented in the remaining sections of this book.)

For instance, in response to the question in (2) above, the administrator might answer:

"Well (head and eyes orient down and to the right, takes a deep breath) I remember one time I was feeling so stuck I was just about ready to totally give up and suddenly (eyes dart to level and left position) . . . I remembered something someone told me once about trusting your intuitions and I began to get the feeling that all I had to do was wait and the answer would come . . . and sure enough in a matter of moments (eyes shift up and left) I flashed on a great solution."

ANALYSIS	*PREDICATES*	*ACCESSING CUES*
Here the person starts out negatively describing an intense kinesthetic sensation that resulted from the testing of previous operations.(K^i_-)	"I was feeling so stuck . . ."	Head and eyes down and to the right. Takes a deep breath.
When the feelings reach a certain level of intensity, however, she has a polarity response auditorily, by remembering something positive someone has told her. (A^r_d)	"I remembered someone told me . . ."	Eyes level and to the left.
A congruent kinesthetic response follows the auditory digital memory. (K^i_+)	"began to get the feeling . . ."	
And a congruent visual response is accessed by the positive feelings. (V^i)	"I flashed . . ."	Eyes up and left.

We would notate this resource strategy as:

$$K^i_{-} \xrightarrow{p} A^r_d \longrightarrow K^i_{+} \longrightarrow V^i$$

Note that we have not specified whether the visual image was one that she constructed or remembered, even though she accessed up and left with her eyes. This is because in our ongoing context, the administrator is remembering the situation and may be accessing a constructed image that was made back then.

Also notice that the steps in this strategy offer a different sequence of representational systems than her previous decision strategy.

The specific utilization of strategies and resources will be covered explicitly in the next section of this book.

Taking our full toolbox of elicitation procedures, let's move quickly through another example.

EXAMPLE B

Consider the following statement, perhaps made by a client, associate, or friend of yours, that is trying to make some change in his life or behavior that is important for him, but who is experiencing difficulty in acquiring the motivation necessary to implement the change:

"I know that I should do it (head and eyes are oriented down and left then shift over to the right) . . . and I really feel that it's the right thing to do, but . . . (reaches up and begins rubbing eyes) at the same time I keep looking at all the times I've tried before (stops rubbing, opens eyes, looking up and to left but head remaining down) and haven't been able to . . . (sighing) it's really a struggle."

Here we are confronted with a case of a multi-representational test:

ANALYSIS	_PREDICATES_	_ACCESSING CUES_
The person begins with an internal dialogue (A_d^i), probably telling them to do the behavior in question.	"I know that . . ." (unspecified)	Head and eyes down and left.
This statement initiates a set of congruent internal feelings. (K_+^i)	"I really feel that . . ."	Head and eyes down and to the right.
These feelings, however, begin to overlap onto a polarity response that occurs visually. (K_+^i /V_-^r)	"at the same I keep looking . . ."	Overlap of cues: (K) head down and right —rubs eyes and looks up and left. (V^1)
The incongruence between these two representations is represented kinesthetically. (K^i)	"struggle"	Sighs (a deep breath).

We can show this strategy as the following steps:

$$A_d^i \rightarrow K_+^i \ /V_-^i \underset{m}{\longrightarrow} K^i$$

Another way to notate it might be:

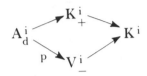

Both of these show that there are two responses to the verbal proposal of the behavior. The final kinesthetic response is about the conflict of the two responses preceding it.

Again, you have a number of options available for eliciting resources for the person:

a. You can elicit a congruent visual representation of making the proposed behavioral change to help reinforce the positive pole of the conflict by asking, "What would it look like if you *could* do it?" Getting congruent representations of an outcome in all representational systems is a very important and powerful resource in assisting people to attain that outcome because (1) it will reduce the probability of a polarity representation if all systems contain a congruent representation that can be accessed by the individual, and (2) it assures that no important information that is necessary for tests or operations involved in securing the outcome is left out of the strategy.

In fact, one elicitation procedure that we often employ and offer to you as a useful tool is that of eliciting a full 4-tuple as a reference structure for each step in the three point process of:

[PRESENT STATE] + [RESOURCES]→[OUTCOME/DESIRED STATE]

This means that you elicit a representation in each representational system, of both internal and external orientation, of what each of these states is or would be like for the individual:

PRESENT/PROBLEM STATE $\longrightarrow \langle A^{e,i}, V^{e,i}, K^{e,i}, O^{e,i} \rangle$

RESOURCES $\longrightarrow \langle A^{e,i}, V^{e,i}, K^{e,i}, O^{e,i} \rangle$

OUTCOME/DESIRED STATE $\longrightarrow \langle A^{e,i}, V^{e,i}, K^{e,i}, O^{e,i} \rangle$

For each of these states or conditions you will want to ask questions eliciting a representation of the experience from each modality. For example, for each state you will want to elicit the following information:

(A^e) What do you *hear* happening *around you?* What does *your voice sound like?*
(A^i) What do you *hear inside your head?* Do you have any *internal dialogue?*
(V^e) What do you *see around you?*
(V^i) Do you have any *internal pictures?* (V^c) What do *you look like?*
(K^e) What is your *tactile or external body awareness?*
(K^i) How do you *feel internally?*
(O^e) What do you *smell?* Are you aware of any *tastes* in your mouth?
(O^i) Are you remembering any *smells?*

Getting these representations will give you explicit information about the neurological nature of each state, and provide you with much insight into the states. Certain representations will be absent and/or out of consciousness and others will be readily available and/or more exaggerated. (As you elicit each of these representations, anchor them in the same place for each individual state, so that you will be able to retrigger them later—see the Utilization and Installation Sections of this book for a definition and exercises for anchoring.)

These reference structures will provide you and your client with an explicit means for getting feedback on the progress of your work, and will also provide explicit information on what kind of resources, in the form of representational systems, will be appropriate.

b. You can also access the positive pole of the conflict by having the individual exaggerate the congruent kinesthetic response to the initial verbalization. This can be most effectively accomplished by having the individual *stop the overlapping of access cues* that contribute to the simultaneous access of the interfering representations.

This exaggeration will also help to initiate a tranderivational search through the kinesthetic system to previous experiences where congruent motivation has occurred.

c. You may again circumvent the problematic strategy by directly eliciting a motivation strategy that you know has been effective in the past by asking, "Has there ever been a time when you were really motivated to do something of importance for yourself?"

Or, to relate it more to the ongoing problem, you might ask, "Can you think of a time when you were really in a conflict with yourself about whether to devote your time and energy to some particular program of behavior that would have profound and lasting importance to you, and when you were able to resolve the conflict in the manner which turned out be the most beneficial to you and all others involved? How were you able to do that?"

Even though the two examples presented here deal with the behavior of single individuals, the same patterns, as we have said, will apply as well to families, groups and organizations. We will present some explicit examples of how to do this as we move onto the Utilization, Design, and Installation Sections of this book.

FOOTNOTES TO CHAPTER III

1. These sensory-grounded indicators or behavioral signals are *potentially* available to the sensory experience of all members of the human species, but we have found that most individuals require a certain amount of training and practice before they become adept at it.

2. The neural set of pathways carrying olfactory information is the only set of pathways of the five senses which does not pass through the thalamus (considered to be one of the "decision centers" by psychophysiologists) en route to the cerebral cortex.

3. It should be pointed out that hemispheric brain research to date has not incorporated the representational system model presented in this book. We suspect that many of the attributes ascribed to the different hemispheres may also be attributed to representational systems. Many of the conclusions of this research should be re-evaluated from the perspective of the NLP model.

4. Digital representations may occur in any of the three major representational systems. The written symbols you are reading now are examples of visual digital (V_d) representations. Braille constitutes kinesthetic digital (K_d) representations.

5. Many of the visceral, emotional and proprioceptive body sensations are mediated primarily by lower and evolutionary older brain structures like the lymbic system, and have no projection to the cerebral cortex.

6. We can show the distinctions we have presented as a set of hierarchic tree structures, beginning at the top with the most basic classifications:

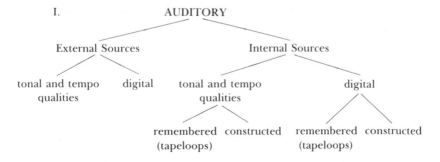

II.

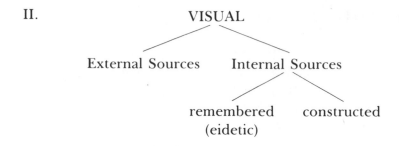

III.

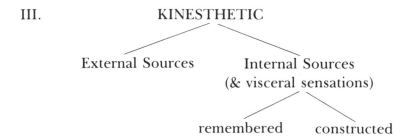

7. One of the authors of this book, Robert Dilts, has conducted research involving EEG and representational systems. Specifically, he examined the correlations between the primary, or most highly valued, representational system and the baseline EEG patterns of the individual, with their eyes alternately opened and closed. Although the research has primarily involved two pilot studies, and the methodology still needs improvement, it has shown a startling relationship between the most highly valued representational system and baseline EEG patterns. The following are generalizations of these patterns for EEG surface electrodes placed over the occipital (visual) cortex of the subjects:

BASELINE EEG DESCRIPTION	PRIMARY REPRESENTATIONAL SYSTEM
Low amplitude beta (over 16 Hz) activity when subject's eyes are open and subject is at rest. Spindles of alpha waves (8–12 Hz) appear when the subject closes his or her eyes.	Visual
High amplitude beta activity with some intermitant alpha activity whether eyes are open or closed.	Auditory
Low amplitude beta whether eyes are open or closed.	Kinesthetic (tactile-motor)
High amplitude alpha waves, whether the subject's eyes are open or closed.	Kinesthetic (visceral)

The following are some sample EEG readings of individuals characterizing the patterns described:

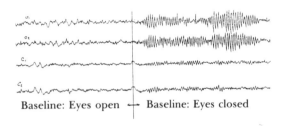

Baseline: Eyes open ⟵⟶ Baseline: Eyes closed

Fig. A   Baseline EEG for
         individual of Primarily
         visual cognitive strategies

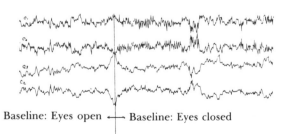

Baseline: Eyes open ⟵⟶ Baseline: Eyes closed

Fig. B   Baseline EEG for
         individual of primarily
         auditory cognitive strategies

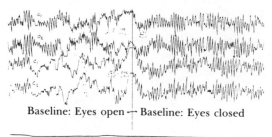

Baseline: Eyes open — Baseline: Eyes closed

Fig. C   Baseline EEG for individual
          of primarily visceral cognitive
          strategies

8. Accessing cues carried out over long periods of time, particularly those involving breathing, posture and muscle tonus, will begin to shape an individual's body. Those who have specialized themselves with respect to representational systems—people who have come to value one representational system over the others for most of their behavior—will remain in particular accessing postures and maintain certain breathing rates and levels of muscle tension. This contributes to the relative atrophy or hypertrophy of certain muscle groups and affects the body's metabolism. We have noticed that certain body types tend to reflect the primary representation system of the individual. These body types seem to be the result of an interaction between the extended use of postural and other anatomical accessing processes and the genetic makeup of the individual.

The patterns we have observed between body types and primary representation systems seem to parallel, in some ways, the work on constitutional psychology proposed by W. H. Sheldon.

a.   *A thin, tense body* (Sheldon's *ectomorph*) is characteristic of a *visually oriented* person.

b.   An *athletic, muscular body* (Sheldon's *mesomorph*) is characteristic of an individual who is more *kinesthetically* (in the *tactile and motor* realm) oriented.

c.   A *full, soft body* (Sheldon's *endomorph*) characterizes a person who is more oriented toward *visceral* or *internal kinesthetics.*

d.   The body of an *auditorily* oriented person tends to be *in between* those identified above, and is more readily identified by the "saxophone" posture described in this section.

IV: Utilization

A poet, it is said, was once strolling through the forest toward dusk when suddenly there appeared before him an apparition of the greatest of all poets, Virgil. Virgil told the awed poet that fate had smiled upon him and that he had been elected to be shown the secrets of Heaven and Hell. By magic Virgil transported himself and the poet, who was still dazed by the suddeness of this experience, to the ancient and mythical river which surrounded the underworld. They got into a boat and Virgil instructed the poet to row them across the river to Hell. When they arrived the poet was somewhat surprised to find the terrain much like that of the forrest they had just left and not made of fire and brimstone nor infested with winged demons and slimy fire breathing creatures as he had expected.

Virgil took the poets hand and led him down a path. Soon the poet could smell, as they approached a barrier of rocks and shrubs, the scent of the finely cooked stew. Mingled with the smells, however, were the eerie sounds of wailing and the gnashing of teeth. As they rounded the rocks they came upon an unusual sight. There was a large clearing in which were situated a number of huge round tables. In the middle of each table was an enormous bowl of the stew the poet had smelled and around each table were scores of emaciated and obviously hungry people. Each person held a spoon which they were using in an attempt to eat the stew. Because the table was so large, however, and the spoons had to be made so long in order to reach the bowl in the middle, the handles of the spoons were twice as long as the arms of the people using them. This made it impossible for any of the hungry people to put food in their mouths. There was much fighting and cursing as each person tried desparately to get even a dribble of the stew.

The poet was so moved by the terrible sight that he finally hid his eyes and begged Virgil to take him away. In a moment they were back on the boat and Virgil instructed the poet which way to row to get to heaven. When they arrived the poet was again surprised to find that the scene did not fit his expectations. This land was almost exactly like the one they had just left. There were no great pearl gates nor bands of singing angels. Again Virgil led the poet down a path where the smell of food eminated from behind a barrier of rocks and shrubs. This time, however, they heard song and laughter as they approached. When they rounded the barrier the poet was much surprised to find a set-up identical to the one they had just left; large tables surrounded by people with oversized spoons and a large bowl of stew in the center of each table. The one essential difference between this group of people and the one they had just left, however, was that the people in this group were using their spoons to feed each other.

Although there are a number of morals that may be drawn from this parable, it is essentially an example of how one group of people were able to turn what was an environmental variable for another group of people into a decision variable. It demonstrates that what is important in achieving an outcome is not so much what resources are available but *how* those resources are utilized. It is the process of how resources may be utilized that will be examined in this chapter.

4. Utilization

Utilization may usefully be described as the process of applying an existing strategy, one that you have elicited, for the purpose of assisting a client (individual, family, group or organization) in achieving some desired outcome, or in securing some outcome for yourself. Using this process, the NLP practitioner assists clients by running new content through the formal representational sequence of an existing strategy by packaging or repackaging the client's experience in terms of the existing structure of that strategy.

One of the major difficulties that people of all backgrounds and disciplines have in transforming the portions of experience with

which they are confronted from the class of environmental variables to the class of decision variables, is that they have no explicit
way of applying strategies and resources that they have used to
successfully complete this transformation in past contexts, to the
ongoing situations with which they are confronted. The process of
utilization provides an explicit operation for making this transformation.

4.1 Form vs. Content.

The power and usefulness of strategies lies in the the fact that
they are descriptions of the purely formal operations of our behavior and are not tied to any particular experiential content. As we
mentioned earlier, the same strategy people use to motivate themselves to get out of bed in the morning may be utilized to motivate
them to work more efficiently, to learn something new, to go
jogging, to sign an agreement or even to buy a car. Our strategies
provide the frameworks within which we incorporate and interpret
the content of our sensory experience.

The behavioral significance of any particular experience we encounter—that is, whether it becomes a resource or an obstacle, a
decision variable or an environmental variable—is totally dependent on how we utilize it within the strategies and operations we
have available to us; we can choose to transform our obstacles into
resources, as in the case of the waterfalls or the bread mold mentioned in the introduction. A particular content fact, is of no use
to us unless we can process it through a strategy to achieve some
outcome. Having the part we need to fix our car is useless to us
if we don't know what to do with it.

Any past or future experience can serve either as a block or
a resource, depending on how you make use of it through
your strategies. Whether learning or coping comes to you with
ease or with difficulty, or is rapid or laborious for you, is determined by the formal frameworks provided by your strategies.

By paying attention to context and by packaging experience in
terms of the most appropriate and resourceful strategies for each
situation, anyone can greatly expand their repertoire of choices
and behaviors.

4.2 Pacing Strategies.

Our primary means of utilizing a strategy is through packaging and presenting the content of the situation or task in question in such way as to pace the steps and sequence of an appropriate strategy that we've elicited from a client. The process of *pacing,* first introduced in *Patterns I,* has been an extremely important part of all of the work we have done.

Pacing is the process of feeding back to a client, through your own behavior, the behaviors and strategies that you have observed in them—that is, by going to their model of the world. You will have successfully paced a person's strategy when you have packaged the information which you are working with (whether it is mathematical formulas, how to work camera equipment, making fiscal policy, information about some product you want to market, a personal problem the individual has, etc.) such that the form of your presentation matches, step for step, the sequence of representations the person cycles through in that strategy.

For example, consider the following strategy for decision making:

$$V \longrightarrow A_d^i \longrightarrow K^i \longrightarrow Exit$$

This is a fairly simple decision strategy. The initial gathering of information involves *looking* at the possibilities (V). This information is then *discussed or described verbally* through internal dialogue, or the individual recalls verbal information (A_d^i) concerning what s/he sees. This is then tested (against other remembered dialogues) and the results are represented through a *kinesthetic* (K^i) response—through the person's feelings about what s/he hears or says inside his or her head. If the feelings are congruent with the words (that is, if they are definitely positive or negative) the individual will decide either for or against acting on the experience that has been proposed. If the feelings indicate an incongruence about the action the individual will operate by looking again at the situation, or perhaps by looking for alternatives (V), and the strategy will repeat itself. Note that we leave off the superscript of the V component of the decision making strategy—if the possibility(s) or alternative(s) to be decided among can be displayed easily externally (e.g. deciding three types of carpets—all available inside the store), then the superscript will be V^e. If the possibility(s) or alternative(s) is difficult to display externally, the formulation would be V^i.

If you are involved in a decision making process with this person, or if an outcome you desire depends on a decision made by this person, and you have elicited this as his strategy, you will want to utilize it by sequencing and organizing the information that you are presenting to be decided upon so that it matches the form of this strategy step for step. That is, you will first want the individual to *see clearly* or get a good *picture* of what you are talking about (rather than go into a long verbal explanation or description, or have him get a feeling for what you are talking about). You will then want to direct him, and give him time, to internally *talk* about what he sees. Finally you will want to make sure that he checks out his *feelings* about these verbal thoughts.

For instance, you might pace the strategy with your verbal communication in the following way: "I think you should really take a good *look* at this, so you can *see* how it will fit into the whole *picture* (V). I'm sure you'll find that it will answer the *questions* we've all been *asking* (A_d^i) *ourselves,* and you'll really be able to *say,* "Yes, this is the one!" You'll *feel* (K^i), as I do, that this is the most *solid* and *grounded* choice available."

At the same time that you are presenting this verbal pace you can strengthen the effect in a powerful manner by pacing non-verbally. First, as you verbally present each of the steps of the strategy you use your hands to direct the person into the appropriate accessing posture. For example, as you say, ". . . really take a good look. . . . you can see . . ." you capture his visual attention by movements of your hand and then move your hand up and to your right. This will cause the person to look up and to his left (assuming you are facing one another), thereby placing the person in the appropriate accessing posture to, indeed, allow him to ". . . take a good look. . . ." At the point where you say, ". . . questions we've all been asking . . .", you would move your hand down and to your right, thereby directing the person's eyes down and to his left. Such supporting non-verbal maneuvers greatly add to the effectiveness of pacing communications.

By packaging information this way you will be making your communications maximally congruent with the other person's model of the world and behavioral strategies. Mirroring a person's thinking processes with your communication will often, in fact, make the outcome that you are proposing through your communication *irresistable* to the individual. *A person can't not respond to his or her own strategies.*

The following are a couple of exercises that we often have people in our seminars practice as a means to learn how to utilize strategies. Try them out for yourself and notice what kind of responses you get so that you may begin to sharpen your ability to identify strategies and use them effectively.

EXERCISE A:

Step 1. Elicit a creative strategy from someone by finding out what his internal processes were at some time when he was being very creative. Through questioning and observation determine the sequence of representational systems applied by that individual that lead to the creative outcome.

Step 2. Have the individual identify some area or incident in his life or current experiences in which he becomes stuck or blocked, or in which he would like to have more choices of behavior.

Step 3. Utilize the creative strategy you have elicited as a resource for the situation by having him reprocess the experiences, either experientially on the spot or through imagination and memory, in terms of his creativity strategy. Direct him through his creativity strategy by having him reconsider the situation through the representational sequence that he runs through when he is creative. In doing so the person will automatically generate, or create, a number of new possible choices.

For instance, suppose the person you are working with is a business executive who has a creativity strategy that goes:

$$\underbrace{V^e \xrightarrow{m} A^i_d \xrightarrow{m} K^i}_{(-)} \xrightarrow{(+)} A^i_d \longrightarrow V^c \longrightarrow EXIT$$

In this strategy the person would begin by looking externally at the significant components in the situation (V^e). He would then begin to talk to himself about the object or components (A^i_d); how they operate together; asking what kind of resources may be required for the situation; perhaps describing some incident from his personal history that was similar to the situation he is facing now. As he talks he gets a feeling about each of the verbalizations (K^i) which indicates to him whether the direction of the thought is appropriate or not to the situation in question. If the feeling is negative, executive will operate by looking back out at the situation, talking about it and feeling out each of his verbalizations. If the feeling is positive, he will repeat the internal dialogue that felt good (A_d^i) and begin to construct internal visual images (or "flash" on new possibilities) that detail the progression of the new behavior (V^c).

Let's say this executive is frequently getting stuck or blocked in communicating or coping with an associate that he spends a lot of time with. He often finds himself irritated with this associate to the point that it interferes with his work, and he would like to have more choices in dealing with it.

(Note that as the executive accesses the blocked experience, he is also accessing the strategy that makes him stuck and keeps him stuck. By paying close attention you will notice that the strategy sequence the person goes through when he gets stuck is very different from his creative strategy and will be missing some of the steps that serve as resources in the creative strategy. The stuck strategy, for example, may occur because the associate of the person you are working with says something in a tonality (A_t^c) that initiates negative internal kinesthetic (K_-^i) sensations (i.e., irritation). The irritation triggers a series of criticisms of the associate inside the head of the executive, through internal dialogue (A_d^i). He then, however, has a polarity response to his own internal dialogue, and tells himself that he should be trying to work together with this associate and not blaming (A_d^i). This makes him feel as though he is failing because he has gotten irritated (K_-^i), and so on. This strategy would be shown:

$$A_t^e \xrightarrow{p} K_-^i \longrightarrow A_d^i \xrightarrow{p} A_d^i \xrightarrow{m} K_-^i \ldots$$

As we can see, this strategy is obviously very different from the creative strategy and is obviously missing the person's visual resources.)

If you were to utilize the person's creative strategy as a resource in this instance you would first have him go back to a situation in which he experienced the difficulty (either physically or through imagination). Rather than allow him to get caught up in the feelings of irritation, direct him to *look* at his associate so that he can *see* him clearly (V^e). When he has focused on the person, direct him to begin to *talk about* the situation to himself—what kind of expression is on his associate's face; what he is doing; what are some possible alternatives are for changing the situation (A_d^i). Have the person choose whichever proposal *feels* the best (K^i) and then have him *look* to *see* if he can find a way to implement that change (V^c). If he draws a blank, have him take another look at the situation outside of himself.

It is extremely helpful to direct the person to the appropriate accessing cues as you lead him through the strategy to make sure that he will be accessing the appropriate representational system. Your major task will be to keep him from getting hooked into the old strategy by accessing the same old triggers.

EXERCISE B

STEP 1. Elicit a motivation strategy from someone.
STEP 2. Identify some simple and relatively inoffensive behavior that the individual is not motivated to do. This could be something like standing on his head, driving around the block, lifting up a chair, taking the garbage out, etc.
STEP 3. Have the person reconsider the behavior in a sequence that paces his motivation strategy. That is, direct the person's processing of the behavior so that it matches his strategy for motivation.

For instance, let's say you have elicited a motivation strategy that takes the form of the following sequence:

$$V^e \longrightarrow V^c_m \longrightarrow K^i_+ \longrightarrow A^i_t \longrightarrow EXIT$$

Here the individual *looks* at the situation in question (V^e) and then makes a *constructed image* of carrying out the proposed behavior. (V^c). He then gets a *positive feeling* about what he sees (K^i_+)

and hears a *ringing* or *humming* in his head (A^i_t). As soon as he hears the ringing he gets up and executes the behavior. If your task was to motivate this person to stand on his head you might direct him to first look for a place where there is enough room to stand on his head (V^e). Then ask him to imagine himself walking over and standing on his head (V^c) and to imagine feeling really good (K^i_+) about doing it. When he can really experience the good feelings that he could get by standing on his head, ask him to hear that hum begin to come up (A^i_t).

What will be important for the successful completion of these exercises is that you (a) make sure all of the steps occur in the appropriate order and (b) make sure the appropriate kind of representation is in each step. If you left out the visual constructed step or put it after the internal auditory tonal (A^i_t) step, you would not get the outcome of motivation in the above exercise. Further, if the constructed visual image were a polarity response —if, for instance, the person constructed an image of walking out the door instead of standing on his head—or if he just constructed an image of a purple cow, he would not get the outcome of motivation. If, however, you are careful with your elicitation and your pacing procedures you will end up with the outcome designated by the strategy. An individual cannot not respond to his own internal processes.

4.21 Identifying and Utilizing Decision Points.

The elicitation of a successful and appropriate outcome from a strategy will depend on your ability to help people satisfy specific tests that they have incorporated to organize and process aspects of their experience. Every strategy will have at least one step that functions as a *decision point* or *choice point*. The decision point in the strategy is the step where the individual decides to a) *exit from the strategy,* b) *operate to change representational value in the strategy,* c) *go on to the next step in the strategy* or d) *switch strategies if the one being employed is ineffectual.* The purpose of all the information gathering and operations that we perform is to allow us to satisfy the tests or decision points in our strategies.

Consider the following diagram of the decision making strategy discussed earlier in this section.

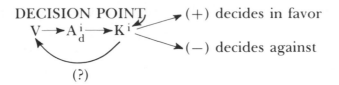

Here, the individual makes a decision by looking at possibilities, describing them to himself and then deriving internal feelings on the basis of those descriptions. The internal feelings constitute the decision point in the strategy. If the feelings are congruently positive $(+)$, the person decides in favor of that particular verbal representation; if the feelings are congruently negative $(-)$, the individual decides against it. If the feelings are ambivalent or incongruent $(?)$, the individual operates by looking back at the options and by describing them again.

Depending, then, on the outcome you are working toward, you will want to emphasize different kinds of content representations at this step. If it is appropriate for the individual to decide in favor, you will emphasize a positive kinesthetic representation $(+)$. If it would be useful for the individual to decide against, you will emphasize negative kinesthetic sensations $(-)$. If you want many alternatives to be considered, then be sure to stress ambiguity in feelings $(?)$.

Decision points, then, are steps in the strategy where different values of the representational system involved in that step (kinesthetic, visual, auditory or olfactory) will trigger different directions in the unfolding strategy sequence. What happens in the representational system at a decision point will have a great impact on the eventual outcome of the strategy.

The creative strategy and the motivation strategy that we used for examples in EXERCISES A and B contained two other examples of internal kinesthetic decision points. In the creative strategy:

$$\text{DECISION POINT} \quad \underbrace{V^e \xrightarrow{m} A^i_d \xrightarrow{m} K^i}_{(-)} \xrightarrow[(+)]{} A^i_d \rightarrow V^c \rightarrow \text{EXIT}$$

the internal feelings about the previous verbalizations either trigger an operation in which the subsequent verbalizations are transformed into constructed images, or trigger an operation in which the individual loops back to the beginning of the strategy and looks at the situation again.

In the example of the motivation strategy:

$$\text{DECISION POINT} \searrow$$
$$V^e \longrightarrow V^c \longrightarrow K^i \longrightarrow A^i_t \longrightarrow \text{EXIT}$$

the internal feelings either initiate the auditory tonal representation and exit to the behavior, or they do not. If the feelings do not initiate the internal tone, no motivation occurs.

Not all decision points, of course, are internal kinesthetic representations. Consider the following learning strategy:

$$K^e \longrightarrow V^e \begin{array}{c} \nearrow V^r \longrightarrow A^r \begin{cases} K^e \longrightarrow K^i \longrightarrow \text{EXIT} \\ A^e \longrightarrow A^i_d \longrightarrow V^r \longrightarrow \text{EXIT} \end{cases} \\ \searrow K^i \longrightarrow A^e \longrightarrow \text{EXIT} \end{array}$$

In this strategy, V^e and A^r are both decision points. The outcome of this strategy is for an individual to learn or incorporate some behavioral patterns. The person starts off by performing somephysical movement or activity (K^e). Then, depending on what the external visual feedback (V^e) is for that action the person will choose between two subroutines. Within one of these subroutines, some remembered auditory experience will also serve as a decision point where one of two other substrategies will be selected.

Notice also that the V^r or A^e representations that appear at the end of two of the subroutines are also decision points that will either trigger an operation in which the strategy loops back on itself again, or moves on to exit.

Another example of a decision point would be the situation below:

$$K^e \longrightarrow V^e \longrightarrow \underline{A}^{\underline{i}}_{} \longrightarrow ?$$
$$A^i_d \longrightarrow V^i \longrightarrow K^i_+$$

Here the decision point is shown as a comparison of steps from two different processings of the same content, with conflicting results, A^i_- and K^i_+ (they feel that they should do one thing, but something tells them to do another). In this situation, most likely, the representational system with the highest signal magnitude will determine what sequence of behavior is to follow.

Your ability to identify and elicit the appropriate representation at the decision point in a strategy will directly determine your success at utilization. In fact, your success at being able to access appropriate decisions at the choice points in a strategy will accurately reflect how well you have paced the individual. Because you are dealing with internal processes it is evident that the more closely you pace the person's strategy the more likely you are to get the representation (and thus the outcome) desired at the decision point.

Successful pacing is irresistible. During our workshops and seminars when we call for a volunteer from the audience to demonstrate a motivation strategy, often several others in the group who happen to share the volunteer's motivation strategy will begin to perform the outcome behavior when we've finished pacing the subject. Or, observers in the audience find that they must consciously restrain themselves from carrying out the behavior because they have become so strongly motivated.

4.22 Rapport

The process of pacing, whether unconscious or deliberate, is undoubtedly at the root of many of the experiences that we label "rapport," "trust," "influence," "persuasion" and so forth. When you pace someone—by communicating from the context of their model of the world—you become synchronized with their own internal processes. It is, in one sense, an explicit means to "second guess" people or to "read their minds," because you know how they will respond to your communications. This kind of synchrony can serve to reduce greatly resistence between you and the people with whom you are communicating. The strongest form of synchrony is the continuous presentation of your communication in sequences which perfectly parallel the unconscious processes of the person you are communicating with—such communication approaches the much desired goal of irresistability.

The phenomena of rapport, trust and influence derive from our ability to observe, understand and use the strategies of those with whom we communicate. Anyone involved in working directly with others (whether parents, businessmen, educators, lawyers, therapists, scientists, government officials, etc.) will know intuitively that a large portion of your successful interactions depend on your ability to establish and maintain rapport. In fact, much of your preliminary encounters with associates each day probably centers around the initial establishment of a certain level of rapport. A knowledge of strategies and the process of pacing will greatly streamline this process for you.

In our other works we describe how the process of pacing can be extended to all aspects of communication. Matching your voice tonality and tempo, vocabulary, posture, gestures, breathing rate and other behaviors to those of the person with whom you are communicating can rapidly and effectively establish rapport with most people (although in particular cases successful pacing can require that you assume a role that is expected of you, one in which your behavior is very different from that of the person with whom you are interacting—doctor/nurse, teacher/student, parent/child, etc.) See *Structure of Magic* II, *Patterns* I and II and *Changing With Families* for further discussion and exercises involving these types of pacing.

Rapport, like many other aspects of neurolinguistic programming, is quite subtle but extremely powerful in its implications and effects. Rapport of some kind is essential to any type of communication. Once you believe rapport has been established through pacing, you should continually test it to make sure you are staying appropriately attuned. The best way to do that is by attempting to "lead" the person. Once you have paced the person you are communicating with and believe you have established a secure rapport, violate your pace and change your behavior—that is, attempt to lead the person you have been pacing into a different behavior. If sufficient rapport and trust have been built up you can make this transition smoothly and easily. If the person doesn't follow you, return to pacing him until you *have* established the necessary rapport. If the person follows your lead, it will be important that you return to pacing him periodically to keep up rapport. Your leading may be as subtle as a shift in breathing rate, eye gaze, tonality or body posture. Make certain that it is sufficiently overt that you are sure you can observe the change.

The phenomenon of leading has, of course, other important implications as well. We have discussed these at length in *Patterns* I and II and in *The Structure of Magic II.*

4.23 Flexibility in Pacing Strategies

As you begin to explore your own strategies and those of clients and acquaintances, you will discover, as you pace and utilize the various steps and decision points, that some steps will be flexible and easy to pace while others will require much greater attention to the details of the contents of the representation. Some decision criteria will require generalization of the content of the representation while others will involve complex discrimination between the content details.

Many of the difficulties people experience with their strategies result from inappropriate or ineffective tests, or decision criteria. Some people are overly flexible or general and unable to discriminate, which can lead to leaving out or failing to gather important information. Others overly discriminate, often with result of missing important information which becomes lost in a sea of irrelevant "facts" (see the Design Section of this book for a more detailed discussion).

Your ability to pace successfully, then, may involve more or less attention to content detail as you are pacing or utilizing a particular strategy. As a general rule you will find that *the more you can control the details of the content of the representations that occur in the strategy, the more you can control the details of the content of the outcome of the strategy*—provided that you have successfully paced the sequence of representational systems in the strategy. For instance, in the sample motivation strategy in EXERCISE B:

$$V^e \longrightarrow V^c \xrightarrow{m} K^i_+ \longrightarrow A^i_t \longrightarrow EXIT$$

If you want the individual to stand on his head, you will want to make sure that a constructed visual image is made of the act at step V^c. If the image is of something else you won't get your desired outcome. If you want him to stand on his head in the bathtub, as opposed to on the lawn outside, you should also detail that in the constructed image. If you want him to wiggle his toes while he is standing on his head, you should detail that, and so forth.

If, on the other hand, you want the individual to be motivated to carry out a more general task, like studying effectively for a test or watching his diet, you will want to be less specific with the details of the image.

In fact, bear in mind that, *in many cases, trying to control the content details will interfere with your pacing of the person.* Often the details you attempt to provide may be incongruent with those already being generated by the person with whom you are communicating. As with all of the other procedures we present in this book, the rule of modeling elegance applies here. That is, *concern yourself with the details of the content of the strategy only as much as is required to get the outcome that you are after.*

Another important area of flexibility in the pacing or utilization of strategies is that of substituting internally generated representations, within a representational system, for those that are typically generated from external sources, and vice versa. *Because internally and externally generated experiences within the same representational system share the same neural pathways, you can often substitute one for the other as you are pacing or utilizing a strategy.* Sometimes this capacity for substitution is a natural property of the strategy, at other times it will be new for that strategy. The same substitution can also be made, of course, for constructed versus remembered experiences. There will be times, however, when this substitution cannot be made because of the structure of the strategy.

What is important for the outcome of the strategy, of course, is the information carried by the representation.

Many of you readers can make internal images that you can see almost as vividly as you can see the words on this page. Others may be unaware of internal imagery unless you are in an altered state of consciousness, but in your normal state you can remember voices extremely clearly.

For some people, such as schizophrenics, the substitution between internal & external experience is all too easily made. For others, the inability to make these substitutions can be very limiting.

The ability to cross-substitute internally generated experience for externally generated experience, and constructed or imagined experience for remembered experience, is a valuable tool for the neurolinguistic programmer and a very valuable resource for your clients. Often when we are attempting to access or elicit experiences and representations from people, to be used as resources, they will respond something like, "I forget," "I don't know," or "I've never had that experience." In such cases we simply say, "Imagine what it would be like if you could (or did)." When a person's imagination or fantasies provide the same information as the actual experience, there is essentially no difference in the significance of the representations.

4.3 Anchoring—Accessing and Reaccessing Representations.

When it is important to control the content of a representational system, as when you are working with a decision point, you will need a way to assure easy access and reaccess to the particular representation associated with that decision point. This is accomplished in neurolinguistic programming through a procedure we call anchoring.

Most of you readers have had the experience, in communicating with a client, friend or associate, of reaching a certain level of rapport and understanding that was a very positive resource to both of you. Later on, however, the flow of the conversation, discussion or negotiation changes. The interaction becomes more tense, strained or difficult, and you wish you had a way of reaccessing the positive experiences that you shared before. Anchoring is a process that allows you to do this.

An anchor is, in essence, any representation (internally or externally generated) which triggers another representation, 4-tuple or series of representations or 4-tuples (i.e., a strategy). A basic assumption behind anchoring is that all experiences are representated as gestalts of sensory information—4-tuples. Whenever any portion of a particular experience or 4-tuple is reintroduced, other portions of that experience will be reproduced to some degree. Any portion of a particular experience, then, may be used as an anchor to access another portion of that experience.

Anchoring is in many ways simply the user-oriented version of the "stimulus-response" concept in behavioristic models. There are, however, some major differences between the two. These include: (1) Anchors do not need to be conditioned over long periods of time in order to become established. That kind of conditioning undoubtedly *will* contribute to the establishment of the anchor, but it is often the initial experience that establishes the anchor most firmly. Anchors, then, promote the use of single trial learning. (2) The association between the anchor and the response need not be directly reinforced by any immediate outcome resulting from the association in order to be established. That is, anchors, or associations, will become established without direct rewards or reinforcement for the association. Reinforcement, like conditioning, *will* contribute to the establishment of an anchor, but it is not required. (3) Internal experience (i.e., cognitive behavior) is considered to be as significant, behaviorally, as the overt measurable responses. In other words, NLP asserts that an internal dialogue, picture or feeling constitutes as much of a response as the salivation of Pavlov's dog.

Establishing an anchor requires the setting up of a synesthesia pattern. "Synesthesia," as you recall, is the correlation between representations in two different sensory systems that have become associated in time and space. As we have pointed out before, a stimulus, or representation is only "meaningful" in terms of the response it elicits in a particular individual.

Natural language is probably one of the most common, yet sophisticated, anchoring systems available to us. The written words "dog," "warmth" and "love" are all visual anchors for internal representations from the reader's past sensory experience. To make sense out of the visual symbol "dog" you have to access past experience (sights, sounds, feelings and smells) of a particular class of mammals, in the form of the 4-tuple. We can show this relationship in the following way:

$$V_d \langle A_t \quad , \quad V \quad , \quad K \quad , \quad O \rangle$$

"dog"	sound of	image of	feelings	smell of
	bark	dog	of hand	dog's fur
			on fur	

This shows that the letters "dog" anchor a particular set of representations. By changing the form of the stimulus, or by adding to it, however, we can also change the representations that are anchored. If we wrote "wet dog," or "spotted dog," for example, different representations would be anchored. Some anchors, depending on the type of anchor and the state of the individual, will not elicit representations in all sensory systems. Phrases like "look at that," "this will send shivers up your spine" or "his voice was so gravelly," each appeal to different representational systems and will anchor representations in those particular systems to a greater degree than the others.

Patterns II contains a good deal of background information on anchoring and our language systems. We suggest that you review the first few sections of the book to sharpen your understanding of the process of anchoring.

Anchors, of course, may become established through any of our sensory modalities. Facial expressions (V), gestures (V), voice tonality and tempo (A_t), touches (K) and odors and tastes (O) can all be anchors for other representations. Internal sights, sounds, smells and feelings will also be anchors for other experiences. A strategy is a string of representations in which each representation is anchored to the one preceding it.

4.31 Anchoring In Action

The following transcript of a typical anchoring demonstration at an NLP workshop conducted by one of the authors ("A") will illustrate the process and uses of anchoring. The volunteer will be represented as "S".

TRANSCRIPT

A: I'd like to do a demonstration of anchoring now. Would someone be willing to come and be a subject? Someone who hasn't
had any experience with anchoring before? (A woman from the
audience volunteers.) Your name is . . . ?

S: Jan.

A: Thank you, Jan. Would you sit here please . . . I'd like to show
a couple of other things with this demonstration as well as anchoring. One of them is how to use your sensory experience to
gather information and get feedback. I'm going to whisper into
Jan's ear and simply ask her to think of a couple of different
experiences. Then I'll anchor them. As she thinks of them,
you're going to notice both subtle and perhaps dramatic
changes in Jan's ongoing behavior. So I want you to tune your
sensory apparatus now to watch and listen to any changes you
may observe in Jan's facial expressions, breathing rate, muscle
tonus, skin color, body posture and eye movements. . . . Okay?
(Whispers in left ear.)

S: (Smiles. Eyes shift up and slightly to the right. Face flushes
slightly. Breathing slightly shallow and even.) UhHuh . . . (Tonality high pitched and somewhat melodic.)

A: (Gently squeezes S's left shoulder.) Okay . . . good. . . . Now
did everyone see all of the changes in Jan's face . . . (Agreement
from the audience.) Where did her eyes go?

Man: I didn't see.

A. (turns to Jan) Jan where did your eyes go when you were thinking of that experience?

S: Huh? . . . Ah (eyes up) . . . I don't remember. . .

A: (Laughs) Thank you Jan, you did that so well . . . did everyone
see that? . . . In order to make sense of what I'm asking she had
to reaccess some of that experience and her eyes went to the
same place. . . . How about her breathing . . . Where was she
breathing from?

Man: I couldn't really tell. I thought it was in the chest.

A: Yes, that's correct . . . Did everyone hear the shift in her tonality? (Agreement from the audience.) Even though you don't
know anything about the verbal content of the experience Jan
was just thinking of, you have a lot of information about what
might have been going on. . . . I want to try another one now.

(Walks over to the right side of the subject and whispers in her right ear.)

S: (Eyes shift down and to the left. Face drops. Lips tightens. Clenches teeth. Sighs slightly. Skin pales. Touches face with right hand.) . . . Mmmhmm . . . (Tonality low and breathy. Volume quiet.)

A: (Squeezes S's right shoulder.) . . . Okay, fine . . . Now you can all see and hear that this is probably a very different experience from the other one, right? (Agreement from the audience.)

A: Her eyes went down and to the left this time, and her breathing changed radically . . . What about her tonality?

Woman: A lot lower.

A: . . . Skin color?

Man: Paler.

A: That's right . . . As we were doing this, I was attempting to anchor her two experiences kinesthetically. So I want you to pay attention as I test these two anchors . . . (Turns to S) Now what do you experience when I do this? (Squeezes left shoulder.)

S: (Looks back and forth from her shoulder to A's face, as if confused.) Huh? . . . Ummmm . . . Well I feel your hand on my shoulder.

A: (Laughs) Okay (Removes hand) . . . Is there anyone here who thinks I've succeeded in anchoring that first experience? (No response.)

A: No . . . That's right . . . What would have happened if I had anchored it successfully?

Man: She would have thought of the experience again.

A: Right . . . And you would have been able to see and hear the same changes in her behavior that took place before. You need to use your sensory apparatus to check and make sure anchors are solid . . . So . . . what do I do now? . . . A lot of people might say, "Damn, anchoring doesn't work," or . . . (Laughter) . . . "Gee, I must have done something wrong" . . . but the best thing that I know to do when you test and find you haven't gotten the desired response yet is to operate again . . . Observe . . . (Whispers in S's left ear.)

S: (Smiles. Face flushes. Eyes shift up. Breathing eases.) UhHuh . . . (Tonality high pitched and melodic.)

A: (Squeezes S's left shoulder.) Look familiar? (Laughter.) (Agreement from audience.)

A: And then . . . (Walks over to right side of S and whispers in her right ear.)

S: (Lips tighten. Color pales. Eyes shift down and to the left. Sighs) . . . Mmmmm . . . (Tonality low and breathy.)

A: (Squeezes S's right shoulder) . . . You should all be able to recognize that one. . . . As you could see, I simply repeated the process again. Now, what I'm going to do is test the anchors again . . . (Walks over to S's left side and squeezes her left shoulder.)

S: (Smiles. Face flushes slightly. Eyes shift up. Breathing shallows.)

A: What's happening?

S: I started to think of that experience. (Tonality high pitched.)

A: And now . . . (Walks over to S's right side and squeezes her right shoulder.)

S: (Eyes shift down and left. Lips tighten. Skin pales. Sighs.)

A: What's going on now?

S: I'm thinking of the other one. (Voice lower and slower tempo.)

A: Okay, it seems like the anchors are working now. But I'm going to test them a couple more times to make sure . . . (Squeezes S's left shoulder.)

S: (Smiles. Eyes up. Etc.)

A: [To audience] This, by the way, will help reinforce the anchors. (Squeezes S's right shoulder.)

S: (Lips tighten. Eyes shift down and left, etc.)

A: Okay. (Squeezes S's left shoulder.)

S: (Smiles. Eyes up, etc.)

A: (Squeezes S's right shoulder.)

S: (Lips tighten. Eyes down and left, etc.)

A: [To S] What is your experience of all this?

S: It's amazing . . . it's like . . . the feelings just happen automatically when you touch me.

A: Okay, good . . . Now, would everyone agree that I've got these two experiences anchored to the touch? (Agreement from audience.)

A: All I really did was to use culturally established verbal anchors —that is, the words that I whispered—to elicit a response— which I checked and stored through my sensory experience. Then I established another anchor in a different system: kinesthetic as opposed to auditory. . . . The anchors didn't take at first, so I repeated the process until they did . . . We are, of course, doing all this on an overt and conscious level, because this is a demonstration; but it works just as well, often even more effectively, when the person doesn't know what's going on. You just keep pairing the anchor with the response . . . you'll be surprised how fast peoples' unconscious minds catch on. . . . Now . . . I want to show you how anchors can be established through other representational systems as well. Notice what happens when I do this. (Shifts tonality slightly higher, steps up in front of S and starts to reach for her left shoulder.)

S: (Smiles, eyes up, etc.)

A: You'll notice that I never made actual contact with Jan, and yet my guess is that I anchored that first experience . . . [To Jan] Is that right?

S: (Smiles) Yes.

A: And now let's try this one (Lowers voice and slows tempo. Reaches for right shoulder.)

S: (Eyes down and left. Lips tighten, etc.)

A: As you can see, that one's anchored visually too. I never made contact, but she can see which one I'm indicating . . . In fact I'll bet I can anchor them just by doing this. (Raises pitch of voice and points to left shoulder.)

S: (Smiles. Eyes up. etc.)

A: You see, just like magic . . . (Laughter) . . . and now . . . (Shifts voice pitch lower and points to right shoulder).

S: (Eyes down and left, lips tighten, etc.)

A: How about this (Looks at left shoulder)

S: (Smiles, eyes up, etc.)

A: And . . . (looks at right shoulder)

S: (Eyes down left, lips tighten, etc.)

A: I've got the experiences anchored kinesthetically and visually . . . and I've got another anchor. Does any one know what it is? (Raises pitch of voice.)

S: (Smiles. Looks up. etc.)

A: [To S] That's right. Your unconscious mind knows, at least . . . What if I start talking like this? (Lowers voice and slows tempo.)

S: (Eyes down and left. Lips tighten. etc.) I experience the other one.

A: You can anchor with the tone, pitch and tempo of your voice as well as verbally . . . Non-verbal anchoring can be extremely profound. Think about it for a minute . . . We anchor things all of the time with our tonal shifts, facial expressions, and gestures. A change in facial expression or a sigh can change the whole course of a conversation or negotiation. In fact probably more often than not the verbal portions of our communication are the least important or significant aspect of the interaction. It's how we say what we are saying and what we are doing while we say it that gives most of the meaning to the communication. . . . Are there any questions about anchors before I go on to demonstrate how to use them?

Man: Yes . . . How long does an anchor last?

A: I guess the easiest way to answer that is to say that an anchor lasts as long as it lasts . . . Some may only last a couple of days, others will last years . . . even a lifetime. Think of language. Many words will serve as anchors all of our lives . . .

A person I hadn't seen for about four years called me up and wanted me to help him with this problem. Now I had an anchor for trance that I'd set up with him years before, so when he came over I had him sit down, and I fired off the anchor and-boom-he was gone just like that . . .

The two major things that determine how long an anchor will last are, one, how unique the stimulus you use for an anchor is and, two, how well you make the association between the anchor and the experience. For instance, people get touched on their shoulders all the time, so the anchors I've set up with Jan aren't that unique and may not last long. If I had grabbed her left earlobe, the association might be more unique and therefore more longlasting. A squeeze on the shoulder will anchor up other representations that have occurred previously when she's been touched there.

One of the reasons that language is such a powerful anchoring system is that sounds we make with our voices have subtle but distinct differences. We all know that homonyms, words that sound alike, are not direct anchors. Words like 'see', 'sea' and 'C', or 'know' and 'no', are ambiguous- that is, they anchor up more than one representation. Kinesthetic and visual anchors do the same thing. Touching someone on the shoulder or the knee can anchor more than one representation because touches there occur so often.

Another thing to keep in mind concerning uniqueness is context. If I say "I sailed the sea," there is much less ambiguity about what kind of representation I'm referring to because I'm putting the anchor "sea" into a context. The same thing works with other anchors. For example, as long as she is sitting in front of this group of people and sitting in this room and I raise my voice like this (raises pitch of voice) and I use this facial expression (smiles) and reach over and touch Jan on the left shoulder so she can see me, I may always get the response that's been anchored today. If I meet Jan on the street three weeks from now and just start talking in a higher pitched voice, I may not get the full response, because there are a whole bunch of other anchors provided by the change in context. That may change, however, if I also squeeze her shoulder and use this facial expression . . . Then I've fired off anchors in all three of her major representational systems.

It's always best to make sure you've got your anchors established in all representational systems, by the way. It really cleans up your work . . . We call that "redundancy" in NLP. Because you've got your anchor or your communications coded in all representational systems, it increases your chance of success.

Making sure that the association between your anchor and your response is "clean" is also very important. This has to do with congruency. For instance, if I am trying to anchor a certain experience in someone and all the time we're going through the process, the person has this voice in the back of their mind that's saying, "What's this guy doing?" or "This isn't going to work," then I'm going to be anchoring that voice, too. And it will be no wonder if my anchoring doesn't work the way I want it to. That's why it's so important to use your sensory channels for feedback, so that you can make sure that the person is completely and congruently experiencing the 4-tuple that you want to anchor.

Timing is also really important. If you want to make a clean, solid association, you'll want to establish the anchor at a time when the person is really experiencing or reexperiencing the state you want to utilize. Essentially, you will want to anchor when the experience or memory is at its peak or highest intensity. This will make sure that you've got only the experience that you want . . . Any other questions? (No response.)

A: Okay . . . Now I'd like to demonstrate one way to use anchoring . . . Once I've got an experience anchored then I can always use that anchor to bring the experience into the ongoing situation as a resource. That is, I can bring that experience to bear on what's going on right now. I've got a way now to be able to access it as a resource for just about any situation I want . . . For example, Jan, what do you experience when I do this . . . (Squeezes left shoulder and right shoulder at the same time.)

S: (Eyes shift up then down left. Breathing shallows. Eyes shift back up then down and to the right. Scrunches left side of face slightly, sighs slightly, looks back up and then down and left and starts to shake her head slightly back and forth) . . . I . . . well . . . I'm sort of confused . . . It's like I'm trying to take that one (Indicates left shoulder) and put it together with this one, but I . . . it's very intense . . .

A: Jan had begun the process of what we call "integrating 4-tuples." By firing off the two anchors at the same time, or "collapsing" the anchors as we say in NLP, I actually forced the two different representations, or 4-tuples, into the same time time and space, neurologically. This forces the creation of a new 4-tuple that is a *combination* or *integration* of the two that are going together. In this way you add resources to the problem state. . . . My guess is, judging from Jan's response to what I just did, that in this case the resources from the experience anchored over here (gestures to left shoulder) were not enough to help Jan resolve what was going on over there (Gestures to right shoulder). That's not at all surprising since they were just two experiences that I picked out, and the resources weren't tailored for the problematic state . . . and I'll show you how to do that in a minute . . .

What I wanted to demonstrate by collapsing these two anchors is the impact it can have. Could everyone tell there was something going on? . . . It was obvious to me through her changes in breathing, the asymmetry of her face, all of those eye movements, and so on, that Jan was doing a lot of internal processing. Most of it was probably going on at the unconscious level. Consciously, Jan experienced "confusion," which is very common when you are integrating experiences, by the way. She knew the two experiences were going together in some way . . . but at the end she shook her head, giving me the indication that she needed more resources to make a satisfactory integration . . . Now Jan, you would like to have more choices about that experience (Gestures toward right shoulder) wouldn't you?

S: Oh yes. It's really frustrating.

A: [To Audience] Up until now none of you have known anything verbally about this experience (Gestures to right shoulder) but I'll bet most of you could guess that it was frustrating for Jan. (Agreement from the audience.)

A: In order for me to help Jan get more choices about this situation I don't even need to know anything verbally about the situation, as long as I have access to sensory experience. In NLP we call working in this way- that is, without content- "secret therapy." A lot of times people are shy, nervous or resistant about giving out the details of a problem, or they literally can't put the details into words, or they don't even consciously know them. Because we work with form in neurolinguistic programming, we can get around all that because in most situations we're not concerned with the content details . . . Now I'll continue working in this way with Jan to show you how it can be done. So what I want to do, to make the demonstration a little easier to follow, is to give this frustrating experience some innocuous, non-referring name . . . like some color, for instance . . . What color would you like to name this experience, Jan?

S: Umm . . . Yellow.

A: Okay, when Jan 'yellows' (Squeezes right shoulder) then, her breathing, facial expression, skin color and so on change to what she is doing right now . . . 'Yellow,' of course, is another verbal anchor for this experience. I've just now paired it with the other anchors we have established for it. Jan, what color would you like to call your resources?

S: Blue.

A: 'Blue.' All right, we'll call your resources 'blue' . . . Now I'd like to show you how to find, at the formal level, the resources Jan needs to get more choices about 'yellowing.' The first thing I want to do is find out what state of consciousness she's in when she's 'yellow'. And the way I'm going to do this is to simply ask her which representational systems she has access to in this state . . . I already have some information about which representational systems she's using. What is it?

Woman: Her accessing cues?

A: Yes, very good. When Jan is 'yellowing' her eyes are down and left which is . . . ?

Man: Internal dialogue.

A: Right . . . internal dialogue . . . good. There is something else. You'll remember that she sighs slightly—breathing from the abdomen—and that she mentioned something about feelings. So I can also bet that there are some kinesthetics involved . . . But let's check this out with Jan . . . Jan, what I want you to do is to put yourself back into an actual situation when you were 'yellow.' And I'm going to ask you some questions about it, okay?

S: Okay.

A: When you're 'yellow' how easy is it for you to see what's going on around you externally?

S: Ah . . . (Looks up and left) not very . . . I could see things if I wanted to, I guess, but I don't look at things very much while it's going on.

A: (Squeezes S's right shoulder) Okay . . . How about internally? Do you use your mind's eye, or make pictures in your head when you are 'yellow'?

S: Ah . . . (Looks up and left, then down and right) . . . No.

A: (Squeezes S's right shoulder) All right . . . How well can you hear what's going around you externally when you are 'yellow'. Do you hear what other people are saying and what their tones of voice are like?

S: (Looks down and left then up) . . . Uhmm . . .

A: (Laughs) You won't find it up there . . . it's over here (Guides S's eyes straight and to the left) . . . [To audience] One of the things I'm doing is watching Jan's accessing cues to make sure that she's accessing and checking out the appropriate representational system, so I can be sure her response is congruent and valid. A lot of times people make pictures, hear voices or get feelings that are out of consciousness for them. So you have to check it out with their less conscious nonverbal forms of communication . . . You have probably also noticed that I've been reanchoring her as she gives each response. This helps to reinforce the anchor . . . Come up with an answer yet, Jan?

S: Well . . . I can hear some things when I listen for them . . . but in general not very much.

A: (Squeezes S's right shoulder) OK . . . How about inside your head? Is there a lot of noise going in there when you are 'yellow'? Do you talk to yourself a lot?

S: (Eyes move down and left. Starts nodding her head) . . . Oh yes
. . . a lot of it . . . I'm saying all kinds of things.

A: (Squeezes S's right shoulder) Aha . . . Okay, let's move to
kinesthetics. Do you have much external tactile body awareness?
Like temperature, texture, pressure and so on?

S: (Eyes up and then down and right) Mmmm, no . . . not at all.
That's interesting.

A: (Squeezes S's right shoulder) . . . How about internal feelings?

S: (Eyes down left and then down right) Oh yes, a lot of those
(Voice very low. Begins to tense up. S grips left hand very
tightly). I get so frustrated . . . I . . . (Lips tighten, clenches jaw.)

A: (Squeezes S's right shoulder) All right . . . come back . . . no
need to access that too much . . . How about smells or tastes?
Are you aware of any of those?

S: UhUh . . . none.

A: (Squeezes S's shoulder) . . . Any internal, remembered smells
or tastes?

S: (Eyes down and left) No.

A: (Squeezes S's right shoulder) . . . OK . . . [To audience] Now
I've got an explicit description of Jan's state of consciousness
that we're calling 'yellow'. I'll map it out visually on the blackboard so you can all see what's going on . . . (Writes the following on the blackboard.)

$$'YELLOW'$$
$$V^e - ?$$
$$V^i - O$$
$$A^e - ?$$
$$A^i - X$$
$$K^e - O$$
$$K^i - X$$
$$O - O$$

A: "X's" mean full access to the representational system. 'O's'
mean no access, or negligible access to the representational
system. And question marks mean partial or questionable access
. . . What this diagram indicates to me is that Jan is losing access
to a lot of potential resources when she's yellow because all of
these systems drop out—notably her visual system but also practically all systems involved in gathering information from external sources. Her internal dialogue and internal feelings override
all of the other representational systems . . .

The reason that we have five senses is because they are all

resources and each one can pick up information that isn't available to our other senses. We can hear things that we can't see or feel; we can see things that we can't feel, hear or smell; we can smell things that we can't hear or see; we can feel things that we can't see, hear or smell; and so forth . . . There are many situations that you can't see your way out of, a lot of situations you won't be able to talk, listen or shout your way out of, other situations you can't feel your way out of and so on.

If you want to be able to deal effectively with a situation you need access to *all* of your representational systems . . . Losing access to sensory resources is probably the primary block to problem solving . . . What I want to do is help Jan get access to those resources in her problem state by anchoring a state in which she naturalistically has access to the representational systems that she's missing when she 'yellows' . . . It's unfortunate, but what generally happens when people come up against a problem or a frustrating or negative situation is that the negative feelings or their internal dialogue or whatever begin to anchor up other negative situations or 4-tuples associated with the bad experience, rather than going right for the resources. They begin to spiral, or loop, in the bad experience, and that keeps them from getting to their resources . . . [To Jan] So, what I'd like you to do now, Jan, is to think of a time when you had your full potential and resources as a person. A time when you had full contact with the world around you as well as access to internal creativity and confidence. A time when you were able to handle anything that came up.

S: (Eyes down and right then up, straight left and up and right. Straightens posture from slumping position to erect, with shoulders back. Breaths smoothly and easily from whole chest. Smiles a broad smile. Color comes to her face.) UhHuh . . . (Tonality strong and resonant.)

A: (Squeezes left shoulder) Now that's what I call 'blue' . . . (laughter) . . . In this state, Jan, that we're going to call 'blue', are you able to see clearly what is going on around you?

S: (Smiles, eyes defocus, nods) Oh yes, very clearly.

A: (Squeezes S's left shoulder) I thought so. How about inside your head, can you make clear pictures in there?

S: (Eyes up and right). Yes . . . But I don't do it all of the time . . . only when I need to think about something or piece something together.

A: (Squeezes S's left shoulder). OK, good . . . How well can you hear what's going on outside of you when you're 'blue'?

S: (Eyes level, shift straight across back and forth.) Oh, fine (nods her head) . . . I'm really aware of what people are saying to me.

A: (Squeezes S's left shoulder) . . . Now many of you may have noticed that I'm using the same anchor that I used for the other resource, that wasn't effective when we collapsed the anchors before. What I'm doing is what we call "stacking" anchors in NLP. That is, I'm making this anchor an anchor for *more* than one resource. I'm really building up the resources on this side by collapsing two positive experiences together . . . You can, of course, stack as many positive anchors as you need in one place . . . You can also anchor the same experiences in as many places or through as many systems as you need . . . In fact, Jan, I'd like you to help me out with this as we go on. And what I would like you to do, as you access the information I'm requesting of you, is to squeeze your left hand into a fist only as tight as you are able to access the state and the information fully and completely. So, the more you are squeezing your hand, the more you are accessing the resources. Okay?

S: Squeeze my hand like this? (Squeezes left hand into a fist.)

A: Yes . . . that'll be fine. But remember, only as intensely as you access the experience . . . Now I just have a couple more questions . . . Do you have any internal dialogue when you're 'bluing'?

S: (Eyes down and left) . . . Umm, Yes . . . but it's real different than when I'm 'yellow' . . . It comments more on what's going on around me when I'm 'blue', rather than trying to tell me what to do all the time like it does when I'm yellow . . . And it's going a lot less of the time. (As S talks she squeezes her fist tighter.)

A: (Squeezes S's shoulder) . . . Very good . . . How about external body awareness. Are you aware of how your body feels?

S: (Eyes down and right. Breathing shifts to abdomen.) Yes . . . I'm generally very relaxed . . . not tense . . . and my body feels very centered. (Squeezes her fist.)

A: (Squeezes S's left shoulder.) . . . All right. Are you aware of internal feelings when you 'blue'?

S: (Eyes remaining down and right, smiles.) Oh yes . . . I feel really confident and excited. (Squeezes fist.)

A: (Squeezes S's left shoulder.) Where in your body do you feel this?

S: Right in here. (Indicates midline area.)

A: (Squeezes S's shoulder.) Okay, do you smell anything, or taste anything?

S: (Eyes straight right, down left then up.) . . . Ahh . . . no, I don't think so.

A: (Squeezes S's left shoulder.) Okay . . . how about internally. Are you remembering any smells or tastes?

S: Not that I am aware of . . . (Squeezes fist.)

A: (Squeezes S's left shoulder.) . . . Fine. (To audience) As you've noticed, this 'blue' is a very different state than the 'yellow'. (Agreement from audience).

A: Let's look at some of the differences. (Writes on blackboard.)

'YELLOW'	'BLUE'
V^e —?	V^e —X
V^i —O	V^i —X
A^e —?	A^e —X
A^i —X	A^i —X
K^e —O	K^e —X
K^i —X	K^i —X
O—O	O—O

A: 'Blue' has a lot of resources that tend to get screened out in 'yellow' . . . (S laughs) . . . What?

S: I've been trying out my anchor (Squeezes fist) . . . I like this one.

A: (Laughs.) Well good . . . Now we can give you a chance to use it . . . I'd like to offer you a context in which to make use of that anchor. You have a particular situation or state that we have called 'yellow' that you'd like to have more choices about. Your present experience of 'yellow' is a very valuable resource for you because it lets you know that you need to 'blue'. And what I'd like you to do right now is to go back to the last time you experienced 'yellow' and put yourself back into that situation until you see, hear and feel what you were experiencing then. (Squeezes right shoulder.) I want you to imagine how it would have been different if you had been able to bring some 'blue' into that circumstance. (Squeezes left shoulder.) And as you do this I'd like you to squeeze your fist together as much as you need to be able to make whatever changes you need to.

S: (Squeezes her fist. Adjusts posture to sit upright. Takes a deep breath. Eyes shift from down left to up left to down right and then up right. Skin flushes slightly. Smiles and begins to nod her

head up and down) . . . Oh yes . . . It's a lot clearer now . . . (Eyes
return to straight ahead position but remain defocused). . . . (S's
eyes become damp) . . . That's very powerful.

A: Satisfied?

S: Oh yes . . . (Nods) . . . I keep flashing (eyes move up & left) on
more and more things that I can do.

A: Good. I'm satisfied that she hit all representational systems. I was
watching for her cues. How about everybody else? Does your
sensory experience check out? (Agreement from the audience.)

A: Every good engineer, of course, will make a set of blueprints
before he initiates a project. What we have done here by reprogramming Jan's experience of yellow is a form, a simple form,
of behavioral engineering. So what I'd like to do now is have Jan
make a detailed blueprint for herself of how her experience will
change the next time she encounters yellow. How her specific
actions will be different. This is called "future pacing" in NLP
. . . Now if you have lots of time and you aren't doing covert
work, you can go over specifics with your client. This can be
done through discussion, role playing, guided fantasy . . . any
number of ways are available to you. I'm just going to have Jan
fill in the details on her own through her own imagination, using
my sensory experience of her nonverbal behavior to make sure,
at the formal level, that all of the pieces are there. Remember
that, because your internal representations share the same
neurology as those that come from external sources, this kind of
blueprinting can be as profound as the real thing . . . Jan, can
you think of a time in the near future when you might come up
against 'yellow' again?

S: (Lips tightening, nodding.) Oh yes . . . Really soon in fact.

A: Okay . . . what I'd like you to do is to imagine, in as much detail
as possible, (Squeezes S's right shoulder) what those circumstances might be . . . and how you will be able to behave differently (Squeezes left shoulder) in this upcoming situation . . .
Squeeze your fist as much as you need to.

S: (Takes a deep breath, squeezes fist) adjusts posture. Eyes shift
from down left to up left, to down right, to up right. Smiles and
nods.) UmmHmmm . . . Yes.

A: Good . . . Now do you think you can do this on your own—
repeat this process whenever you need to and use your resource
anchor?

S: (Smiles and nods.) Yes.

A: Great . . . By the way some of you may have noticed that I did something a little bit tricky when I established Jan's resource anchor. How many of you noticed that when Jan was talking about her frustrating feelings during 'yellow' that she squeezed her left hand into a fist? (Audience agreement.)

A: By incorporating this naturally occurring gesture as a resource anchor, I built in a powerful backup anchor as well. So if for some reason Jan's future pacing isn't successful, and she begins to loop in the 'yellow' again, at some point she'll probably begin to clench her fist naturally and unconsciously. But since it has now become programmed as an anchor for resources it will automatically begin the process of accessing resources . . . Are there any questions before we move on?

Woman: Yes . . . What happens to the anchors now?

A: That's a good question . . . When you collapse two anchors, they, and the experiences they elicit, essentially become anchors for one another. They are "integrated." So Jan will still know what experience I'm referring to when I lower my voice (Lowers voice) and touch her on the right shoulder. But the 4-tuple has changed . . . Just what does happen, Jan, when I do this? (Squeezes her right shoulder.)

S: (Eyes shift down and left, to down and right to up and right.) Well . . . I think of the yellow experience, but I also think of how it's different now . . . It's a lot more comfortable now. I don't have to feel bad about it anymore.

A: A metaphor that I like to use to explain the process, that is probably actually the physical basis for integration, is the response of single brain cells to stimuli presented simultaneously. Let me map this out visually first so it'll be a little easier to follow . . . (Draws on blackboard):

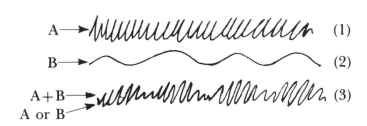

A: A group of neurologists were studying the responses of single brain cells to external stimuli, using micro-electrodes and found something like I've shown here. When they presented stimulus

"A" they recorded a certain firing pattern in that cell. Let's say the pattern looked like wave (1) that I've drawn on the board. Stimulus "A" could be a tone, a light flash, a touch, etc. . . . One way to think about it is that stimulus "A" anchored waveshape (1) . . . When the experimenters presented a different stimulus, "B", they got firing pattern (2) from the same cell . . . So this cell had different responses to different stimuli, or anchors. Then what they did was to present the two stimuli simultaneously. When they did this, they got firing pattern (3), a combination of the two previous firing patterns (1) and (2). And what is interesting is that thereafter, when they presented either stimulus "A" or "B" again by themselves they got the third pattern (3) . . . That's my understanding of what happens to the anchors after you've collapsed them . . .

This doesn't mean that Jan won't ever be frustrated again. She will always be able to access that state independently if she wants to by tuning her physical state & her accessing cues, and by anchoring it somewhere else. We could probably even anchor it in the same place again if we changed the context . . . Collapsing the anchors won't take away Jan's ability to be frustrated it simply gives her another choice. Frustration's an important resource. The ability to be upset and angry is just as important as the ability to be happy or confident. Each of them gives us important information about what's going on. It's what we do with that information that will ultimately make it positive or negative for us . . . By the way, Jan, you can go back to your place now. (S returns to her seat.) Now this is the same pattern—putting together resources with a problem state that we use, with some alterations, in helping students get through "blocks", or helping people with phobias, or helping athletes get over slumps or deal with being psyched out. We use it to help business executives solve both personal and company problems. It's a very simple but powerful pattern—adding resources to a problematic state . . . In some cases where a specific outcome is desired we will make the blueprint for the desired state first, and anchor it of course, so we can use it as a way of choosing the appropriate resources to access . . . This simple anchoring process can increase your ability to do things and help other people do things, no matter what it is that you do . . .

As we mentioned at the beginning of the transcript, this is an example of only one use of the process of anchoring. We will be covering a number of other uses throughout the remainder of this book—especially in the Installation Section.

Anchors and accessing cues will be your major tools in the utilization of strategies. They will provide a systematic means of being able to trigger the appropriate representations at the appropriate slot in the strategy. Before you go on to the rest of the book, we invite you to think about experiences that you have had in which you have been anchored: certain tones of voice, words, facial expressions, touches and so on, that trigger powerful or subtle experiences in you. Also consider ways in which you have, perhaps unknowingly, anchored experiences in other people: when you've said something or done something that elicited a response in another person that you didn't expect. Perhaps you've had an experience in which someone showed great warmth toward you because you looked or sounded like a close relative or friend of his, and this anchored feelings of closeness in them. Or perhaps you have developed a special saying, facial expression or gesture that you can always use to get a smile or chuckle out of someone you know.

The words "Mary had a little . . ." are probably an anchor for the word "lamb" for many of you—as well as an anchor for the melody that accompanies the lyrics.

Before proceeding further, practice the following simple anchoring exercises to help you begin to get some conscious skill in using them:

EXERCISE A—Establishing An Anchor for Yourself.

This exercise is designed to give you a personal feel for the process of anchoring and to help you distinguish between various states of consciousness in yourself. This is essentially an exercise in biofeedback—where the feedback comes from your own sensory channels.

PART I—The "Uptime" Anchor.

Step 1. Find a place, either indoors or outdoors, where you can sit or walk around for a while and enjoy the world around you.

Step 2. As you observe your surroundings, practice focusing and tuning your awareness of your external environment to each of your representational systems:

a) *seeing* things—using both panoramic and detailed viewing of the various objects, colors and movements in your environment.

b) *feeling* the temperature of the air, the textures, shapes and hardness of the objects around you, and the feelings of your skin and muscles as you sit or move through the environment.

c) *listening* for the differences in the tones and location origins of the various sounds around you—and for the changes in your breathing and the pitch and tempo of any voices near you.

d) *smelling* the air and the objects around you—noticing which smells are sharper, which are more subtle—and, if you wish, take note of any changes in the taste in your mouth.

As you access each of these systems, you may screen out your other channels by closing your eyes and plugging your ears and nose in various combinations. Be sure to access each system as completely as possible without any internal dialogue, internal pictures or feelings.

Step 3. With your right hand grab hold of your left wrist. As you judge that you are able to access each system in succession, squeeze your wrist—only as tightly as you are able to completely access the sensory channel you are using. The more you can see, hear, feel and smell clearly the experiences around you, the tighter you squeeze your wrist.

Step 4. Begin to tune into all representational systems simultaneously so that you attention is completely focused outside of you through all of your channels. Squeeze your wrist only as tightly as you are able to do this successfully.

Step 5. Keep repeating the process until all you have to do is reach over and squeeze your wrist and your attention automatically begins to turn outside of you to your external environment, without any conscious effort.

PART II—The "Downtime" Anchor.

Step 1. Find a place where you can sit or lie down and be completely alone with yourself.

Step 2. Turn your attention inward and practice accessing each of your representational systems internally:

a) *Listen* to any internal voices, dialogues, tunes or sounds in your head. Practice making up tunes and conversations as well as remembering things that you've already heard.

b) *Look* through your mind's eye at scenes and details of objects and events that you've made up and that you've actually seen before.

c) *Get in touch* with internal feelings. Pay attention to the similarities and differences between emotional and visceral body sensations and memories of things that you've felt with your hands and skin. Make up things to feel in fantasy.

d) *Smell* and *taste,* in your imagination, things and places that you remember and fantasize.

Again, access each system as completely and separately as you can. You may want to try a simple task, like imagining yourself getting up from your place and opening a door, utilizing each system by itself, in succession. That is, first limit yourself to only fantasizing the action visually; then go back and just talk yourself through it, or do it by sound; then go through just the feelings of the action and so on.

Most of you will probably notice, with this exercise and with Part I, that you are able to access particular representational systems with varying degrees of ease—it may be easier for you to get in touch with feelings than to tune in to internal dialogue or to make internal pictures; or vice versa. You can feel free to use this as feedback for which systems you need to develop or enrich, or practice with.

Step 3. Fold your hands. As you judge that you are able to access each representational system as completely as you can, squeeze your hands together—only as tightly as you are able to completely access that system.

Step 4. Begin to access all systems internally at the same time (you may put all of your senses to work on a single experience, or tune each system to a different experience—seeing one thing, talking to yourself about something else, feeling something new, and smelling something that doesn't have anything to do with the others). Squeeze your hands together only as tightly as you are able to do this successfully.

Step 5. Keep repeating the process until all you have to do is sit down and clasp your hands together tightly and your focus of attention automatically turns inward without any conscious effort.

As you do this exercise, pay attention to the cues and distinctions that allow you to access and discriminate between the representational systems you are accessing and the states you are creating. These anchors will be very valuable to you as they will give you quick access to full sensory experiences externally oriented for gathering information (that is, "uptime"); and internally oriented for extended processing of information ("downtime").

You may also wish to establish anchors for yourself in this way for other states or experiences such as relaxation, creativity, motivation, etc. The pattern of this process is that embodied by all biofeedback: A certain state picked and identified. As the individual accesses that state he is given feedback for it by way of a particular stimulus—the tightness of the grip in this case (K^e); it is done through tones (A^e), or by intensity or color of light or the position of an arm on a dial (V^e) in other biofeedback processes. After a while the feedback stimulus and the target state become associated (the stimulus becomes an anchor for the state) so that the mere presentation of the feedback stimulus anchors and contributes to to the development of the target state.

You may wish to experiment with internal anchors as well. For instance, if you wish to be able to access a state of relaxation easily you can begin by imaging a color vividly in your mind's eye. Begin to allow your body to relax as much as possible, lowering your breathing and relaxing any tense muscles. As you reach the state you desire, watch the color change to a color that most exemplifies that state for you (from orange to blue for example). You may also wish to allow the color to change configuration (watch it drip down into your stomach as it changes color). Keep practicing until you are able to access the state of relaxation by simply imagining the color. Then, when you notice you are tense or anxious, and you wish to have a choice about the condition, all you need to do is simply close your eyes momentarily, take a deep breath and imagine the color, and it will access the desired state.

Many forms of meditation involve auditory anchors like mantras and chanting to access downtime states or relaxation. The words or sounds are repeated as the individual enters the state. Later, repeating the sounds will readily anchor up the designated state.

Incidentally, if you ever want to reprogram or "get rid of" any anchors you have established, all you need to do is collapse the anchor with some other anchor or experience. For example, you

could squeeze your wrist at the same time you fire off some other
anchor or when you are experiencing some other state. Remember, though, that when you fire off the anchor you wish to reprogram it will influence your ongoing experience, so that when you
are reprogramming yourself be sure to pick anchors, states and/or
experiences that are of equal intensity and strength to the one you
are changing.

If you wish to strengthen an anchor be sure you pick a stimulus
that you can keep fairly autonomous and that won't be accidently
fired off and integrated with others.

EXERCISE B—Collapsing Anchors With Someone Else.

This exercise will help you to get a feel for consciously using
anchoring with someone else.

Step 1. Sit down with someone you can be comfortable with and
ask him to tell you about a time when he was particularly resourceful, creative and confident.

Step 2. As the individual remembers and recounts this experience,
reach out and kinesthetically anchor it by placing your left hand on
his right knee. Use your sensory abilities as feedback to be sure that
you are only touching the person's knee when he is accessing the
experience he is describing.

Step 3. (Optional). Get a full 4-tuple for the experience by taking
the person through each of his sensory systems, focusing both
internally and externally, and checking which are operating during
the state. For example:

How do you feel inside when you are in this state? (K^i)

Do you have any external body awareness? (K^e)

Where and how fast are you breathing when you are in this state?
(K^e)

Do you have any internal dialogue? (A_d^i)

How well do you hear what's happening around you? (A^e)

What does your own voice sound like when you are in this state?
(A_t^e)

Can you see clearly what is going on around you? (V^e)

Do you see anything in your head? (V^i)

How well can you smell in this state? (O^e)

Are you remembering any smells or tastes? (O^i)

Use your sensory experience to make sure that they are checking each of these systems, and calibrate to make sure all accessing is of the same intensity. As they access each portion of the experience anchor each one on the left knee. You will then have anchored the entire 4-tuple. We can notate this in the following way:

$$\text{\large ⚓}_1 \longrightarrow \langle A^{e,i}_1, V^{e,i}_1, K^{e,i}_1, O^{e,i}_1 \rangle$$

This shows that anchor number one, " $⚓_1$ ", elicits state number one.

Step 4. Continue to test and reinforce the anchor until you are satisfied that it has been solidly established. It is not necessary that the individual know consciously what you are doing for the anchor to be effective. Nor will the person's awareness of what you are doing interfere with the process, unless it is keeping him from accessing the information you want. It will be up to you to decide whether to tell the person what you are doing or not. (You may also wish to have the person establish a self controlled anchor as a resource.)

Step 5. Next, ask the individual if there is some situation or task in which he typically find himself inefficient or blocked. As the individual discusses the situation, anchor it by reaching out with your right hand and placing it on the person's left knee. Again, use your sensory experience to make sure you are anchoring at the appropriate times.

Step 6. (Optional) Repeat the process of getting a full 4-tuple representation of this second state, anchoring each aspect of the 4-tuple as you observe it come up. You will then have an anchor for the problematic state:

$$\text{\large ⚓}_2 \longrightarrow \langle A^{e,i}_2, V^{e,i}_2, K^{e,i}_2, O^{e,i}_2 \rangle$$

Step 7. Keep testing and reinforcing the anchor until you are satisfied that it has been solidly established.

Step 8. Reach out with both hands and touch off both anchors simultaneously. This will force the two patterns of behavior (as represented by the 4-tuples) into the same time and space neurologically such that a third 4-tuple (or sometimes a set of 4-tuples) will be formed that integrates the other two. The resource experience will be combined with the inefficient experience in such a way that the individual will typically spontaneously generate new choices of behavior in the situation that has formerly been a problem.

We can notate the process of integration as:

$$\text{⚓}_1 + \text{⚓}_2 \longrightarrow \langle A^{e,i}_{(1*2)} , V^{e,i}_{(1*2)} , K^{e,i}_{(1*2)} , O^{e,i}_{(1*2)} \rangle$$

This shows that at the simultaneous firing of the two anchors, the 4-tuples combine to make a third. The star function, "*", represents a function of combination of the sensory parameters of the two states. The manner in which this combination takes place will, of course, not be simply additive but will depend on the strength and content of the representations, and the neurological attributes of the individual.

This exercise involves the use of tactile anchors. We suggest that you also go back through the exercise with a different person (or with the same person, using different subjects) and repeat the process using visual, auditory and olfactory anchors. You can generate these anchors through your own behavior, with gestures and tonal and tempo changes, and also use other available stimuli.

For example, you may use almond and vanilla extract as olfactory anchors. For a visual anchor you may instruct an individual to fold a piece of paper in half and on one side have the person draw a picture representing himself in a problematic state. The kinds of questions listed earlier would be asked to elicit a full representation that would become anchored to the drawing. Then have the individual turn the half-page over and draw a picture representing a resourceful state, and again elicit a full representation. Finally, have the individual open the paper so that both sides are showing simultaneously. This will visually accomplish the same result as the simultaneous firing of the two kinesthetic anchors.

The same process may also be undertaken by having the individual choose two songs or pieces of music that are representative of the two states in question, by eliciting a full representation as the song is being played, and then playing both of the songs simultaneously.

EXERCISE C—Creating Experience Through Anchoring:

In the same way that 4-tuples may be integrated by anchoring them together, various representations from completely different 4-tuples may be anchored together to create a new 4-tuple. Because internally generated experience utilizes the same neural pathways as externally generated or "actual" experiences, creating new 4-tuples in this way can be as powerful and effective as if the individual had "really" had the experience.

In this process the external sensory parameters of one 4-tuple (identifying the external context of the experience) are generally tied with internally generated representations (making up the individual's internal response) of another 4-tuple.

Step 1. Sit down with an individual and ask him if there is any situation in his life that he recurrently finds himself in that he isn't comfortable but would like to have the choice of enjoying.

Step 2. As he describes the situation reach out and touch his left knee *only* when he describes the external aspects of the situation. Ask questions about the external context of the situation—what the situation looks, sounds, feels and smells like *externally*—and anchor them. We will call this situation "1". This process can be notated as:

$$\langle A_1^{i,e}, V_1^{i,e}, K_1^{i,e}, O_1^{i,e} \rangle \longrightarrow \overset{\varrho}{\psi}_1 \langle A_1^e, V_1^e, K_1^e, O_1^e \rangle$$

Step 3. Ask the individual to describe something that they enjoy. Anchor only those representations that are indicative of the individual's internal response by placing your hand on their right knee. Ask questions concerning *internal* dialogues, images, feelings, tones and smells and anchor each respectively. We can show this visually as:

$$\langle A_2^{i,e}, V_2^{i,e}, K_2^{i,e}, O_2^{i,e} \rangle \longrightarrow \overset{\varrho}{\psi}_2 \langle A_2^i, V_2^i, K_2^i, O_2^i \rangle$$

Step 4. Simultaneously touch off the anchor for the external representations of the context which is typically unenjoyable and the anchor for the internal response to the situation that is enjoyable. This serves to pair the representations such that the external representations can trigger the enjoyable internal representations. If the individual has recreated the external circumstances closely enough, then when he or she returns to that environment it should also serve to trigger the enjoyable response. This can be shown as:

$$\Psi_1 + \Psi_2 \longrightarrow \langle A_1^e, A_2^i, V_1^e, V_2^i, K_1^e, K_2^i, O_1^e, O_2^i \rangle$$

As an added measure, you may ask the individual to imagine what the experience would be like if he were able to enjoy himself in that situation as you "fire off" the anchors in unison. You may also ask the individual to think of some time in the future when he will encounter this situation and, as you hold both of the anchors, ask him to describe how his experience will change in this instance. This kind of process is called a *"future pace"*, and helps to insure that the response becomes wired to the appropriate stimuli. NOTE: It is obvious that some of those representations that we have superscripted "e" in our representations of the 4-tuples will actually be internally generated memories at the point in time that you are eliciting them, rather than external events in the individual's ongoing environment. We have used the superscript "e" to establish the difference between what was generated internally and externally in the context or state in question, as that is very important information. Any possible mix-ups may be avoided, of course, by having the individual reproduce the effect of the experience in the ongoing context before you anchor it. For instance, you can ask, "Can you see me as clearly as you saw that other person in the situation you are talking about?"

4.32 Anchoring and Utilization.

Anchoring and accessing cues (you can think of accessing cues, incidently, as self-established anchors), as we have said, are a means to elicit the appropriate representation or representational system at the appropriate position in the strategy. They offer an often surprisingly powerful means to influence the outcomes of strategies. If, for example, you would like someone to decide in favor of something you can ask him if he has ever made a decision that he was very sure of and that generated positive results for him. As he accesses the experience, ask him *how* he knew to decide in favor of the proposition (what you are asking for here is what value in the representational system is required for a positive response at the decision point in the strategy). As the person accesses the representation (it may be "Well, I said to myself...", or "I got this flash...", or "It felt right...") anchor it in whatever means is most appropriate for the situation. Later, as you are pacing the person through his decision strategy, fire off the anchor when you get to the decision point in his strategy. This will exert a great deal of influence toward a positive outcome from the strategy. Sometimes, if you get a good anchor, you can simply elicit the appropriate decision value in the person and get the outcome without the having to go through the rest of the strategy.

You can accomplish the same thing through instructions, like, " ... as you continue to see that image, take a deep breath and think of a time you felt really good ..." Or you can do it indirectly by presenting the content in question and then switching the subject to something that the person enjoys, so that the content you are discussing becomes associated with positive experiences.

Most classical conditioning involves the establishment or over-riding of the choice value at the decision point in an animal's or a person's strategy, through external sources. This is an example of using anchoring to influence a strategy. Let's consider a Pavlov's dog example. Let's say our dog has been conditioned to push a lever for food pellets at the sound of a bell. We will hypothesize a strategy that goes:

$$A^e \longrightarrow K^i \longrightarrow V^e \longrightarrow V^i \longrightarrow K^e \longrightarrow Exit$$

In this strategy the animal hears the bell (A^e) which anchors the internal kinesthetic sensations of hunger (K^i). This in turn anchors up the next step in the strategy which involves looking at the lever (V^e). The dog then sees internally a replay of itself pushing the lever and receiving food (V^i), and this initiates the action of doing it (K^e). If an experimenter wanted to decondition this program or recondition it to avoidance, he would typically use some negative kinesthetic stimulus like an electric shock. The shock would be administered as the animal is carrying out the strategy so that it overrides the ongoing step in the strategy—let's say as it is approaching the lever. It continues getting shocked until it assumes some other behavior. Putting in the negative anchor (the shock) will eventually reprogram the strategy so that looking at the lever may access an internal kinesthetic representation of the shock (K^i) instead of the image of pushing the lever. The representation of the shock initiates the new behavior that has been anchored to it. Eventually the strategy may become streamlined to the point that the bell itself anchors the new behavior, without the other steps in the strategy. We will go into the programming and reprogramming of new strategies in the installation section of this book. In this section we are primarily concerned with the utilization of already existing strategies and experiences.

Anchoring during utilization will generally involve extablishing triggers for previously occurring motivation, creativity and learning states. At the end of this section we will present a number of content examples of how strategies may be utilized in a variety of different fields, including education, business, therapy and law.

4.33 Covert Anchoring and Pacing.

Because consciousness is a limited phenomenon, there will be times when you are pacing and anchoring an individual or group overtly, within their conscious awareness, and times when you are doing it covertly, outside their span of awareness (and sometimes your own).

In overt utilization the programmer paces by making sure the client is consciously experiencing each step that he and the programmer are going through. The programmer makes them aware of the steps in their strategy and shows them how to utilize the representational sequences to achieve new behaviors.

Covert utilization involves pacing and anchoring which are performed completely or partly outside of the client's conscious attention. This type of situation tends to occur the most often naturally during utilization because it is difficult (and often a hindrance) for an individual to be consciously aware of all of the steps in their strategies—particularly if these steps have reached the level of an unconscious TOTE. Covert pacing and anchoring often lead to the most effective results because the strategy is allowed to remain an unconscious TOTE, where it is able to function more readily and swiftly without conscious interference.

Most covert work will usually take place through the client's least conscious representational system(s). That is, through the sensory channels that the person is least aware of.

Covert anchoring is something that many people have to practice to be comfortable with. Beginners often experience themselves as being "manipulative" when they first start anchoring covertly. This results in breaking their rapport with the client (the client picks up on the programmer's discomfort) and reduces the effectiveness of their work.

A good example of covert anchoring that you may wish to practice can be drawn from a demonstration that we occasionally present in our workshops. In the demonstration a subject is asked to recall a number of instances in which he has forgotten something. For instance, we may ask the following series of questions:

Can you think of a time you forgot someone's name? What was that experience like?

Can you think of what it's like to have something important right on the tip of your tongue but not be able to get it out?

What is it like when you know that you know something but just can't remember what it is?

As we observe the subject's facial expression, skin color, breathing, and tonal and tempo changes as their 4-tuples for "forgetting" come up, one of us will anchor each of them with a clearing of the throat (an A^e anchor to which most people pay no conscious attention). Eventually, the subject is asked to remember something that should be readily available to him—such as his telephone number, his mother's first name, or to repeat what they just finished saying. As soon as the question is asked, however, one of us will clear his throat, triggering the strategy for forgetting. The subject will often experience an unusual and convincing amount of difficulty in the recall task. If one of us keeps clearing his throat, the individual may be unable to recall the information for extended periods of time.

In one workshop one of the authors noticed that a participant had a primarily auditory recall strategy. She was asked to recall a song that she was particularly fond of, which she did easily and readily. The author anchored the song with a finger gesture (subtly moving the finger as if directing an orchestra). Because the woman was tuning in to her internal auditory system her external visual experience was outside her awareness. The woman was then asked what her home address was. She quickly supplied the answer. Immediately after she finished saying her address she was asked to repeat it. This time, however, the author fired off the anchor for the song. For a full thirty seconds the woman could not answer the question—until the music stopped. She was very confused at what caused the difficulty, even though she knew it had something to do with the song. The process was repeated several times for other simple tasks, such as remembering her phone number, children's names, etc., until she was finally made aware of the visual anchor.

Demonstrations like these often bring up the question of the negative aspects of manipulation: an important issue. We, of course, urge you to use your full discretion in using and applying the information we are providing in this book. We want to remind you, however, that these utilizations are influence tactics and do not magically "make" people do things—especially things that they don't want to do. As Milton H. Erickson, M.D., (one of the persons from whom this model was derived) said, "If I could make people do things that they didn't want to do, there would be a lot more well people in this world today."

We suggest you keep in mind that the events and procedures we are describing here are constantly occurring *all the time* in our everyday lives. Most people just aren't aware of them. An excellent example of this can be seen in a film about Carl Rogers, a man who epitomizes non-manipulative, client-centered therapy. In one portion of the film Rogers is "feeding back" to the client a statement that she made of a conflict she was having (we will refer to the two aspects of the conflict as X and Y). Paraphrased, the interaction goes something like this:

Rogers: I understand you have this choice X (gestures with left hand) . . . and you have this choice Y (gestures with right hand) . . . Now I don't know which one (gestures with left hand) you will choose, but I'm sure it will be the one (gestures with left hand) that is best for you. . . .

The client, not surprisingly, decided to go for choice X (anchored by the gesture with the left hand). Certainly, though, Rogers had no conscious intention of influencing the client's decision in that way. Perhaps at an unconscious level he chose which way would have been best for himself, a choice revealed by his hand gestures. Both Rogers and the client were so tuned to the auditory external (and probably kinesthetic internal) portions of the ongoing communication that neither of them were conscious of the subtle gestures picked up through the external visual system.

It is not possible to prevent these kinds of subtle anchors, nor would it be useful as the more powerful channels of communication are those nonverbal channels which lie outside of awareness. If you consciously attempt to avoid anchoring with your hand gestures and words, you may begin to anchor instead with your breathing, tonality or facial expression at the unconscious level. If you pay attention to these variables in an attempt to stop them, you will lose track of others that will communicate your unconscious decisions. It is better that these subtleties be brought out in the open than to remain hidden in such a way that people become victims of their own (and others') unconscious processes. You cannot not influence someone.

4.34 Requisite Variety

In cybernetics there is a principle known as the law of requisite variety. This law states that in any connected interactive system, the element that has the widest range of variability in behavior will be, ultimately, the controlling element.[1] No matter what field you are in, you will probably have come to the realization that the top people in that field are those who have the most variety in their behavior, those who have choices of behavior that their colleagues don't have. Any time you limit yourself with regard to some choice of behavior, you are working against yourself and letting others get the competitive edge. The objective of NLP is to provide the human species with more behavioral choices. We believe that the more choices and possibilities the members of our species become aware of and make available to themselves, the more we will advance as a whole.

The greater your ability to respond to any situation in a variety of ways, the more effective you will be at utilization and at getting the outcomes you want.

4.4 Ideas and Examples: Areas of Application for Strategy Utilization

In the following subsections we will show how the material discussed thus far in this book may be applied to different fields to expand the possibilities for their growth and development. Obviously the examples we have selected represent particular options for utilization that could be expanded upon or reorganized in a variety of ways. By applying your own strategy for creativity when you go back through this book to review and outline procedures useful in your field, you will obtain a unique pattern specifically oriented for your own purposes of strategy utilization.

4.41 Education

The field of education is an obvious place to start, as the establishment of synesthesia patterns, strategies and anchors is precisely what the process of learning is about, not only in the classroom but in interactions among teachers themselves, between teachers and parents, teachers, administrators and school board members, district school officials and personnel in each state office of education, and so on, up to and including interactions with the Department of Health, Education and Welfare at the federal level. Learning is a lifelong process, and although we will concentrate on classroom learning in this subsection, you can easily apply your imagination to the enormously positive potential inherent in using NLP in exchanging and enhancing teaching strategies, troubleshooting personnel problems, settling salary negotiations, harmonizing with parents and parent organizations and so forth.

For teachers, one important application of strategy utilization is to pace students' learning strategies in the classroom. By identifying the steps through which a student naturally incorporates new information and behavior, and by presenting the material to be taught in that form, teachers can greatly facilitate the learning process. Through adapting information to the representational systems with which a student is most adept, a teacher utilizes the student's natural skills and resources most effectively, whether at the kindergarten or college level.

For example, an electrical engineer in one of our workshops, who primarily used internal kinesthetics in his strategies, described how learning to read electrical schematics was at first very difficult and boring for him. He had a hard time making sense out of the mass of lines and symbols he saw in his textbook. He couldn't "connect" with them and found circuits extremely difficult to interpret until one day he began to imagine what it would feel like to be an electron floating through the circuit he saw diagrammed in front of him. He would imagine his various reactions and changes in behavior as he came in contact with the various components in the circuit, symbolized by visual characters on the schematic. The diagrams immediately began to make more sense to him and even became fun to figure out and to design. Each schematic presented him with a new odyssey. It was so enjoyable, in fact, that he remained with electronics and went on to become an engineer—all because he found a way to utilize his strategy effectively in the learning process.

In our experience, "good" teachers use the process of pacing intuitively. Teaching is much more difficult if you have to constantly fight your students' models of the world to "reach" them.

A remarkably astute understanding of strategies was shown by a teacher in one of our workshops who had taught special education classes for several years. In her algebra class for slow and handicapped students, a large and muscular black student was having a very rough time working any of the problems on the board or on paper. (Remember that the athletic muscular—or mesomorphic—body type is indicative of a person with primarily tactile kinesthetic (K^e) strategies.) Another member of the class was blind—so all of the material presented in the class was also available in braille and raised surface diagrams. As a project, the teacher had the "slow" black student learn to read braille (K^e_d). Not so surprisingly the student's ability to pick up algebra using the braille and raised surface material was many times more rapid than when he attempted to do it visually. The braille paced his natural abilities and strategies with his tactile system (we have often suggested the use of braille and raised surfaces for sighted but kinesthetically oriented persons when we have consulted for special education groups).

Generally, kinesthetically oriented students have a difficult time in the classroom. Feelings, especially those from external sources, don't lend themselves well to what we call "academic" subject areas. One of the classic stereotypes in education is that of the athlete who has a difficult time in the visual and auditory world of lectures, blackboards and books; and likewise the thin, tense "A" student who has difficulty in the kinesthetic world of athletics. Written tests and the classroom environment are visually and auditorily oriented. In our experience many young people who have been labeled "slow," "handicapped" or "disabled" in this context are far from "stupid"—they simply have different strategies for learning that are not utilized by present techniques of education.

In most cases K^e individuals end up in manual or mechanical occupations like construction, farming or gardening, athletics, assembly line work, auto repair and other jobs where they can utilize their kinesthetic skills.

The teacher mentioned in the preceding example also pointed out that many of her students (most of whom were black) had elaborate "tapping" systems for doing arithmetical operations like addition and multiplication, in which they would perform and keep track of their calculations by tapping their fingers on their thighs or desks ($A_t^e \longrightarrow K^e$), a process resembling the use of the abacus. When the students were forced to do problems without tapping in this way they were unable to get the correct answers.

It has been our experience that one distinguishing characteristic of black culture is an orientation toward auditory external (A^e) and kinesthetic external strategies and attributes. This would account for many of the difficulties experienced by Blacks in educational institutions established and controlled by white western cultures.

People with efficient auditory strategies often have difficulty writing. In fact many of you readers may notice that your writing style and strategy are very different from the way you talk. Both involve externalizing internal experience in a digital form, but speaking and listening are different from writing and looking. One method that we often suggest to people who get blocked easily while writing is to dictate their work first, or to tape record discussions with friends. This can help overcome any inertia that they have toward writing in that they can always begin the process of writing by transcribing the recorded material. In essence they would be employing a strategy that goes from A^e to V^e. The inverse of this strategy for people who have difficulty speaking is, of course, to write or take notes on their material before they present it orally.

In many contexts it will be difficult to pace the strategies of each individual—especially in large group situations where time is limited. When addressing groups it is important to gear your presentation to include the three major representational systems. Make sure you can present your ideas through each representational system, so that people can hear it, see it and get a feel for it. Being able to communicate your material through each of these different systems is what we referred to as "redundancy" earlier. It greatly decreases chances of miscommunication as well as assuring that you are presenting the material in a representational form that will pace, at some point, everyone in your audience. Lectures and discussions (A^e), demonstrations, diagrams, written outlines and other visual aids (V^e), and experiential exercises and examples that involve audience participation (K^e), tend to make the most well rounded presentational format. Using anecdotes, questions, examples and directive vocabulary (involving sensory specific predicates) that require an individual to access internal experiences in all of his systems will help to insure that you reach all of the members of your class or audience.

Organizing students into various study groups of different orientations, groups that pace different learning strategies, can accelerate group learning processes. One group with an emphasis on discussion, another using experiential exercises, and another concentrating on observation, would be one way of doing this on a general scale.

4.411 Anchoring and Reinforcement in Education.

Anchoring is important in the learning process. The establishment of bad anchors and negative feedback loops is one of the major problems within institutionalized education. For many students tests become anchors for stress or anxiety, and if these are not utilized positively in recall or creativity strategies, then chances are they will inhibit test performance. Because many people are unable to access their resource strategies in this context tests are not a meaningful indicator of how much they have learned. Teachers who use group relaxation exercises before tests or who establish a group resource anchor that can be fired off at the beginning of the test find that test scores improve for many students.

By pairing learning situations with positive 4-tuples (by incorporating jokes and anecdotes, for instance) teachers can strategically program learning to be a positive experience.

In the example given earlier in this section, the teacher who had her slow student learn braille bypassed any negative anchors that he may have associated with learning algebra visually. For some learners simply sitting in a classroom or looking at a blackboard is an automatic negative anchor. We have known people with excellent strategies for mathematics who, when presented with a "word problem" as opposed to an equation, don't access their most effective strategy, because they process problems in word form with a different strategy.

A person in one of our workshops had taken beginning French a total of five times over a number of years, failing the tests each time. He was not a poor student and did well in his other classes. He kept taking French because he needed a foreign language to graduate, and he figured that surely, because he had taken it so many times before, he would eventually pass the class. Besides, his ability to use it outside the classroom kept improving, and certainly this was an indicator that he was learning. Utilizing the process of transderivational search, we discovered that at the beginning of each of his tests, when he was handed the test sheet, an extremely negative 4-tuple would be anchored up, a memory of his first French teacher, whom he despised. This would, of course, short circuit his strategies for recall. As he grew anxious at the thought of failing the test again, the two negative experiences would form a two point loop, each anchoring the other. The effect snowballed such that he could not adequately complete the test. Because this had happened at every test, it also became a self-fulfilling prophecy. Every time he studied for or took a French test an internal dialogue would be triggered that said something like, "Oh no, what if I fail this test . . . I probably will". Because this kind of dialogue and his negative feelings were solidly anchored to the test context he was continually blocked from accessing his usually effective resource strategy.

$$\left\langle A^i, V^i, K^i, \emptyset \right\rangle \; \underset{\longleftarrow}{\longrightarrow} \; \left\langle K^{\underline{i}} \right\rangle$$

Negative 4-tuple   Anxiousness
of first French teacher   about test

His condition was resolved by integrating the negative 4-tuple and the dialogue with other resource experiences, and by giving him a well conditioned anchor for relaxation and for eliciting his recall strategy.

4.412 Polarity Strategies and Negative Motivation Strategies in Learning.

Negative kinesthetic experiences are not always a block to learning or to accessing resources. Many people access their resources only when the situation makes them grow stressful or anxious. Some become motivated by harsh auditory commands and hard looks. There are students who put off an assignment until they say to themselves, "I'll never be able to do this on time now," to which they immediately have a polarity response and do the assignment easily and well.

People who operate best under pressure may have a difficult time operating where there is no pressure (or "challenge"), because the situation does not access the representations that trigger their most effective resource strategies.

These strategies are not limited, of course, to people in the context of education but occur in many other contexts and tasks. Very often people who have negative motivation or polarity strategies have a high tension level and may end up with stress related physical ailments common in this culture. We will discuss these strategies and how to deal with them in more detail in the Design Section of this book.

4.413 Feedback

It will be important for anyone involved in the process of teaching to tune their sensory channels to pick up feedback from students. Non-verbal cues like head nods, breathing changes and other systematic minor body movements will indicate which people are following the presentation and when. Observing eye movements, tonal shifts and other easily available accessing cues will let you know which systems and strategies students are using.

The typical written test is only one way of getting feedback for how much students are picking up (though probably the most common). It is also, as we have shown previously, limited in both the kind and reliability of the feedback it gives. For example, it reveals nothing about the strategy a student is employing (excepting, in some cases, to an NLP trained teacher, depending on the type of written test). Many students who take foreign language courses are able to pass written exams with A's or B's but learn little of the spoken language. One important task of education is for students to learn to achieve the designated outcomes of learning assignments. Too often what happens is that written test performance becomes the primary measuring process and outcome of the educational institution.

Setting up tests that provide useful, accurate feedback is crucial to the educational process. To do this educators must decide what kind of outcome to test for. One of the initial distinctions in outcomes to make is whether (1) you have a specific set of contents you must teach—that is, do you have to teach X number of people N amount of information or (2) you want to teach learning skills specifically targeted for the subject matter of your courses. In the first case you will want to *pace* and *utilize* your students' existing learning strategies and feed in the content you want to teach. In the second case you will want to *install* in your students the strategy most appropriate for the task or behavior in question. There is a wise saying which states that "If you give a man fish you have fed him for a day, but if you teach him *how* to fish you have fed him for the rest of his life." NLP provides the technology with which to make this generative *how* process explicit.

The distinction we are making is that between *Learning I* and *Learning II* (learning to learn). In his essay "The Logical Categories of Learning and Communication," Gregory Bateson discusses and defines the differences between types of learning:

> "*Zero learning* is characterized by a *specificity of response,* which— right or wrong—is not subject to correction.
> *Learning I* is *change in specificity of response* by correction of errors of choice within a set of alternatives.
> *Learning II* is *change in the process of Learning I,* e.g., a corrective change in the set of alternatives from which choice is made, or it is a change in how the sequence of experience is punctuated."

The example Bateson gives of the two processes at work is the following:

". . . you can reinforce a rat (positively or negatively) when he investigates a particular strange object, and he will appropriately learn to approach it or avoid it. But the very purpose of the *exploration* is to get information about which objects should be approached or avoided. The discovery that a given object is dangerous is therefore a success in the business of getting information. The success will not discourage the rat from future exploration of strange objects."

Finding out which objects to avoid is the content of the process at the level of Learning I. It is essentially the procedure of establishing anchors and making connections appropriate to the achievement of an outcome. In this case an animal or person "learns" when a stimulus anchors a particular behavioral response or program (going when the light turns green, or learning multiplication tables, for example).

The strategy for discovery (the process of exploration) employed by the rat comes from a different level of learning. Learning II is establishing or changing the *strategy* by which you are gathering information and establishing the anchors and connections through which you achieve outcomes. This kind of learning would involve changes in representational systems and sequences. The rat, for instance, may explore visually, by looking at objects; olfactorily, by sniffing at them; auditorily, by listening to them; or kinesthetically by touching them with its nose. The rat may also sequence these modes of exploration. It may be to the rat's benefit, in some situations, to look at and sniff an object before touching it with its nose. How the rat establishes these patterns takes place through a different process from that of Learning I.

A chemistry professor may be "good" at chemistry, in terms of knowing the formulas, when and how to apply them and what will result, but may have had a difficult time learning it when he was in school. In other words, he knows the content very well (successful Learning I) but has a poor strategy for learning to learn it (Learning II). This person may, of course, have had very effective strategies for motivation and tenacity, but if your outcome is to teach people to learn chemistry easily and efficiently you will not want to install this professor's strategy for learning. Instead you would want to elicit and install the strategy of someone who is able to pick up and be creative with the content of chemistry very quickly and smoothly (like presumably Linus Pauling, for instance), or design one that is more suited to that outcome.

Most educators, as we pointed out earlier, are unaware of strategies and either don't teach them at all or else they unconsciously reinforce for their own strategies, which may not be the best suited for the material they are working with. An elementary school teacher may have a great strategy for dealing with children, but a poor spelling or reading strategy.

It will be very important, then, when you design tests to gather feedback from students to make this distinction in what to test for. The process of designing, installing and testing new strategies will be covered in the remaining two sections of this book.

4.42 Business and Organizational Development.

There are many aspects of business and organizational interactions that we could consider, and we will single out specific areas as we go through this section. But there will be general applications of NLP elicitation and utilization procedures for this field that hold for all situations in which communication between human beings is involved, which we can generalize across all of these aspects.

The most important resources of any business are the people that make it run. Being able to organize and deal with people effectively is the principal task of almost every executive, supervisor, manager and administrator, no matter what kind of business is involved. There are four essential steps in doing this successfully:

A. Rapport

Establishing rapport with the individuals you work with will pay off by greatly cutting down unnecessary resistence to the job you are trying to get done. Your approach with each individual will powerfully influence the course of the interaction. By pacing the person's strategies and other behavior, picking up his vocabulary, mirroring and feeding back his voice tonality and tempo, facial expressions, posture and gestures, it will be possible for you to establish a rapid and worthwhile rapport.

Investing the necessary time to establish positive anchors and resource anchors at the beginning of a communication inter-change can profitably assist in speeding up progress toward the desired net outcome of the interaction.

B. Information Gathering

Knowing what information you need and how to get it will greatly assist you in getting things accomplished rapidly and suc-cessfully. Grounding this information as much as possible in spe-cific sensory based language (that is, so that it is in terms of things that everybody can explicitly see, hear, feel and smell) will be well worth the effort in streamlining any plan, procedure, negotiation or operation. By using the meta-model, paying attention to non-verbal cues, organizing your information gathering tactics in terms of the three-point process and putting emphasis on form and pro-cess, you will quickly pinpoint what changes are required to elimi-nate costly or time-consuming problems as you discover what strategies are required to open profitable and dynamic new pos-sibilities of action. The minimal information to be gathered for any decision making, problem solving, change or transition process to be properly engineered would consist of:

What do you want? (Desired/outcome state.)
What is happening now? (Present state.)
What stops you from getting what you want? (Problem state.)
What do you need in order to get what you want? (Resources.)
How would you know if you were moving adequately toward your goal? (Feedback.)
Have you ever got it before? What did you do then?
(Resources.)

These are purely process questions. You will want to get other evaluative (meta) information at some point as well (i.e. a cost benefit analysis), such as: What will it cost? What is it worth? Do I (we) have the resources?

Pacing, described in the step on rapport, is a quick and efficient way of gathering information. Pacing gives you rapid access to information about the model of the world and the strategies of those you are working with. By simply feeding back an individual's behavior you will actually begin to pick up naturally many of the details of their strategies and operations.

C. Delivery/Presentation

By packaging the delivery and presentation of your ideas and suggestions in a way that is consistent and congruent with the strategies and models of the people you are dealing with, you will make those ideas maximally acceptable to them. In presenting several alternatives you may choose to package only the alternative you identify as most beneficial to you and your client in the form which matches their unconscious strategies. By so doing, you exert a powerful influence on the decision. In either case these tools achieve their effectiveness by using information about the patterns of personal organization which lie outside the conscious appreciation of the person being addressed.

D. Feedback

It is always necessary to get feedback on how your communications are affecting the individual or group you are dealing with. One of the basic presuppositions of NLP is that *the response you get from the person or group you are communicating with is the meaning of your communication, regardless of what you intend the meaning to be.* That is, people may not interpret your communication in the way you intended; but it is up to *you* to observe what response your communication is eliciting from them and to respond appropriately—i.e., to vary your behavior until your intended meaning is conveyed to the other party. Feedback lets you know when and to what degree what you are doing is working; when to continue what you are doing and when to change your behavior. Your ability to make refined sensory distinctions will be an invaluable and time saving resource for you with this process.

4.421 NLP in Sales

In the area of effective sales work, we begin with the assumption that sales personnel are trained to qualify their customers. By qualifying their customers or clients, we mean that the sales representative is committed to offering their company's product or service only to clients who would actually benefit from such a product or service. To fail to match the product or service to each unique customer is to run the risk of buyer's remorse. Most new business is the result of word of mouth referrals by satisfied customers.

The tools we offer here are powerful enough to sell without qualifying clients. Thus the step of qualifying customers becomes even more important as a safeguard for both the customer/client and the business involved.

Let's consider an example of how NLP principles could be applied in the area of sales. Let us suppose that a salesperson from Superior Electronics (SP in the following dialogue) has previously laid the groundwork for a sales meeting with the purchasing agent (PA) for ZX Computer Corporation by thoroughly researching what kinds of computers ZX sells, how well they are performing and selling and by leaving a sample power semiconductor with ZX's Engineering Division to be tested and "qualified." That is, SP has accomplished his information gathering and knows his product meets ZX's performance specifications before he walks into the meeting.

SP: Good morning, Mr. Edwards. I'm George Smith with Superior Electronics.

PA: Oh yes, I remember talking to you on the phone. (After handshake, sits, leans back in chair, crosses left leg over right, points to chair beside his desk.)

SP: (Sits, mirrors PA's voice tonality and portions of his posture unobtrusively.) Mr. Kurtz in your Engineering Division tells me your ZX-12 personal computers are really moving along in sales. . . .

PA: (Smiling.) We've picked up a big chunk of the market in the past two years. We're certainly pleased with the customer response the ZX-12 is getting.

SP: (Pacing PA's tonality and posture more strongly.) Are you satisfied with its power supply performance?

PA: Oh yes . . . We've used a lot of Solitar products in getting off the ground, but . . . (Looks down and right) we're interested in staying in contact with what's available in terms of quality and price.

SP: Your feeling is that you'd be interested in system components that would add to the sales momentum you've established for the ZX-12?

PA: Yes . . . That's right.

SP: (Tests establishment of rapport by shifting to slightly new posture. PA follows, indicating that rapport has been established. SP then begins to gather information about PA's buying strategy.) Do you think you made a good decision buying your initial components from Solitar?

PA: Yes . . . considering our marketing options at the time.

SP: What made you decide to buy from Solitar?

PA: (Eyes move up and left.) Well . . . as I said . . . Solitar looked good to us from our perspective at the time. We knew we could be comfortable with their overall price package and still get a foot in the market door with a moderately priced personal computer.

SP: Solitar components looked like they would fit the bill when you were just starting out with the ZX-12. . . .

PA: That's right . . . Of course, that was before we'd established the marketing advantage we have now. . . . (Eyes move down and left, then shift to down and right.)

SP: (Picking up on kinesthetic accessing cue.) How did you feel about that?

PA: (Eyes remaining down and right.) Oh, I felt it was obviously the best move for the company at the time . . . so I approved that buying decision. (SP covertly anchors the decision point visually by lifting his eyebrow and making a hand gesture. SP now postulates that PA's buying strategy goes $V^e \longrightarrow V^c \longrightarrow A^i_d \longrightarrow K^i \longrightarrow$ EXIT. That is, PA will look at SP's sales package proposal, construct an image of how SP's power semiconductors would fit into the ZX-12's competitive market situation, talk to himself about it, then get an internal feeling from his internal dialogue. SP then tests this postulate by asking about another buying experience.)

SP: The housing units that make the ZX-12 look so good—those are made by Zuniga aren't they?

PA: (Smiles.) Yes, they are. Our engineers designed them, and

Zuniga manufactures them to our specifications. Zuniga's a good outfit.

SP: (Returns the smile.) They sure are. How did you decide to go with Zuniga?

PA: Well . . . (Smiles and shakes head) . . . as soon as we saw samples of the housing units they were making for Tricon portable TVs, I pictured how impressive the ZX-12 would look wrapped up in a package like that, and I just said to myself, "Zuniga's the right outfit to bring that off for us . . ." and I felt so strongly about that feature that I could hardly wait to get our engineering people working on design specs! (PA's eyes begin up and right, shift down and left, then down and right—confirming SP's postulate of PA's buying strategy. SP again anchors the decision point by lifting an eyebrow and making the same hand gesture as before.)

SP: (Opening his briefcase to begin his own presentation.) I'm sure that we can offer you an excellent price/quality package on power semiconductors for the ZX-12 power supply unit. (Lays out display material on PA's desk.) As you can *see*, these semiconductors outperform Solitar's. You might *imagine* how this component will lower your warranty repair and replacement costs and give you that extra edge on customer confidence, and you can *say to yourself* that the package is just right for ZX because . . . (lists features and benefits). It's a good *solid feeling* to know that with a more reliable power supply unit, using our semiconductors, you can push the ZX-12 marketing strategy to really build on what you've already accomplished. (As SP speaks, he paces the tonality and gestures that PA used while describing his strategy earlier and fires off anchors for the decision point by raising his eyebrow and gesturing with his hand.)

The salesperson has paced the buying strategy elicited from the customer in casual conversation. By packaging his presentation so that it paces the customer's natural decision making processes, it is much easier for the salesman to communicate the value of whatever product or service he is marketing. Because the presentation matches, step for step, the sequence that the customer naturally uses to gather, process and act on his experience, it is much more likely to fit the customer's needs, wants and expectations. Equally as important, it is much less likely to bring up objections or resistence. For those customers who have polarity steps in their strategy, though, objections will be an extremely important part of the pace. Salespersons should intuitively recognize this kind of strategy—where it is important that you actually try to discourage the customer from buying in order to make them want to buy. Some customers will also want to play devil's advocate and raise a number of objections before they are willing to buy.

If you make sure the person goes through each step and satisfies all of the tests within his strategy or TOTE for buying, the product will approach irresistability to the customer, regardless of what that product is.

This same procedure, of course, could be employed equally well by a sales executive attempting to convince the five members of the board of directors to buy a training package, organizational development package, or sales package, etc. The sales executive would want to gather information like "Have you bought a program like this before?" "Were you satisfied with it?" If not, "Did you think you were going to be?" "How did you make that decision?" As the group responds to these questions you will be able to gather information about how they make a decision as a group (in order to answer the questions they will make a decision about how they make decisions) and about how they make decisions individually. It is very helpful, when possible, to question each member of a group individually as well as observing the group function as a whole, because your presentation to each one is going to be different. Once you have identified the strategies of each person you mark out the portions of your overall presentation to him nonverbally through eye contact or by pacing his individual tonality, etc. (The amount of information you can gather on the strategies of the individuals and the group will depend on the amount of time you can spend and the degree of rapport you have with the group members.)

Consider the example of a woman sales executive, (S), who, by asking a few short questions and by observing the predicates and eye movements of the group members as they respond, determines that of the group of five (A,B,C,D and E) A and B have a decision point in their strategy that is primarily based on visual information; C has a decision point primarily based on auditory digital information; and D and E have decision points primarily based on internal kinesthetic information. S could structure her presentation as follows:

S: (Begins by marking out A and B by looking back and forth at them as she speaks, and by assuming the somewhat tense and nasal tonal qualities of A, and by gesturing unobtrusively toward each of them with her hands and fingers as she speaks.) I think that if you really *look* closely at the situation we've been discussing you will *see* that there is a *clear* need for this program . . . (S continues talking, using primarily visual predicates and descriptions, and also brings out visual aids and diagrams) . . . (S then changes her tonality to match the even tempoed and controlled voice of C, and shifts her eye contact to C) And I think it's very important to *listen* to what other people in this organization are *saying.* One of the first things that I had to *ask myself* was, "What does this situation have to *say* about where we are going as an organization?" . . . And I suddenly remembered what the president had once *said* about . . . (S continues talking, recoding what she has just essentially communicated to A & B substituting auditory predicates and examples.) . . . (S then begins to make eye contact with D and E and lowers her voice to match that of E) It's a great *feeling* to know that you've got a practical and *solid* program design (looks at D) *and* that you're able to stay in *touch* and flow with the *feelings* of the majority of your employees . . . (S continues, recoding what she has already said to A,B & C, substituting kinesthetic predicates and expressions.)

What she does, then, in this relatively simple and generalized example, is to present the same content recoded into the language of each of the three major representational systems. She marks out and directs the appropriate coding to the person with that strategy and paces each person she addresses, even though at the same time she is maintaining the structure of a group presentation. S will use any feedback she receives to direct and amplify the strength of her presentation. If E (whose decision point was discerned as kinesthetically oriented) should begin to look up and left consistently and begin to shake his head slightly as S is speaking to him with kinesthetic predicates, she would know that she had lost rapport and would immediately begin to switch her presentation to pace him.

If she'd had time to elicit the full decision strategy from each of the group members her task would be slightly more complex, as she would, for maximum impact, want to pace the entire representational sequence that each member cycled through during their decision processes.

Those readers familiar with group decision making will recognize that such complexity would rarely be required. Rather the more typical group will have developed (unconsciously) some group level strategy where the various functions are distributed among its members. For example, one group member will be extremely active in questioning the factual basis of the presentation, while another will make comparisons with alternative products or services. Frequently, the group will have the decision point function assigned to a single group member. When that member's tests are satisfied, the group has decided. The individual who has sharpened his sensory acuity will recognize the signals and package for the sequence specified by the group strategy with special attention to the individual decision strategy of the member who serves as decision point and exit.

One of the major obstacles to success for many salespeople is the lack of what we have called *requisite variety*—that is, the ability to vary their behavior in response to feedback from different kinds of customers. Many salespeople present only one particular form of packaging that will pace some percentage of the population but will be ineffectual with the rest. They rely on volume coverage rather than repackaging their communications to pace each individual appropriately. High pressure tactics will pay off with some people but not with others. Any particular existing sales technique will work—but only for a limited percentage of the market population. One effective use of NLP for sales would be to determine which of the existing techniques, that work well, paces which class of representational strategies. The salespersons may then adjust their behavior to access the most effective approach for each buyer's strategy so that statistically they will succeed with a larger percentage of customers. Hence, any particular technique will continue to succeed where it has been succeeding, but you will know exactly which kind of people to expand with. After a period of time, since there will not be that many different categories of buying strategies, the salesperson will know the moment someone walks in the door which category he falls into and which tactic to use.

4.422 Implications of NLP for Advertising.

Advertising agencies and personnel have utilized the pacing of strategies since advertising began (although they probably never thought of it that way). Consider the following example of an advertisement, paraphrased almost word for word from a popular magazine:

"When I shop I like to *ask* a lot of questions. That way I can *feel* sure that I've *seen* all of the options, and am really making the best choice. Product X has the best quality I've *seen* . . ."

The strategy of the person making this statement is obviously $A_d^e \longrightarrow V \longrightarrow K^i \longrightarrow EXIT$. The strategy is essentially one for information gathering in which the person asks questions, and is shown samples of the product, which are then evaluated kinesthetically with respect to the sample size required for the person's decision strategy. This ad would, of course, pace to some degree anyone who shared a similar strategy. The ad also contained a photograph of the person allegedly making the statement—dressed in stylishly modern clothes. Such a picture might also serve to pace the image a person has of themselves, or an image they aspire to achieve.

A statement which would pace a different shopping strategy might go something like:

"I don't like to *feel* pressured when I'm shopping. When I *see* someone really coming on with all that phony *show,* I just keep *telling* myself, "Who needs it?" and get out of there as fast as possible. The people at company X have never tried to put on any *glitter.* It's a good *feeling* to *see* people that really care. I can *say* from the bottom of my heart, "They know how to treat their customers . . ."

This statement would pace a strategy that went:

$$V^e \longrightarrow K^i \longrightarrow A_d \Big\langle \begin{array}{l} \nearrow \text{leave} \\ (-) \\ \searrow \text{buy} \end{array}$$

$$(+)$$

In this strategy the person derives feelings from what they see and then makes a verbal evaluation which leads directly to the outcome.

One effective approach in advertising, since there are different buying strategies, is to discover the most general or pervasive classes of strategies and create an advertisement pacing each one.

Most successful advertising involves all of the representational systems in the 4-tuple, generally placing an emphasis on one or two—depending upon the nature of the product. The essential desired outcome of any product advertising is to establish overt and/or covert anchors linking the product to positive 4-tuples and to the motivation and buying strategies of consumers, such that anchors will be triggered when prospective buyers enter a context in which that product is sold. For this reason it is important to include visual or auditory cues in the advertisement that will also be present in the buying environment. Audience participation in the advertisement (the involvement of the viewer/listener), such as showing what the observer will see through his or her own eyes, or hear on the scene, establish effective anchors associated with the product and its market environment.

Another important step often left out of advertising is that of telling the customer what to do to buy the product—giving him explicit directions about where to go and how to buy.

Tailoring your vocabulary to the culturally established dialect or idioms of the target population of your advertisement is another very effective and often amusing means of pacing that may be employed by sales and advertising personnel. One of the authors, for example, was recently consulting for a floral brokerage. The primary marketing targets of this company were florists, whose very job demands sensory refinements (olfactory) not common in the general population. One of the recommendations made to them, as a means to help their sales department branch out to new areas, was to mix in an assortment of floral idioms and terms, and olfactory predicates, into their advertising and sales arrangements. This would provide an enjoyable way to pace customers, to keep rapport from wilting and to insure healthy growth. It would also provide a fresh, fertile and satisfying environment for the creativity of sales personnel to blossom and even help morale to grow. A sample list of floral terms easily transplanted into everyday speech could include:

smell	process	wilt	moist	assortment
mix	bloom	shrivel	light	fertile
sort	blossom	rot	petal	fresh
transplant	arrange	fade	root	firm
grow	stem	fragrant	arrangement	texture
budding	branch	odor	bouquet	nip in the bud

Specialized vocabularies like this, that provide overlap into everyday speech, are available in most businesses and fields and can provide extremely useful and powerful advantages in communication.

4.423 Recruiting and Selection.

Neurolinguistic programming is a valuable and practical asset to those involved in the recruiting, selection or training of personnel. It should be obvious intuitively that the strategies that make a good sales executive will be different from those which make a good personnel manager or engineer. For anyone involved in the recruiting or selection process there are basically two choices available:

1) If you already have within your organization a person who is naturally skilled at the job you are recruiting for (that is, if the person already has the necessary strategies) and you want find someone else to recapitulate this person's behavior, elicit the strategies of the person who is naturally good at the job and record them. Once you have recorded the person's strategies for decision making, motivation, learning, creativity, etc., conduct a series of interviews in which you elicit the natural strategies of the applicants. You will want to choose, of course, the applicant whose natural strategies most closely match those of the employee you have chosen to model.

2) After you have elicited and recorded the strategies of the person who is naturally skilled at the job you are recruiting for, you can choose to install those strategies in an existing employee or applicant (installation will be discussed in detail in the last section of this book).

You can also recruit an individual with three out of four of the necessary strategies and then install the fourth. Depending on the nature of the task, and your available time, you may find it more profitable to opt for one or the other of these choices. If the task is not highly technical and doesn't involve a great number of sophisticated strategies, it will be easier to recruit people. If the task is technical and sophisticated, there will be less likelihood that you will find someone who already has the necessary strategies, and it will be easier to install the strategies in someone who most closely approximates the job requirements.

If you don't already have a highly qualified person in your organization who can be modeled for your selection process, you can always locate someone who is skilled in another company or organization and model their strategies. Rather than trying to "steal" or "buy" that employee, you can take him out to lunch or engage him in a social setting to covertly elicit their strategies and record them for later installation in somebody else.

You may choose to implement career development or employee development programs designed to develop representational systems or strategies in existing employees. We have successfully implemented several human resource development packages designed around this simple principle. Such programs help to encourage and fortify natural abilities in employees and to develop those who are deficient.

4.43 Medical and Health Professions.

Many studies in recent years have shown that a suprisingly high percentage of modern illnesses have stress related causes. A significant percentage of heart and circulatory problems, ulcers, arthritis, migrane headaches, eye problems and other physical symptoms have been shown to be directly related to stress, a natural outcome of many people's existing strategies. Stress can be very functional (it is not inherently "bad") as a motivator and as a test mechanism.

For us "mind" (neurological processes) and "body" (the machinery governed by these neurological processes) are an interconnected part of the same biological system. Strategies are not merely cognitive activities within our representational systems. Our representational systems interface with other neural systems such that the neurological outcomes of our strategies affect our motor responses, respiration, autonomic control of glandular secretions, body chemistry, heart and blood pressure, metabolism and even the immunity system. The neural activity in one part of our biological system can't *not* have some effect on the rest of the system.

Neurolinguistic programming is a powerful resource for preventive medicine and in the treatment of psychosomatic illness. Psychosomatic illnesses are, by definition, not "all in the mind," but are the result of real interactions between biological systems.

By changing the way people guide and organize their behavior neurologically, through their strategies, (which involves changes in accessing cues and outcomes) people reorganize themselves physiologically. In our therapeutic work we have encountered instances, time and again, in which people we have been working with have had physical symptoms improve, clear up or go into remission when they have changed an old strategy, installed a new one, or utilized a forgotton resource strategy. Symptoms have ranged from minor colds, coughs, infections and warts to arthritis, nearsightedness, tumors and cancer.

Psychological attitude has long been recognized in the medical and health professions as a contributor to the ease and speed with which someone is able to recover. With NLP we are dealing with processes more encompassing and profound than simply attitude. Using NLP we have helped people to interrupt strategies that were contributing to the ailment and to design and implement strategies used to control and regulate major aspects of their physiological ailments. We have found (not surprisingly) that people who have similar strategies are prone to similar illnesses, and that one can predict the kinds of sicknesses a person with a certain set of strategies is most likely to get.

One effective tactic is to find an individual who has been able to recover easily and rapidly from a particular illness and model his strategies (for motivation, self feedback, etc.) Then teach these strategies or install them in others with the same sickness. In our workshops we sometimes conduct an exercise in which people who have completely recovered from former chronic ailments such as allergies or poor eyesight are paired up with individuals confronted with the same problem the others used to have. The task for the person who would like to get over his allergies, headaches, nearsightedness, etc., is to elicit the strategy that his partner has used. Once this is accomplished, it is his partner's task to help him install the strategy he have just elicited. (Installation procedures will be discussed fully in the final chapter of this book.) We have had many startling successes with this exercise.

We are in no way, of course, trying to discourage people from seeking proper medical assistance for physical ailments. What we are trying to communicate is that surgery, medication and other forms of chemotherapy, treat physiology directly and may fail to utilize fully the potential effectiveness of self regulation or control, or other avenues of symptom treatment. The cause for many physical symptoms can be traced to behavioral patterns and can be alleviated through alterations in behavior. The advent of biofeedback has produced abundant evidence that people can control autonomic physiological processes to a much greater degree than was believed possible a few years ago. There are many areas where culturally and institutionally accepted limitations can be successfully and usefully challenged. The primary goal of NLP is, as we stated in the introduction, to continue the evolutionary process of challenging limitations and to move more and more parameters of our experience from environmental variables (those outside our control) to decision variables (those within our personal control). When given the choice we would always opt for the avenue of treatment emphasizing internal personal control over those involving external factors outside of our control.

Innumerable accounts of the placebo effect seem to indicate that there are classes of symptoms and pathological processes that people may be able to cure on their own, without the use of active drugs.

Certainly, much can be done behaviorally to prevent illness. The development and installation of strategies that encourage finer discriminations in, and a larger vocabulary for, proprioceptive feedback (this will come through K^i, and synesthetically through internal representations in the other systems) can assist in gaining more direct access to forms of self examination and regulation.

Pacing motivation and learning strategies can be used effectively to encourage and promote good health habits. In fact, health professionals could utilize the same tactics described in the advertising section of this book to promote health care plans and preventive programs.

4.431 Informed Consent and Bedside Manner.

As with any profession, there will be a division of labor in the medical field with respect to strategies—that is, some strategies will be more suited to certain tasks than to others. There will be a difference between a strategy for diagnosis and one for surgery. A good diagnostician may have a strategy designed for gathering information concerning symptoms from the patient, and then internally checking through lists of symptoms and textbook pages until he begins to find similarities or patterns between the recorded symptoms of other patients and the one he is confronted with. Such a person may do well as a medical school professor but poorly as a general practicioner because his strategies for establishing rapid rapport with individuals on a one-to-one basis are underdeveloped.

The ability to discern strategies and establish rapport can be critically important for many of a physician's duties like prescribing treatments to the patient and for informed consent, where the doctor must tell the patient the risks of his or her operation or treatment. The strategies of an individual patient will determine how you should package the information to be communicated to him. Some people, if you tell them there is a greater than 50% chance of death or serious impairment, will become depressed, apathetic or fatalistic (their strategy tends to carry out the weaker part of a statistic). Such persons may incorporate the statistics as self-fulfilling. For patients who have a polarity strategy, however, it may be useful to tell them they could die, to stimulate them to flip polarities to access the resources they need to recover from or change their condition.

Some patients will suddenly adopt symptoms if you describe them in too much detail or with too much emphasis.

If a heart patient uses stress (K^i_-) as a motivater, he will also build up stress as a means to motivate themself to relax and exercise more! (This is the "hurry up and relax . . . or else" syndrome.)

It is important, then, for the physician to establish rapport with patients and gather information about patients' strategies before presenting them with consequential information. It is always a good idea to elicit and anchor a resource strategy with the patient. The strategy may then be reaccessed and utilized in situations that may be difficult or important.

4.44 Law

One of the primary tasks of an attorney is representation. The attorney's ability to gather information and establish rapport with clients, witnesses and judges will determine to a large degree his professional success. If a lawyer needs to present a brief or a case to a judge for a decision, for example, it will be extremely useful to know that judge's decision making strategy. By packaging your presentation so that it paces the judge's strategy, it will be easier for him to appreciate the value of your argument. The same principle applies, of course, to juries.

Because of their training in the use of language, we have found most lawyers and judges to be remarkably (though unconsciously) explicit in describing their internal processes through their speech. One of the authors was recently a plaintiff at a small claims trial. As the author waited for his case to be called, he listened to the judge and identified his decision making strategy. Every time the judge decided a case he would give an account of how he came to the decision, describing the form of his internal processes each time. For example, the judge might say, "Well, Mr. X, as I *look* over these records I *see* that this is not your first time in this courtroom, and I have to *ask myself* "How much longer will this go on? . . . How many more times?" I really *feel* that it's my responsibility to make sure that this doesn't happen again." This indicates a decision strategy of:

$$V \rightarrow A_d^i \rightarrow K^i \rightarrow EXIT$$

When it came time for the author to present his case, he packaged his presentation to pace this strategy. A skeletal paraphrasing of this presentation might go—"Your Honor, as you *look* over the case in front of you, you will clearly *see* that the defendant did not complete the work he contracted to do . . . And you'll have to *ask yourself,* 'Given the available information about the amount of work completed and the agreement made by the defendent, what is the best course of action?' . . . And I'm sure you will *feel,* as I do, that this matter should be decided in my favor."

After hearing the arguments the judge favored the author but questioned the amount of the claim presented (the author was asking for a full return of what he had paid the defendent even though the defendent had completed half of the work). The author again presented his argument in a way that paced the judge's strategy. The appeal was to the following effect: "Your Honor, I had to *look* at the amount of work the defendent did in *perspective* with the amount of time, difficulty and delay it cost me personally . . . and I had to *ask* myself, 'Is it fair to ask for compensation for all of the extra trouble I've been put through?' And I *felt* that the claim I was making was a reasonable compensation for all of the *tension* and *frustration* I had to go through."

The judge agreed and decided the case in the author's favor—for the full amount of the claim. Note that even though the author used himself as the referential index in this last argument—he talked about his own internal processes rather than directing the judge as he did earlier—it still served to pace the judge. The judge had to access the same sequence of representational systems to make sense of what the author was saying.

The arguments in this last example were paraphrased simply, and most of the content details were left out so that the form of what was being done would be more obvious. Most of the content involved in this kind of utilization will be provided by the situation, and, of course, should be fed back into the appropriate slots. Content considerations like picking up and pacing the appropriate legal terms and vocabulary, and relevant precedents, will also be extremely helpful, but as we have pointed out many times, the packaging is more influential than the content.

The same tactics used by the salesperson for a multi-person presentation, described earlier in this chapter, can be utilized by an attorney making a presentation to a jury. Information about the strategies of each individual jury member may be gathered through questioning during jury selection and by observing their eye movements and other accessing cues as they respond during trial procedings. Then, by using analogue (nonverbal) markings, minimal cues and embedded commands (see *Patterns I and II*), direct your presentation at individual members of the jury and pace their strategies. In some cases you can be as direct as walking up to a jury member and talking directly to him.

If you want to convince them of a particular point, package your communication to match their belief strategies. If you want to influence their decision, utilize their decision making strategies. If you know their strategies well enough, you will know what conclusion they will arrive at, given the available information, so that you can predict and to some degree control what will happen when they are no longer in your presence. You will be able to predict how people of various strategies will interact with one another. And by observing accessing cues and other minimal cues (slight unconscious head shakes or nods, sighs, breathing changes, etc.) you will get feedback for how individual members are responding to your presentation and that of your opposition. You may know that person 1 responded positively to verbalization "X", and will probably be arguing in its favor; person 2 got feeling "Y" from the verbalization and will probably be leaning in a different direction and so on.

It will make your utilization a lot less complicated if you are able to select jury members who all share the same strategy—preferably your own. (Background, sex, political beliefs, and other content differences should be secondary to strategies as selection criteria.) If the opposing attorney shares your strategy, however, it may be better to select a jury of different strategies and rely on your own flexibility in pacing. It may also be to your benefit to hang a jury. In such a case you would want to select jury members of widely varying or opposing strategies. It would be possible to accomplish this by selecting part of the jury to have strategies which pace that of the prosecuting attorney, and the other part to have strategies pacing those of the defense attorney.

Covert anchoring and nonverbal communication can be extremely effective in courtroom situations. Courtrooms are a unique environment for communications because conscious attention is placed overwhelmingly on the digital (verbal) content of the communication (for instance, only the verbal portions of a trial are recorded and later considered). This leaves most of the nonverbal interchanges to take place covertly. Although a great deal of nonverbal intimidation and rapport building occurs in courtrooms, it is generally consciously ignored as significant to the final decision making process. Intimidation or rapport can be strengthened by covertly establishing negative or positive anchors. For example, one of the authors once accompanied a friend to a hearing (a jury was not involved) to observe the proceedings. During a few relaxed moments before the official procedings had begun, the judge knocked over some objects on his desk accidently. The court

recorder made a witty remark about the judge's "heavy handedness" which immediately set the judge back at ease and even induced genuine laughter from him. The author seized the opportunity to establish a covert anchor for the positive experience by
clearing his throat in a unique but innocuous manner that was loud
enough to be within the audible range of the judge. A number of
other cases were called before that of the author's friend, which
gave the author time to reinforce the positive anchor by reproducing the unique clearing of the throat anytime the judge exhibited
a noticeable positive response during the procedings. When the
author's friend's case was called the author cleared his throat a
number of times as his friend was being initially questioned and
inspected by the judge, and frequently during the court proceedings (although not so frequently as to seem out of the ordinary).
A quick rapport was established between the judge and the author's friend which lasted throughout the proceedings, which were
eventually settled in favor of the author's friend.

Simple tactics like this could be (and are) used just as easily, and
more effectively, by the attorneys participating in trials.

Most capable attorneys, of course, will do the majority of their
work by settlement out of court, which is generally much more
efficient and economical than going to trial. The same rapport
building, information gathering and influence tactics may be applied in out-of-court negotiations as well (other techniques, procedures and skills for negotiation will be presented in later portions
of this book). If you can elicit the motivation, convincer, decision
making, and buying strategies of your client, your opponent and
your opponent's attorney, you can utilize each of their strategies
to bring about the most rapid and satisfying solution to the negotiation. For instance, if you could elicit the buying and decision
making strategy of your opponent's attorney, you could influence
him to accept a plea bargaining or a settlement as being more
efficient than going to court.

Analogue marking and covert anchoring will be extremely useful
tools in such processes.

4.45 Implications for Psychotherapy

We have already described in this chapter a number of ways in
which strategies and anchoring could be applied therapeutically.

The essential basis of therapy and change is the three-point process—(1) eliciting and applying personal resources to a (2) present
or problematic state to assist the client in (3) achieving a desired
state. In the transcript on anchoring presented in this chapter we
showed how this could be done by integrating, (through collapsing
anchors), the client's stored representations of his or her problem
state and some relevant resources. Resources consist of reference
structures for success from the client's personal history or new
4-tuples created internally by the client.

Problems and resources are defined and identified in relation to
the client's abilities to access representational systems and gather,
process and respond to information gathered through the sensory
channels. The more access a client has to the information provided
by all of his representational systems, the more resources he will
have. This kind of flexibility will contribute greatly to the adapta-
bility of the individual. The individual's ability to gather and discriminate information about his environment and access the appropriate strategy with which to respond in that environment will
be his other major resource. This involves the sequencing of one's
behavior in the form of strategies.

Problems occur when an individual gets caught up in one representational system or a strategy that loops, and when he is kept
from observing and responding to important cues in the environment. Problems also occur when an individual accesses a strategy
or response that is inappropriate for the context.

The therapeutic procedures of neurolinguistic programming are
outcome oriented—that is, the client's behavior is engineered to
achieve specific outcomes. The essential therapeutic procedure
presented thus far in this book is the elicitation and utilization of
an appropriate resource strategy of the client's through anchoring
and pacing. The programmer, as therapist, would require the same
skills for achieving therapeutic outcomes as he would for getting
outcomes in any of the other fields discussed so far. Specifically the
programmer should be practiced and capable in each of the following:

1. *Building Rapport*—You will have established rapport with your
client when you have elicited in him the kind of behavior that is
generally labeled "trust," "responsiveness," etc. Rapport, as we
have pointed out, is essential to the success of any communication,
interaction or relationship. You will know when you have achieved
rapport when you can smoothly and easily lead the client into new

experiences. The programmer builds rapport by being sensitive to and by pacing the client's strategies and macro- and micro-behavior such as vocabulary, tonality, tempo, posture, breathing rates, facial expressions and so on. Quickly establishing anchors for resources and positive experiences will contribute to the building of rapport. Therapeutically, rapport serves to help eliminate resistence and speed up the process of change.

Programmers should be warned, however, especially those in the field of therapy, that you should not always pace all aspects of your clients' behaviors. It can be physically and mentally maladaptive to pace the behavior of many individuals. In most cases you will want to pace the client only enough to establish the rapport necessary to be able to work to achieve his desired outcomes.

2. *Information Gathering*—Through questioning and the observation of accessing cues and other minimal cues the therapist will gather information about the client's strategies and sensory abilities, to be used in the three-point process. The therapist will want to find out what natural resources the client already has available, which resources and strategies are missing and which are needed. Some clients may need a strategies to *motivate* themselves to change old behaviors, establish new patterns of behavior or to access resources that they already have. Others will need to *learn* new strategies and behaviors to be utilized in their present situation. Still others may need to employ the process of creativity or to make consequential decisions to clear up crippling incongruencies in their behavior. Many times, a number of these processes are involved. To make this determination the therapist will need to gather from the client the following information about the present state, desired state and resources of the client:

a) Desired Outcome—What do you want or need for yourself? How would you know if you got it?
b) Present or Problem state—What is happening now? What is causing you problems? What is stopping you from getting what you want?
c) Resources—What do you need (what would have to happen) in order for you to get the outcome you want? Have you ever got this outcome before? What did you do at that time?

To be relevant and utilizable to the programmer the answers to these questions need to be in terms of sensory based reference structures from the client's model of the world (although the client need not have a conscious appreciation of such answers), and the sensory observations the programmer makes of the client's behavior and strategies. "Sensory based" means specific and non-interpretive. For instance, for someone to say that he wants to be "happy" is not a sufficient answer to define a desired outcome. You need to have definite images, sounds, feelings and smells for what specific changes will be made in their behavior and their environment for them to have that kinesthetic experience. As we have said before, we highly recommend that you study the meta-model (in *Structure of Magic I*) to acquire skill at eliciting this type of answer.

3. *Therapeutic Procedure and Delivery:* Repackaging and re-presenting the client's problem in a form that matches an appropriate resource strategy that he presently has available is the primary therapeutic procedure discussed thus far. Utilizing a resource strategy in this way serves to add in abilities that have not yet been brought to bear on the client's problem state. Anchoring is another way to accomplish this.

In the coming chapters of this book, methods for the therapeutic design and installation of new resource strategies will be covered in detail.

4. *Operating Off of Feedback:* The only way you have of knowing whether what you are doing is working is by the feedback you get from your client. Only a small part of this feedback will be the conscious verbal reports of your client. The majority of it will be changes in the client's ongoing accessing cues and minimal cues, which will all be rooted in your immediate sensory experience.

No technique will magically and automatically bring about change. There are many, many conditions brought to bear on the process and results of a therapeutic interaction. It will be an absolute necessity for you to continually check your work at each step of the way. We have said before that *the meaning of your communication is the response that you elicit, regardless of what you actually intend.* You should never presuppose your behavior will always have the same effect. An anchor that you have established in one context may be inoperative in a different context. Constantly use your sensory awareness to test the outcomes of your communication in your client. If you find that what you are doing is not working, try something else. If you have proved to yourself that it won't work, why repeat it? There will always be another resource you can elicit, or another strategy to try. If you find that you are running into resistances, interference or incongruence, re-establish rapport and gather more information. (For other methods of dealing with interference phenomena, see the Installation Section of this book.)

We can represent the behavior of the client and programmer, involved in a successful interaction, as two TOTEs:

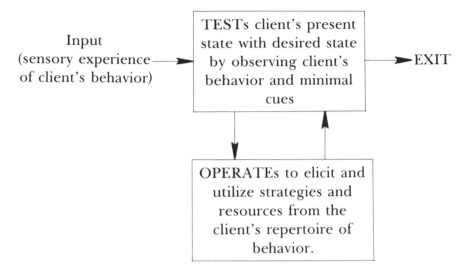

This shows that the programmer is continually testing the client's present state against the desired outcome and operating to access more resources in the client until the present state and desired state are finally one and the same (that is, until the client has exhibited the desired outcome). The programmer's tests are based on sensory information gathered and stored through all of his/her representational systems.

2) Client's TOTE:

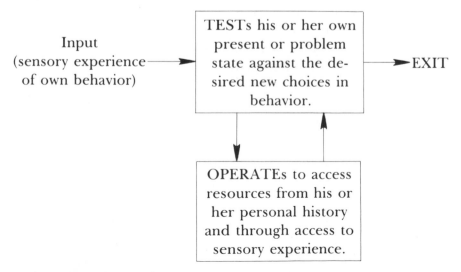

The client must also have a way to test his own progress so that he may continue or initiate the process if necessary at some point when the programmer is not around. Also the client may need to access and utilize information concerning his present state and desired state (perhaps at the unconscious level), information that is not necessary for the programmer to know. All that the programmer needs to know is the result of the test. The client's representation of his present and desired states will consist of 4-tuples and strategies that compose the two states. The client operates to access personal resources until the desired outcome is reached.

One interesting phenomenon we have noticed about many therapists who have participated in our seminars is that, though they have a good TOTE for therapy and can help other people to access resources, they have difficulty accessing resources in themselves when it comes to dealing with their own problems. This is because most of the strategies they have developed for accessing and utilizing resources are triggered by their *external* auditory and visual experience of their clients' states (a valid strategy for working with other people). Their experience of their own problems, however, is primarily in terms of *internal* kinesthetic, auditory and visual representations, and fails to trigger their programs and strategies for accessing resources. We humorously refer to this as phenomenon as "therapist's syndrome." When confronted with their own internal experience therapists often have no ready resource programs with which to deal with them. This leads to other negative kinesthetic experiences like "guilt" and "frustration" because the therapist thinks if he can't even handle his own problems, how can he reasonably presume to be assisting someone else?

A good example of how NLP utilization procedures may be used therapeutically is provided by the following account of how one of the authors assisted a therapist in overcoming such a situation during one of his workshops. Outside the therapeutic context of her office when she was working with her clients, this particular therapist would have a strong phobic response to any mention of blood or gore, or in response to any threatening gesture or tonality regardless of whether the gesture was feigned or an actual threat. The response was so strong that she would actually keel over forward, holding her face in her hands. This response had been accidentally elicited a number of times by the other participants in the workshop as they went through exercises, and it was greatly interfering with her ability to participate and learn in the context of the workshop. Because of the severity of the problem the author decided to work with her in a demonstration during the workshop.

The author began by first eliciting a resource strategy—specifically, the strategy that she used to work with her clients. It was a fine strategy for therapeutic work which included two basic subroutines. When a client would come in the therapist would first carefully observe him visually and auditorily ($V^e + A^e$). As she observed, she would begin to pace him posturally, gesturally, and with her breathing (K^e). As she did so, she would begin to get internal feelings about the client and would have the experience of somehow stepping into the client's body (K^i). If the feelings she got from this were too negative or too intense, she would access an operation that involved a dissociation from her feelings by refocusing her attention completely on external visual and auditory experience ($V^e \longrightarrow A^e$). She would then ask herself or talk to herself about what could be done with this client (A^i_d) and begin to remember images of what she had done with previous clients (V^r). When the image reached a certain degree of clarity she would implement physically with the client (K^e) what she had seen. She would then test the result of her actions through her external sensory channels and repeat the process of pacing as a test to find if the intense kinesthetic feelings had begun to subside. If they hadn't she would repeat this subroutine. If the feelings had lessened enough she would begin a second operation which involved a continued pacing of the client's posture, gestures and breathing (K^e) and would start to operate on the feelings she got from them (K^i). These feelings would access constructed images of possible interventions she could make (V^c) which she would immediately implement (K^e). She would then return again to the beginning of the strategy and test the results of her intervention by observing the client's response through her external sensory channels. In her estimation, this operation was much more creative than the other. Represented in its entirety, we could show this strategy as:

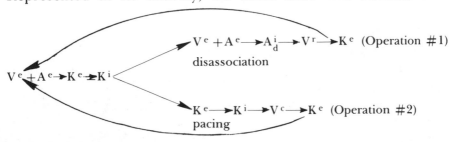

The author noted that as the therapist discussed this strategy her posture was erect and her shoulders were thrown back. Her head was tilted slightly upward and she breathed evenly from her chest.

The strategy in operation during her phobic response was a simple but powerful $V^i_- \longrightarrow K^i$ synesthesia. The external triggers would access a rapid internal visual image which would immediately anchor a strong kinesthetic reaction. In this state the posture of the therapist was slumped forward, head to her knees, eyes closed and watery with her hands covering her face. The elicitation procedures uncovered that the image was one of herself as a child, where she had been consistently and severely mistreated and beaten by her parents.

The following is a transcript of how the author ("A") utilized the therapist's ("T") resource strategy to help her overcome the phobic response. The transcript begins after the author has re-elicited the phobic response so that he may work with it. He has previously established a resource anchor with the therapist (self-initiated) in which the tighter she squeezes his wrist the more she can access a particularly positive reference experience.

TRANSCRIPT

(T is leaning forward with her head on her knees—A interrupts the ongoing strategy by having her change posture and other accessing cues.)

A: Now if you want to get over this thing it will be important that you follow all of my instructions . . . I want you to sit up straight . . . okay? . . . (helps T into upright position) . . . now open your eyes and look at me until you can see me clearly . . . come outside so that you are no longer hooked into all of that internal stuff . . . look at me.

T: (Sobbing slightly) I'm trying . . . (starts to slump over again).

A: Stay sitting up straight (holds her in upright position) . . . Squeeze my wrist.

T: I'm trying to . . . it's hard . . . my body keeps wanting to go back down there . . .

A: I know, but it's important that you stay up straight . . . now I want you to breath up here in your chest . . . Just concentrate on that for a while.

T: (Begins to breathe regularly and finally gets control over her posture.)

A: That's right . . . keep squeezing my wrist . . . Does it help?

T: UhHuh. (Sobbing has stopped.)

A: Okay, now tilt your head back . . . and I want you to look up there for a minute and see, and I only want you to see it, . . . see that image that you see right before you get that re-action.

T: (Begins to close eyes, wrinkle face and slump over.)

A: Squeeze my wrist now . . . open your eyes and look up there . . . Do you see it?

T: (Voice beginning to break) Yes . . .

A: Now I want you to look at that image carefully . . . and I want you to imagine that this little girl has just come into your office . . . Can you still see her?

T: (Tonality steadying, posture becoming more upright) Yes.

A: Can you hear her voice?

T: (Beginning to close her eyes and cry) . . . She's calling for help.

A: Now keep your eyes open and look up there at her . . . keep breathing . . . (wiggles his wrist until T begins to squeeze it) . . . Now I want you to imagine putting your body into her position and to feel her feelings . . . ($K^e \longrightarrow K^i$).

T: Ohhh . . . (Closes her eyes and slumps over).

A: Okay, that's enough, come back here with me . . . Sit up . . . Open your eyes and look at me . . . Squeeze my wrist . . . (Waits until T has recovered—then begins to utilize T's operation involving dissociation from the client). . . . Now this time I want you to just look at the child and listen to the tonal qualities of her voice . . . Continue squeezing my wrist as much as you need to . . . As you continue to look at her I want you to ask yourself (A_d^i) what you could do to help her . . . Can you see (V^i) anything to do to help her?

T: What I can do? (Holding back tears.)

A: Yes . . . What can you do to help her . . . What would you do if she were a client of yours? (Directs T's eyes up and left.)

T: (Looking down and left, then up and left) . . . Well . . . (long pause) I could go over and hold her.

A: Okay, good . . . I want you to imagine the body sensations of going over and taking that child in your arms and holding her . . . (K^e) Can you do that?

T: (Eyes shift down and right, face flattens) . . . UhHuh . . .

A: Now look at the child . . . (V^e) How is she responding?

T: (Voice hesitant as if somewhat surprised) . . . She feels better . . .

A: Is she saying anything? (A^e)

T: Umm . . . No . . . She wants to be inside herself . . . so she can heal.

A: If you were to mirror her body posture now, would you be willing to take on her feelings . . . ($K^e \longrightarrow K^i$)

T: (Stares down and right, defocuses) . . . No . . . She still has so much pain . . . (Begins to cry again and slump forward.)

A: Sit back up . . . (helps her into upright position) . . . Look at me . . . that's right . . . Squeeze my wrist . . . Come back . . . and just look at the girl again . . . (V^e) and ask yourself what else you can do . . . (A_d^i) (T's eye move down and to the left) . . . That's right . . . Now can you see anything else that you can do to help this child? (V^i)

T: (Eyes flick up and left) I can reassure her . . . and tell her to breath . . . she isn't breathing very much . . . and I can just hold her . . . that's what she says that she wants the most . . . and I can tell her that it's okay to look at me . . .

A: Fine . . . Now imagine the feelings of what it would be like if you were actually doing that . . . (K^e)

T: (Eye position changes a number of times and eventually ends up down and right) UhHuh . . . Okay . . .

A: Look at the child . . . how does she respond? (V^e)

T: She's relaxing a lot . . . She isn't crying anymore . . . (T's eyes have moved back up and to the left.)

A: As you look at her, I want you to tell me whether or not . . . if you were to mirror her body . . . whether or not you'd be willing to take on her feelings yet? ($K^e \longrightarrow K^i$)

T: (Looks up and left, then down and right, then back up and left) Ummm . . . UhHuh . . .

A: Okay . . . Great . . . Now I want you to begin to mirror her (K^e).

T: Okay . . . (Adjusts her posture by drawing her arms and legs together, and tilting her head down and to the right.)

A: Now I want you to step inside her for a moment so that you know how she . . . feels (K^i) . . . and after you've done that . . . I want you to see (V^c) if there's anything else you can do to help that child with those feelings.

T: (Looks up and right and readjusts her posture to an upright position) I can take her out of the place that she is . . . I can take her somewhere new . . .

A: Can you see where yet?

T: (Eyes shift back and forth from up right to up left position) . . . Yes . . .

A: Imagine the feelings of taking her there . . . and look at her and listen to her to see how she is responding.

T: (Eyes move from up and right to down and right to up and left) . . . Good . . . (begins to smile and nod her head) . . .

A: Now I want you to step inside her again ($K^e \rightarrow K^i$) and see (V^c) what else she might need to do.

T: (Looking down and right and then up and left) She needs to open her eyes and look around and see all of the beautiful things around her . . .

A: Imagine yourself having her do that . . . (K^e) How does she respond?

T: (Eyes scan back and forth from up left to up right, smiles and takes a deep breath) She loves it . . . it's like she's in a new world . . .

A: Does she need anything else?

T: No, she's happy there.

A: Okay . . . Now I want to leave her there for a moment . . . and I want you to come back here with me so that I can ask you a question . . .

T: Okay . . . (Looks at A)

A: From now on when you see those gestures that have scared you or hear those words that cause that reaction . . . What can *you* do?

T: (Pauses) Ummm . . . I can open my eyes and look around?

A: (Smiles) That's right . . . That's the only way you're going to
be able to tell if you're in real physical danger . . . And what are
you going to do if one of those things happens and you're not
in danger (Makes a threatening gesture at T by clenching his fist
and scowling.)

T: (Face pales and flattens. Hesitates momentarily, then color returns.) . . . I . . . I . . . I did it (laughs) . . . I didn't go away
. . .

A: That's right . . . (smiles) . . . you can laugh and feel good
. . . and anytime you need to you can always look up there and
see that little girl with her eyes wide open . . . observing carefully
everything around her . . .

The author went on to help T devise tests for being able to
tell when she was in truly dangerous situations, and to design
operations for dealing with those situations. He also tested her
responses to the formerly problematic words. All were satisfactory.

In this example of utilization the author simply directed
the therapist, step by step, through her own strategy for effective therapy, substituting internal representations for those
that were normally external. The therapist essentially did
therapy on her own internal representations, transforming
them from anchors for a powerful negative kinesthetic state
into an anchor for resources (opening her eyes and looking
around).

The therapist completed the remainder of the workshop without interference, and, in fact, after this reference experience, was
able to incorporate the material extremely rapidly. Within a
few weeks after this workshop, her work with her clients had
improved so dramatically that her client load had tripled as a
result of client referrals. So marked was the increase in her client
turnover rate that it created somewhat of a furor with the
other therapists in her agency who had no idea about what
was going on or what had occurred. She eventually left the
agency, and has conducted a successful private practice ever
since.

Footnotes to Chapter IV.

1. The exact formulation is given by W.R. Ashby in *Introduction to Cybernetics* (1956), p. 206 and p. 245. The generalized form offered in the text assumes no element has a structurally dominant position.

V. Design

We all know what "design" means—or at least we pretend we do. In order to achieve a certain outcome that can't be immediately produced or that hasn't been done before, we devise a plan or design a strategy to accomplish that particular outcome—such as starting a new business, inventing a better mousetrap or bringing surface samples back from Mars. Strategy design is most effective when all appropriate sensory channels are used to survey available resources, including all relevant environmental variables and decision variables, and to decide how to utilize them effectively in generating the desired outcome.

Consider, for example, a simple topological problem. The outcome objective is to connect the nine dots below using only four straight lines without lifting your pen or pencil from the paper. Give it a try if you want to—look at it, check your feelings and talk to yourself about it.

```
    •   •   •


    •   •   •


    •   •   •
```

If you were successful, congratulations. Very few people are able to complete this design problem successfully because they assume one or more decision variables are in the domain of environmental variables. (See the next page for the solution.)

In our experience we have found that maximum effectiveness in design is achieved by making the fewest possible assumptions about contextual constraints—those features of a particular behav-

ioral environment that only *seem* to be environmental variables—
and by making creative and efficient use of available resources.

The most frequent assumption with this problem is that one's
pen or pencil must not be moved away from the pattern of dots,
in which case five straight lines are required to connect all dots. A
second and less frequent assumption is that pen or pencil lines
must not cross. The solution is:

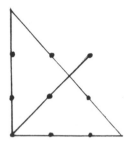

5. Design

Sometimes the organization or individual with whom the programmer is working will have no strategy immediately available;
for a particular outcome or, possibly, no strategy at all for securing
the desired outcome. Others may have strategies, which, although
achieving the outcome, are very cumbersome and inefficient. Still
others have developed strategies which achieved an outcome that
was important and adaptive in one context in the organization's or
individual's personal history, but which have been generalized to
contexts in which the outcome is no longer appropriate. In this
case, the strategy very often becomes streamlined and efficient but
the outcome becomes maladaptive. Since the strategy is so streamlined that it is entirely unconscious, the individual or organization
loses some of the requisite capability to discriminate in the test
phase and, since everything happens so quickly, there is little room
for flexibility. The person or organization becomes ineffectual.

In each of these instances the programmer may be called upon to
help design a new strategy for the individual or organization in question. Some cases require a design for more appropriate tests; others-
need more effective and efficient operation designs. In cases where
there is no existing strategy whatsoever, the programmer will have
to design from scratch an entirely new sequence of representations.

5.1 Streamlining

Streamlining is required for strategies that are cumbersome or inefficient in achieving the desired outcome. For example, we have noticed that people who were good at reading aloud when they were children, or who are still good at sight reading, have a difficult time with speed reading. This is because they have developed a strategy that includes an auditory digital step in their processing of the written word; that is, they have a verbal translation phase in their reading strategy. Very fast readers do not have this step—the visual symbols making up the word directly access internal representations without the auditory digital step.

Words, as we have pointed out, are anchors for 4-tuples of experience and only have meaning for us in terms of the experiences they elicit. Persons with an auditory digital step in their reading strategies must say the words to themselves before they will have any meaning (before they access the relevant stored experience). The strategy goes:

$$V^e_d \longrightarrow A^i_d \longrightarrow \langle A^i_t, V^i, K^i, O^i \rangle$$

| the printed word | saying word in- ternally | experience that gives the word "meaning" |

The speed reader's strategy goes directly from seeing the written word to accessing the internal 4-tuple:

$$V^e_d \longrightarrow \langle A^i_t, V^i, K^i, O^i \rangle$$

| printed word | stored experience anchored by the word |

For most people who subvocalize or verbalize the word internally, the synesthesia pattern becomes so strong that they actually can't understand written language just by looking at it—they must say it to themselves (transform it to auditory digital) before it makes any sense; otherwise it may as well be in a foreign language.

Although the strategy involving the verbalization step is a fine strategy for the outcome of sight reading aloud, (which is generally reinforced in grammar school), it is inefficient for reading quickly. It is possible to see whole sentences and paragraphs at once, but internal verbalizing requires pronouncing words in sequence, one at a time, and the information gathered by such a procedure is redundant since it contains the same digital information already present in the written material. For the outcome of rapid reading the sight reader's strategy would need to be streamlined by pulling out the unnecessary A_d^i step. This will generally involve the rehearsal and development of a synesthesia pattern working directly from V_d^e.

Speed reading courses generally have you rehearse the speed with you gather the visual information, but do not work directly with the strategy. Of the people we've talked to who have taken speed reading courses, those who already have the $V^e \longrightarrow \boxed{A,V,K,O}$ synesthesia pattern as an existing natural resource benefit the most from the training. Readers who have a strong $V^e \longrightarrow A_d^i$ synesthesia pattern learn to look at the words faster but become very frustrated at their high loss of comprehension, until they've stuck with the process long enough to reprogram the strategy themselves. The effectiveness of speed reading courses is tied to their tendency to force the reader to establish a V_d^e synesthesia pattern, because the reader doesn't have time to say the words internally. For the highly auditory reader, however, this essentially involves relearning the language which can be very difficult. The process is much easier when the individual rehearses the new strategy at the same time he or she is learning the mechanics of speed reading. In the Installation Section of this book we will provide methods you can use to assist with the installation and development of various synesthesia patterns.

Another possible method of streamlining, depending on the kind of strategy you are dealing with, is to have the individual simply practice the component parts of the strategy more and more until they become chunked as an unconscious TOTE. It is also possible to switch the modifiers between the steps in the strategy so that it works more efficiently (i.e., switching a polarity response to a congruent response).

5.2 Redesigning Maladaptive Strategies and Outcomes.

In cases where strategies produce outcomes maladaptive for the contexts in which they occur, the programmer will modify the strategy or design a new one such that a more appropriate outcome is reached.

Phobias are interesting examples of such cases. A phobic response is an outcome of a strategy that was most likely adaptive for the individual at the establishment of the behavioral pattern. The negative kinesthetic response and withdrawal were probably important for the survival of the individual at some time because of other elements in the situation. And even though the quick phobic response will always insure survival, it becomes problematic in contexts where it is unnecessary or unwanted. More appropriate responses, such as uptime and alertness, are more efficient at insuring adaptive outcomes.

Certain phobic responses are established when a very negative outcome, a result of the specific circumstances of an experience, becomes anchored to a certain situation or behavior that is then generalized to later situations or behaviors. Whenever the person is in a similar situation the negative experience is accessed, although there is no actual danger of a reoccurrence of the negative outcome.

One of the authors once worked with a woman who had a phobia of balloons. Using the elicitation procedures described earlier in this book, the author uncovered the following sequence of of representations: The person, a woman in her mid-twenties, would see a balloon externally (V^e); this would trigger a rapid unconscious visual image (V^r) of a scene that occurred when she was a child at a birthday party where a balloon had burst in her face; this would anchor up strong negative visceral feelings (K^i_-) and she would attempt to get away (K^e) from the balloon she was seeing externally.

Her strategy, then, went: $V^e \rightarrow V^r \rightarrow K^i_- \rightarrow K^e$.

The remembered visual image of the scene from the past and the negative feelings led to an outcome which, though it may have been appropriate at the party when she was a child, was no longer useful. It was evident to the author that, in order for her to have a more effective strategy, the woman needed a more appropriate and effective test with which to assess her present environment when in the presence of balloons. This would involve the design of a more accurate external visual check.

In place of the visual image of the scene from the past, the author installed, through anchoring and rehearsal (see the next chapter for installation procedures) an internal voice that said,

"Look and see if it is going to pop." From this A_d^i step she would then look again externally at the balloon in her immediate environment and the surrounding context to see if there was any chance that the balloon might pop (V^e). If there was, the voice would tell her to step back (K^e) a safe distance (as opposed to running away as she had done earlier) so that it would not pop in her face. If she wasn't sure, the voice would tell her to take one step back and look again more carefully. If she could see there was no chance of the balloon popping, the voice would tell her that it was okay to relax and feel comfortable (K^i).

This strategy contains a new test (V^e), a new set of operations and a new decision point (A_d^i):

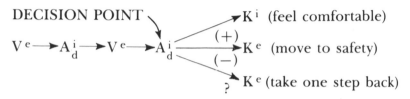

After rehearsing and testing the strategy a few times in the presence of the author, the woman was able to completely banish her former phobia of balloons.

5.21 Designing Context Markers and Decision Points.

In some cases, where an older existing outcome and accompanying strategy have become inappropriate for a majority of circumstances, they may still remain effective for some contexts (even though these contexts may be extremely rare). The programmer will then want to leave the individual with the *choice* of accessing the old strategy as well as the new one. In these cases the programmer will want to install a test or decision point in which some representation serves as a context marker to indicate in which situations which strategy is appropriate. If such a measure is not taken, interference may occur as a result of ambiguities or overlap between the two contexts, which will tend to access both strategies at the same time. The person may not know which strategy to apply and may become immobilized by responding to both strategies simultaneously. Something *tells* him to do one thing but another *looks* or *feels* as if it would be more appropriate.

The representation that serves as a marker may take on any content. It could be a certain threshold of tonality, a particular word or class of words, a positive or negative kinesthetic sensation, or some visual image or distinction picked up in the environment. The purpose of the cue is, as shown below, to differentiate which context is appropriate for which strategy:

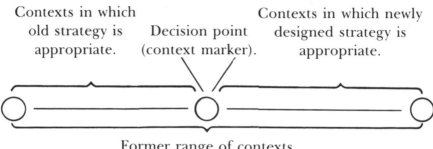

Contexts in which old strategy is appropriate.   Decision point (context marker).   Contexts in which newly designed strategy is appropriate.

Former range of contexts
in which old strategy
was applied.

As a simple example of this, let's say you are working with a manager who has a strategy, when she sees one of her personnel making a mistake, of telling him (A^e) that that isn't the way the job should be done, after which she shows him how to do it properly (V^e). You design a new strategy which involves her pacing the employee posturally first, then explaining to the employee how she feels about the way the job should be done ($K^i \longrightarrow A^e_d$), and finally walking him through what she feels to be the appropriate behavior for the task (K^e). The old strategy is still appropriate, of course, for employees whose strategies are more visually oriented. The new strategy will be more effective with kinesthetically oriented personnel. The decision point, then, should involve a test that allows the manager to discriminate between individuals to determine which strategy would be more effective. A quick decision such as this can be readily based on a momentary observation of the body type, voice tonality, predicates and available accessing cues of the employee (V^e/A^e). The strategy that the manager chooses, then, is based on her observations of the employee.

Another example of this involves a situation similar to the phobia example presented earlier. A woman in her mid-thirties with whom one of the authors was working was having many problems with the man she lived with and was experiencing a lot of pain because she had a strong negative emotional response every time he raised his voice at her, even slightly. She would become overwhelmed by feelings of fear and would want to leave the room even though her partner was not at all angry or threatening. She didn't want or understand this response, and didn't know what to do about it.

Upon eliciting her strategy, the author discovered the following sequence for the woman's strategy: She would hear the rising volume of her partner's tonality (A_t^e) and access the sound of her father's voice (A_t^i), which was in many ways similar to that of her partner. This anchor would then access an image of her father (V^r), who had beaten her severely as a child, approaching her with an angry facial expression. This would then reaccess all the feelings of fear and hopelessness that she had experienced as a child.

The author designed and installed a new strategy in which, as soon as she heard the volume of her partner's voice approaching that of her father, she would immediately look at him and compare the look on his face to the remembered threatening look of her father (V^e / V^r). If the two matched, then she could legitimately feel in danger and access her old response. If the two did not match (which was, of course, almost always the case) then she was to ask her partner to lower his voice (A_d^e) so it would be easier for her to communicate with him. If she wasn't sure, she was to walk across the room until she could look at him and feel that there was a safe distance between them ($K^e \longrightarrow V^e \longrightarrow K^i$), and ask him to lower his voice (A_d^e). A certain pairing between tonality and facial expression, then, was used as a context marker or decision criterion to choose which operation or strategy to access. Another way to think about this is that certain combinations of tonality and facial expression are programmed as anchors for different responses. We can show the newly designed strategy as follows:

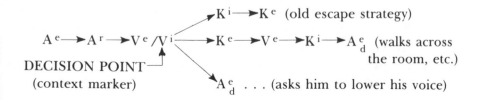

5.3 Artificial Design.

The purpose of artificial design is to create a strategy that will secure the designated outcome or outcomes in the most efficient and effective manner when there is no appropriate strategy immediately available. This requires that the strategy contain all of the necessary tests and operations needed to sequence the behavior and gather the information and feedback involved in obtaining the desired outcome.

One useful method of designing effective strategies is to find a person, group or organization (depending on which you are dealing with) that already has the ability to achieve the outcome you desire to attain, and to use their strategy as a model for your design task. If you want to be able to do well in physics, find someone who already has that ability and use his strategy as a model from which to design your own. If you want to be able to get outcomes in the fields of therapy, management or law, find the people who are already able to do this and use their strategies as a model.[1] This way you will be assured that the strategy you are designing will be effective.

This method of design has many implications for the field of education. We have pointed out before that many teachers don't actually have a good strategy for the subject they are teaching. A creative writing teacher, for instance, may have a good strategy for reading and criticizing literature, but not for generating it. By finding the the strategies of a number of people who are good creative writers, the teacher could improve the quality of his course, beginning each term by teaching and installing, during the first few days of the class, the effective creative writing *strategies.* Once she has done this, the teacher would then procede with the content of the course. This will increase the effectiveness of students' writing abilities. The same procedure will work for all subjects—if the *strategy* for incorporating and handling the material is taught first, the learning of the *content* will be more easily and effectively accomplished.

When consulting for educational institutions we have often organized a series of study groups for students set up in the following way. Students are covertly divided up on the basis of their ability to achieve outcomes in the particular subject in question, into fast, medium and slow students. Each study group is composed of two students from each division (two fast, two medium, and two slow). After we teach them about representational systems, pacing and accessing cues, the students elicit and swap strategies with one another for a number of subjects. Invariably, students who are slow in one task have a better strategy for some other task, and each of the students is able to offer a resource to the group. Because each benefits from the others a support network with mutual rapport tends to be built. The process of eliciting and swapping strategies is also fun. And this kind of grouping will keep students, especially of grammar school age, from being labeled and reinforced as "slow" or "stupid." In many of the places where we have set up such a program there have been dramatic improvements in the performances of the "slow" students within a matter of days.

One should be careful, of course, when designing strategies through modeling, that you don't get stuck or stagnated with one particular model for doing things. Challenging the old limitations and models and creating new ones is the basic means for improvement available to us as a species. The neurolinguistic programming model itself is continually changing, transforming and improving itself.

In designing strategies there will be some cases where *any* new sequence of representations you design will be more effective than the existing one. You may even wish to experiment by changing around various sequences for a particular strategy just to find out how the outcome will be affected.

When you are trying to tailor a specific strategy for a specific task and for a specific client it will be important, in addition to taking into account which kinds of discriminations in which representational systems are required for the task, to take into account the natural abilities of the client to access, gather information, and make discriminations in the various represntational systems. The design of your strategy will have to take into consideration which resources are missing and which are present in your client's existing repertoire of strategies and abilities. Some individuals, for instance, may have very limited abilities for accessing and making discriminations in one of their representational systems, and the programmer may have to first help the individual develop the representational system so that it is useful, before he can design it into a strategy. Such training may sometimes consume a considerable amount of time and energy, and the programmer may want to make a "cost-benefit" analysis as to whether it will be more beneficial to develop a particular representational system or synesthesia pattern to fit the requirements of a strategy, or to redesign the strategy to fit the existing resources of the individual.

Some people have strong and inflexible synesthesia patterns that divert or interfere with a designed strategy sequence. An individual, for example, who has a highly developed visual-to-kinesthetic synesthesia pattern may have a very difficult time performing that operation in reverse—that is, going from feelings to images. In such cases much time may have to be spent interrupting the inflexible synesthesia pattern and rehearsing and developing the new one(s).

The time spent on developing representational systems and flexibility in synesthesia patterns, however, is generally well worth the trouble. Teaching somebody to access and gather information through an underdeveloped representational system can bring about dramatic changes.

One of the authors was once working with a person who had been diagnosed and institutionalized as a paranoid schizophrenic. The author quickly noticed that the person had one essential strategy for decision making, motivation, remembering, etc. This strategy was to take any of the experiences in his other representational systems and transform them into internal kinesthetic sensations. Although this was limiting in itself, it was complicated by the fact that the person was only able to make three basic distinctions in his kinesthetic experience—"anger", a kind of neutral calmness and a kind of "fear/paranoia". All of the person's ongoing experience was interpreted and boiled down into one of these three categories, with a primary emphasis on "fear/paranoia," of course. As therapy, the person was simply taught to make more and more distinctions in his kinesthetic experience and to practice different synesthesia patterns. As his ability to discriminate feelings improved, his repertoire of behavior increased rapidly (much to the surprise of the hospital staff) because it was no longer always channeled through the previous kinesthetic bottleneck of three feelings. As the person's feelings and choices of behavior expanded so did his ability to get along with the staff, and he was eventually discharged from the hospital.

People who are depressive often share a strategy similar to that of the person described above; only the content of their feelings is different. All of their strategies end up in negative K^i which tends to create a self-fulfilling and reinforcing belief system, or strategy, that everything is negative. They can always validate this belief by tacking on a negative K^i to any particular ongoing experience. Therapists often have a difficult time helping depressives because it is hard to access resources for them. If you try to persuade them to think of a time they felt good, they may be able to remember the experience but end up feeling worse because they are unable to feel that way now. They may feel that they were once able to be happy but that it's all gone now. Typically, they will have a polarity response to any positive experience you attempt to access as a resource.

Their problem is not, of course, that they really don't have resources—everyone has experiences that can serve as resources, no matter what his personal history has been like. Nor is their problem the inability to access resources—anyone who can see, hear or feel can do that. The root of the trouble is in their strategy for responding to the given context—the therapeutic context, for instance when asked to make a decision about whether they have pleasant memories, or whether they have the ability to recall such memories. Some depressives will have a polarity response to qualitative (interpretive/judgemental) words but not to sensory specific description. For instance, if you ask them if they ever had a *good, positive* or *happy* experience, they will have a polarity response. If, on the other hand, you ask them if they can think of a time when they could see clearly, were breathing fully and regularly in their stomach, etc., no such polarity response occurs.

If you find that a person you are working with has a strong polarity response you can always utilize it by "playing polarity" with them. You can say, "You know . . . I don't think there's any hope at all for you . . . you have absolutely no resources or positive abilities that I can tell . . . You're a hopeless case . . ." If the person has a polarity strategy, they will have to have a polarity response to this statement, too and come up with resources.

Another way to deal with these cases, of course, is to bypass the person's existing strategy by designing and installing a completely new strategy. You will generally want to do this covertly so the person will not have a chance to process the new strategy through their old strategy before it has been installed. You may also need to interrupt their existing strategy in order to install the new one (for information on how to do this see the Installation Section of this book).

Once one of the authors was working with a depressed person and encountered a strategy such that whenever the man tested his internal feelings and found that they were positive, a voice would trigger in his head and say, "This can't last . . . I always end up feeling bad again eventually . . . so I might as well start feeling bad now . . ." The author redesigned the content of the strategy so the test and the verbalization were reversed, and installed it in place of the other strategy. With the new strategy, everytime the person found himself feeling bad, he would say to himself, "This can't last . . . I'll end up feeling good again eventually . . . so I might as well start now . . ."

5.31 Well-Formedness Conditions for Artificial Design.

As we have stated, the goal of artificial design in strategy work is to create the strategies that will most efficiently and effectively secure a particular outcome. This requires that the programmer discover: 1) what kind of information (for both input and feedback purposes) needs to be gathered, and in which representational systems, in order to achieve the outcome; 2) what kind of tests, distinctions, generalizations and associations need to be made in the processing of that information; 3) what specific operations and outputs need to be elicited by the individual or organization in order to achieve the outcome; and 4) what is the most efficient and effective sequence in which all of these tests and operations should take place. When you are tailoring your design to a specific client, it will be necessary to find out which abilities and resources are already present within the client's repertoire of behavior, which are missing and which are needed. We have developed a set of four general well-formedness conditions for design to help you find what is present, missing or needed in your client's existing strategies, and which, if the conditions are met, will insure that the strategies you design will be efficient and effective:

1. THE STRATEGY MUST HAVE AN EXPLICIT REPRESENTATION OF THE DESIGNATED OUTCOME. If the strategy does not identify and get the specified outcome then it is useless.

The test phase of the TOTE, as discussed in Chapter II, requires that the organism compare a representation of where they are now with where they desire to be. For this an explicit representation of the outcome is essential. How many of you readers when you've tried to help someone make a decision or implement some new behavior, have asked questions like, "What do you want out of this interaction?" or "How will you know if you've (changed, made a good decision, etc.)?" or "Where are you trying to go with all of this?" and received answers like, "Well, I'd be happier," "I'd just feel differently," "Things would be better," or "Things wouldn't be the way they are now." None of these responses provide enough information from which to build an adequate strategy. It is no wonder that such persons have been unable to achieve their "goals."

When somebody simply says, "I would feel different," he has represented his desired outcome only in the kinesthetic channel and may not have any idea how things would look, sound or smell when change has taken place. Such a person doesn't have any way of devising operations utilizing these sensory modalities.

Choosing the sensory systems with which to represent the desired outcome is a crucial step in the design of any strategy. Sometimes a person may overspecify his outcome. A person, for instance, may construct a visual image of how he thinks his friends and family and associates should look and act in order for that individual to have secured his outcome. If the individual begins to carry out operations to make his friends, family and associates look and act that way, everybody involved may experience a great deal of discomfort and frustration—a so-called disappointment strategy. In some cases you will want to leave some aspects of the outcome unspecified until you have gathered more information. There are some aspects of particular outcomes that sometimes cannot or should not be decided ahead of time. In instances where this is the case, however, an explicit operation to get feedback and to gather information from which to build or modify a representation of the outcome should be included in the strategy. Implicit in this well-formedness condition, of course, is the requirement that the strategy secure the desired outcome it has represented.

2. ALL THREE MAJOR PRIMARY REPRESENTATIONAL SYSTEMS (V, A and K) MUST BE INVOLVED IN THE STRATEGY SEQUENCE. Each of our representational systems is capable

of gathering and processing information that is not available to the others. We can perceive and organize things visually that we cannot do kinesthetically or auditorily. We can sense and process things kinesthetically that we cannot do visually and auditorily and so on. This condition will insure that the resources of each system and therefore of the organism are at least potentially available.

3. AFTER "N" MANY STEPS, MAKE SURE ONE OF THE MODIFIERS IS EXTERNAL. This means that after so many steps in the strategy the individual should tune one of his/her representational systems to the external environment. This is to insure that the person or organization is getting feedback from their external context so they will be able to detect what effect the progression of the strategy is having and so they will not become caught up in their own internal experience. "N" will be determined by the kind of task being performed. If it is important to the carrying out of a task (such as basketball or therapy) that you gear your responses on the basis of actions taking place in your external environment, then put in an external check often. If the task requires more internal processing (like writing down an incident from memory or solving a complicated math problem) your external checks can take place less often. If you are not certain how many external checks are required for a task, a good rule of thumb is is, "When in doubt, put one in."

An alternative way of satisfying this requirement, especially in the context of tasks which require extensive internal processing, is the use of "counters." For example, suppose you are attempting to make a decision among several alternatives and your strategy involves a three point loop

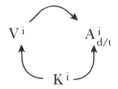

$$V^i \qquad A^i_{d/t}$$
$$K^i$$

for each alternative. Specifically, you look at each alternative (V^i), comment to yourself about it ($A^i_{d/t}$) and check to determine how you feel about it (K^i). Your strategy allows you to cycle around the loop to edit the pictures (V^i) based on the comments ($A^i_{d/t}$) and feelings (K^i) you have in response to them in order to arrive at the best visual representation of that particular alternative. The danger here is that you could become trapped in the editing and stay in the loop too long. This well-formedness condition is designed to protect against such an occurrence. The condition of including an external check would require interrupting the internal processing each cycle around the loop to determine, for example, how much time has passed. Equally effective and more natural would be the maneuver of introducing a counter on the loop. There are two easy ways of accomplishing this: (1) In the V^i step, you introduce a visual representation of a counter—that is, the first time through the numeral "1" is affixed visually to the starting image; each time the loop returns to that step (V^i) the visual counter is incremented by 1, so that consecutive cycles are visually noted 1, 2, 3 . . . etc. Using this approach, the decision maker would determine, prior to beginning the process, the number of edits to allow for each alternative. When that numeral appears, the strategy kicks in the next alternative and resets the visual counter back to 1. (2) Introduce a K which is outside the loop

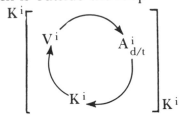

The K^i is timed—that is, the decision maker determines prior to beginning the decision making how long to allow for constructing and editing each alternative. K^i is set for that length of time. When that time period (kept kinesthetically) has elapsed the K^i outside the loop switches the decision maker into the next alternative to be considered.

4. THERE SHOULD BE NO TWO POINT LOOPS IN THE STRATEGY. A two point loop is a loop in the strategy where the individual cycles or spirals between two representational systems, the usual result being that the loop doesn't exit. The loop is kept from exiting due to an inadequate test or because the operate phase (which only involves one representation system) is too minimal to make any significant change in the value of the representation being tested for. Loops that do not exit can be established in strings of representations that display more than two points, of course, and these should be avoided as well. But the majority of spiraling cases occur in loops of only two points because they do not generally access enough information or behavior to form an effective TOTE. An example of a two point loop would be if,

during some strategy, an individual triggers an internal voice that criticizes him in a high pitched, blaming tonality. The blaming voice, in turn, triggers negative visceral feelings. The voice then blames the individual for feeling bad, and this causes the person to feel even worse. The voice then becomes further agitated and blaming, and the loop spirals between auditory and kinesthetic: $A_d^i \rightleftharpoons K^i$. The same sort of interaction can happen among people in a family, group or organization as well. Notice that a change in any of the modifiers in a particular representational step qualifies as a new distinction. A change from auditory internal (A^i) to auditory external (A^e) would have kept this sequence from becoming a two point loop. A change from tonal to digital, from remembered to constructed or from a polarity response to a meta response would each qualify as a legitimate difference in representational quality.

As an illustration of these four well-formedness conditions, consider the following example of a decision making strategy which violates all of the well-formedness conditions. One of the authors was working with a woman who was experiencing a great many unnecessary problems in her life because of her inability to make decisions. The author elicited her decision making strategy and found that it essentially consisted of one two point loop. Whenever it was necessary for her to make a decision she would begin by proposing one of the possibilities to herself verbally. She would then get a feeling about what it would be like to be doing that particular activity. As soon as she got that feeling, however, she would have an auditory polarity response in which a voice would tell her that she should do something else which the voice would then specify. Just as she would get a feeling for doing the second alternative proposed by the voice, the voice would cut in again and tell her she should be doing something else. She would wind up bouncing back and forth among the various options available to her but would never be able to choose any of them because of the polarity loop, until some external experience would finally force her into choosing one of the alternatives. If there was no external intervention, however, she would sometimes spend days at a time literally immobilized, either lying in bed or sitting around her house.

Obviously the strategy did not contain all of the representational systems, nor did it achieve the outcome of successful decision making. It contained no external checks and represents a classic example of the two point loop:

$$A_d^i \rightarrow K^i$$
$$\searrow_p$$

The author designed a new strategy for the woman that contained two visual steps. She was to begin the strategy by looking externally at a clock and at other conditions in her external environment (V^e). She was next to tell herself how much time she had to make her decision (A_d^i); this was based on what kind of decision was to be made but was not to exceed an hour unless there were unusual conditions. She was then to make an explicit internal image of the clock in her mind's eye, showing what time it would be at the completion of her decision (V^i). After getting a feeling for the amount of time she had (K^i), she would check the clock to see how much time had elapsed (V^e) and propose her first option to herself verbally (A_d^i). The following step was to make an image of what would be involved in the task and outcome (V^i). After she could see these details she would get a feeling for what it would be like to carry out that option (K^i). Then she was to check the clock again (V^e) to assess her progress in relation to the time limit, and propose possibility number two to herself verbally (A_d^i), picture (V^i) what was involved and check out how she felt about what she saw (K^i). She was to check the clock again (V^e) and repeat this operation until she saw that time had run out, at which point she was to tell herself (A_d^i) that time had run out and that she would now make her decision. She was to look at all the images she had made of the various possibilities (V^i) and begin to carry out the one that felt the best to her (K^i). This new strategy proceeded in the following manner:

$$V^e \rightarrow A_d^i \rightarrow V^i \underset{m}{\rightarrow} K^i \rightarrow EXIT$$

The strategy was installed and tested on the spot by having the woman utilize it to make an important decision that she had been putting off for weeks.

5.311 *OUTCOME SEQUITUR.*

In many cases where a person is looping in a strategy between a number of possible alternatives, as in the instance just cited, or when a person is having motivational problems, we will design into his strategy a representation we call the "outcome sequitur." The term means that which follows the outcome—what happens after the outcome has been achieved.

For instance, rather than simply designing and installing a strategy for a student to achieve the outcome of writing a term paper, we might also include a representation of what his experience would be like *after* the paper is finished as part of the outcome. Similarly, instead of having an alcoholic concentrate on the outcome of stopping his drinking habit, we would have him consider what he would be doing if he weren't drinking—as part of his outcome. This type of maneuver can often automatically positively reframe the person's experience of the specific task he is trying to accomplish by putting it into perspective with a larger train of events.

Considering the implications or outcomes of a particular outcome you are attempting to secure also has important ecological value especially if you are involved in working with businesses, organizations, families or in political situations where every outcome will propagate a series of responses from others involved in the system. The ability or inability to achieve an outcome may be based on secondary gains or contextual conditions that are not uncovered until the outcome sequitur is explored. These ecological considerations will be covered in more detail in the next section of this book.

5.312 *RULES OF THUMB IN DESIGN*

The purpose of design is to maximize efficiency and ease in achieving a particular outcome. There are other considerations that, although they are not well-formedness conditions, you should keep in mind while designing strategies: 1) When possible, *choose the strategy that has the fewest steps*—this is the *modeling elegance* rule again; don't complicate the strategy if you don't need to. 2) *Having a choice is, in general, better than not having a choice*

—this goes back to the law of requisite variety mentioned earlier; variability in behavior is essential to adaptation. This also refers to the point we made earlier that the old strategies you are redesigning may still be useful in some contexts. When working with NLP you should never have to "get rid" of anything, only contextualize maladaptive behavior and design and install effective strategies. 3) When possible, *opt for positive motivation when designing strategies.* This is essentially an ecological consideration. Many individuals, and some institutions and organizations, have strategies that utilize negative motivation for achieving outcomes. Some people, for instance, have motivation or decision strategies that have tests that require a certain level of stress to be reached before the person will operate to access resources. The strategy keeps looping until enough stress is built up to anchor in a resource strategy. Others use punishment systems and aversive conditioning methods as motivators. And, although these methods are sometimes quite efficient and effective in securing outcomes in the short run, ecologically, because of the physiological effects of prolonged stress, pain, anger, and other negative visceral representations, they will often end up being detrimental to the health of the person or system. Also, we have found that negative anchors have a propensity to extinguish if not reinforced. Positive anchors, on the other hand, build in their own reinforcement.

5.313 Meta-Outcomes.

The topics of negative motivation and requisite variety are only two of a number important ecological considerations that occur in strategy design. One of the most important questions to ask yourself when designing a strategy or choosing an outcome is, "Will it violate personal or organizational ecology?" Make sure that the strategy you design does not go directly against any other strategies that the client has. Sometimes there will be important reasons why an individual or organization hasn't achieved some particular outcome or developed a particular strategy.

Any given specific outcome or task is framed within the context of a higher order outcome, an organizing principle or *"meta-out-*

come" for the system (ie., the individual or organization). A meta-outcome is one that organizes the behavior of the system in terms of general goals like the preservation and survival, growth and evolution, protection, betterment, adaptation, etc. of the system. To be ecological, any other outcome or strategy must contribute to these basic outcomes. Most naturally occurring strategies and outcomes are geared for achieving the adaptive meta-outcomes, but it will be important to test to make sure those that are artificially designed are congruent with these meta-outcomes. Gregory Bateson in *Steps to an Ecology of Mind* discusses some of the dangers of what can happen if outcome oriented behavior is not kept ecological. (See his article, "Conscious Purpose versus Nature" pp. 426–439)

One should take note, that, as with the case of the phobic response discussed earlier in this section, some strategies and outcomes which contributed to one of these meta-outcomes at one point in time and/or in a particular context may actually be counterproductive to the achievement of that outcome in other circumstances, and it will important to include specific context markers in your design.

Often, establishing the meta-outcome first will help you in the choice and design of specific outcomes and strategies.

5.32 Applying Artificial Design in a Group Situation.

Designing a strategy for a group or organization draws from the same basic principles as individual strategy design. The purpose is to accomplish an outcome in the most effective manner possible. In an individual's strategy, the elements that you sequence to perform tests and operations are the representational systems—in an organization the elements that you sequence to perform the various tests and operations are the people. As in a strategy for an individual, a strategy for an organization will be composed of the following parts: 1) gathering and inputting information, 2) processing that information by making tests, associations, generalizations and discriminations, 3) operating and outputting in response to the outcome of this processing, and 4) gathering feedback on the effects of the operations and outputs. We can diagram these visually in the following way:

INPUT—►PROCESSING—►OUTPUT/OPERATIONS

FEEDBACK

An organization is in essence a TOTE in which people are the elements that perform the test & operate functions instead of representational systems. In designing a strategy for an organization you will need to take the same things into account that you do when designing a strategy for an individual:

a) What is the desired outcome of the strategy? DESIRED STATE

b) How will you know if you have achieved it? FEEDBACK

c) What specific elements and functions are required to achieve the outcome? REQUIRED RESOURCES (division of labor)

d) Which of these are already available in the organization you are working with and which are missing? PRESENT STATE (Cost-benefit analysis: Should you try to obtain the missing resources, or design the strategy with what you already have?)

e) How do you sequence and schedule your elements and functions to achieve the outcome in the most elegant and efficient way possible?

Let us demonstrate how neurolinguistic programming principles and strategy technology may be used to engineer an effective group strategy by means of an example showing its application to team building, decision making and brainstorming procedures. The example is drawn from our consultation work with businesses and organizations.

Suppose you are consulting for a group of five executives involved in a decision making process (for instance, let's say they are based in New York and are trying to decide whether to expand to Pennsylvania and to initiate several specific new programs). The executives are having a difficult time, however. Each has a strategy that operate in such a way that his or her behavior tends to negate that of one or more of the others. They are out of rapport and end up mostly arguing with one another. The conflict is delaying and distracting them from achieving their outcome. Using NLP principles you would set about organizing the situation in the following way:

1. The programmer establishes him/herself in meta-position—having no committments other than insisting on a high quality outcome, independent of the content of that decision.

2. The programmer elicits and states as explicitly as possible (skill with the Meta-Model will help greatly here) the desired outcome (O_1) of this particular session.

In this example O_1 is to decide whether the program for expansion into the state of Pennsylvania is sound.

3. The programmer then frames this outcome by putting it into the context of the corporate or meta-outcomes (O_M).

Meta-outcomes in this example might include:

(1) to increase company revenues.

(2) to provide a high quality product and service to customers in Pennsylvania which increases

   (a) the absolute size of the industry market.

   (b) their company's relative share of the market.

4. The programmer and the executives are then to specify (for feedback purposes) what specific elements will constitute an adequate O_1. This will be the outcome sequitur of the particular meeting they are involved in. The information gathering process should also include a consideration of the outcome sequitur (the results of achieving the desired state they are deciding upon) for O_1.

For example, O_1 is achieved when the program has been reviewed by all group members and either:

(1) a decision has been made that the entire program is sound and its implementation is the next step, or

(2) a decision has been reached that the overall program is sound and some portion(s) of the program

   (a) requires further information.

   (b) the information required is identified—sources for the information are identified—the cost of securing such information is adaquately offset by the expected value of such information (cost-benefit analysis).

   (c) the assignment to secure the information is made and the next meeting scheduled.

(3) O_1 is judged unsound and O_M has again been validated. Assignments to develop alternatives to O_1 in achieving O_M are made (including feedback to arrange a next meeting at which O_2, O_3, ... O_n will be presented as ways of achieving O_M).

It will be very helpful in all procedures if all information relevant to the decision making process is available or translatable into all representation systems (verbally, pictorially on graphs and flip charts, and in a way that is relatable to feelings).

5. The programmer should then assess the present state capabilities of each of the participants in the decision making process. Specifically, the programmer should identify what strategy is functioning for the task he is trying to accomplish. This can be accomplished:

(1) from the observations the programmer has made of their interactions before he began his interventions.

(2) by eliciting an appropriate strategy from the individual's personal history (e.g., "Think of a time that you were able to make a good decision that involved a number of complex issues").

Let's say that the programmer has chosen option (1) and observed the interactions of the executives as they initially attempted to make the decision. From his observations he has been able to determine the following:

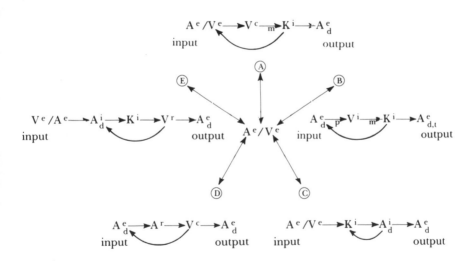

Each circle represents one of the people involved in the process. Each is inputting the external visual and auditory signals of the others. The strategy sequence nearest them indicates the strategy that has been observed in them by the programmer.

PERSON A has been able to take the visual and auditory input (V^e/A^e) from the others and *see* at least fifteen *new* possibilities (V^c) that he *feels* (K^i) would increase the revenue of the corporation, and has described these images to the others (A_d^c).

PERSON B, when he has gotten person A's auditory output, has had a polarity response to it and accessed remembered images (V^r) of situations similar to those that A is proposing where something has gone wrong. He finds fault with all of A's proposals and has strong negative feelings (K_-^i) about what he sees as a possible disaster. He expresses these feelings to A in a hostile tone of voice (A_t^c) which has precipitated a number of arguments between he and A.

PERSON C feels that an expansion is necessary (K^i) but does not have any clear ideas on what specifically needs to be done, but she keeps telling herself (A_d^i) that she'll know it when she hears it.

PERSON D, through remembering a number of ideas she's heard and picked up, (A^r), is able to modify the faults that that B has found in A's proposals so that it looks (V^c) as though they may work.

PERSON E has been able to figure out how to possibly implement some of both A's ideas and D's revisions by asking himself if it could be done (A_d^i), beginning to sense himself going through the motions (K^i) and then remembering ways similar things were done in the past (V^r).

From the information he has gathered the programmer can determine that A's strategy tends to be specialized for creativity but is not always practical. B has an effective critical strategy good for testing ideas for possible faults but tends to lack the creativity needed to operate to modify ideas to make them workable. C's strategy is without a visual component and is not particularly useful in terms of creativity. She will make a decision on the basis of her feelings. D has a good strategy for modifying input and making it more practical. D also possesses some creativity. E has a good strategy for implementation but lacks the ability to be creative or to modify.

6. The programmer's task now is to sequence the interactions of these five people into the most effective order for obtaining the outcome. He may choose to either:

(1) spend time developing and designing more effective and versatile strategies for each of the participants, installing them as added resources, or

(2) sequence the existing strategies in the most useful order given the existing outcomes of the strategies. This would involve

organizing the interaction so that the output of one individual's strategy flowed easily and usefully as input to the strategy of another—to set up a system in which each of their strategies is maximally utilized for what it does well.

Let's say, for the purpose of this example, that the programmer chooses option (2). He has already made a determination of the special abilities and deficiencies of the strategies the persons involved. The task now is to

(a) Number each participant and schedule them to present their ideas for a specified time (eg. five minutes). Each is to take the output of the one that has come before them and to process it through his or her strategy. Each must let the others talk without interruption.

The trick, of course, will be to find the the sequence that best fits the natural resources of the participants. You may, for example, want to design your sequence such that A starts with his creativity strategy. Then you schedule B to critique A's suggestions. Then you schedule D to modify the faults that B found and make A's proposals useful again. Then you schedule E to figure out ways to implement the modified proposals. And finally you schedule C to feel everything out and decide if the proposals and implementation procedures are appropriate.

You are assigning them to do what they have done before anyway. Their problem has been, however, that their sequencing was somewhat random and, because of conflicts, nothing was ever really allowed to develop. They did not have a framework structured to take full advantage of their abilities. By scheduling them you reframe the situation so that B is no longer "insulting" A by finding fault, but carrying out a necessary function. Each person's strategy is framed as a resource (which indeed it is) and each is respected for his or her skill. Person A generates ideas specifically *so that* B may test them and find where they need to be modified and made even better. The time becomes maximally utilized and each time block is used for one function at a time. One major difficulty with many group decision making processes is that the people jump from considering and defining present state to desired state to problem state to resources, and often the content gets jumbled. One important function of scheduling is that when you are considering a desired state you stick with desired state until it has been specified in detail. These details may later be modified on the basis of other information—but the process of initially defining it is not interrupted.

(b) The programmer must also control for adverse nonverbal or interpersonal interactions, whether they are intentional on the part of the participants or not. Sometimes one member of the group will use a certain tonality, for instance, that triggers negative feelings in another, even though the person using the tonality is merely excited and does not mean to intimidate. If the programmer observes such a response s/he can take steps to neutralize that tonal anchor and repeat what she or he has just said over again.

By making such an intervention, the programmer can assist the executives into each contributing their strategy as a part of a larger decision making strategy, so that the overall decision they make together is better then any could have made alone.

FOOTNOTES TO CHAPTER V.

1. We have been making plans for some time to organize a project in which the twelve people who are best able to achieve outcomes in each of the major divisions of the sciences and the arts will be modeled for their strategies. This would result in a battery of the most effective strategies for many fields or sectors of organized human behavior.

VI. INSTALLATION

As we approach the final section of this book, we are approaching the end of what may be viewed as the second act in a three-act play. Some appropriate portion of your life experience prior to reading this book is act one, in which the main characters are introduced, the plot is established, and the tempo and pitch of the action have risen to create exactly the right degree of anticipation for act two. "Live" theater, for over 2,500 years, has provided one of the most powerful and exciting forms of entertainment available to the human species. The sensory encounter with living people—surrounding us in the audience as well as on stage—allows us to experience a range and variety of synesthesia patterns that we've learned to appreciate and value in the context of that altered state of consciousness commonly called "vicarious" experience.

In the second act of our play—this book—the characters and their interactions are revealed to a depth and extent not available to us on the level of act one, generating new levels of meaning to the dialogue, gestures and facial expressions of the characters and setting the stage for the launching of the most powerful act in the drama . . . act three. Under the impact of the insights, dialogues and outcomes of act two, the action in the third act takes a quantum jump to a new dimension of experience, leading the protagonist to the denouement of your choice—a meta-choice if you wish.

For weeks prior to the first public performance of a stage play, the actors and actresses of the cast rehearse their lines before the watchful eyes and ears of the director, who may insist on certain body movements, gestures, facial expressions, tones of voice, rate and volume of dialogue delivery and so forth to generate maximum effect in the eventual presentation before a "paying" audience. The function of a director, in part, is to recognize, elicit and utilize the talent resources of each member of the cast to maximize his or her performance. A discriminating theater-goer decides to attend a play as much on the basis of who the director is as well as the cast and author.

During rehearsal members of the cast anchor their on-stage entrances, exits, movements and dialogue lines to particular cues —words or actions immediately preceding their own "parts"— until each scene and act flow as smoothly as the ongoing life experience it represents and emphasizes. The purpose of all pre-liminary work is to embed, to disguise, to render magically invisible in the flow of the performance another and more fundamental set of cues: a sequence of culturally rooted visual and auditory stimuli that evoke appropriate combinations of audience 4-tuples. By controlling the sequence, tempo, timing, variation and magnitude of audience internal kinesthetics during a stage play, the actors and actresses play their audience much as a musician plays an instrument. If it is done well, both the audience and the cast thoroughly enjoy their shared experience.

Whether art imitates life or life imitates art, effective installation is like the preparatory work that is integral to a successful performance. The NLP practitioner, like the director of the play, insures that all cues are appropriately anchored and that each member of the cast has rehearsed until his performance is exactly tuned to achieve the desired outcome—only in this case you will write the script for your own third act.

There are two basic ways to install a strategy sequence that you have designed: (1) through *anchoring* and inserting the steps of the strategy and (2) through having the client *rehearse* (a form of self anchoring) the strategy sequence. Although these two methods will be treated separately as we initially present them, they are best utilized in conjunction with one another—firing off the anchors you have established as you "walk" the person through the strategy.

The goal of installation is to make the strategy you have designed function as naturally and automatically as the existing strategy you are replacing. Each step in the strategy must automatically trigger the next. There are two major well-formedness conditions for installation that you will be testing for to insure that you have done effective work:

1. The entire strategy sequence must be available to the client as an intact unit—so that each step is automatically tied to the next.

2. The strategy sequence must be tied to the appropriate context —so that it is wired (anchored) to some stimulus (context marker) within the context that will initiate the strategy when that stimulus is introduced. This is to insure that the strategy will initiate itself at the appropriate time.

To install a strategy effectively you will have to interrupt or break the existing strategy at the appropriate place so that the new one may be inserted. Generally this is just a matter of timing, so that you begin the new strategy at the place in the existing sequence where the old strategy would have gone into operation. Sometimes, however, you will have to purposefully interrupt the existing strategy (if the synesthesia patterns are too ingrained or the strategy operates too quickly) before the new one can be effectively installed.

As you install the strategy you will also want to test its ecological fit. (This can be done by finding the outcome sequitur). If you try to install a strategy that is somehow inappropriate or maladaptive for the client you will encounter interference phenomena such as resistence to the strategy or "sabotage" of the installation process.

6.1 Installation Through Anchoring.

In the Utilization Section of this book we discussed how anchors could be used to establish and elicit either full 4-tuple representations of an experience, or could be used to selectively access one particular portion of a 4-tuple. The use of anchors in strategy installation involves the anchoring of a selective sequence of individual representations over time. Just as anchors may be used to access either one or more parts or the whole of a 4-tuple, in the utilization of strategies, so may they be used to access either parts or the whole of a particular strategy sequence for installation purposes. An entire strategy sequence may be anchored with a single anchor, or the programmer may selectively anchor single steps or subroutines (synesthesia patterns).

A major difference, however, between the use of anchoring in utilization procedures and the use of anchoring in installation is that, in utilization, you want to use anchoring for controlling the content of particular strategy steps. In installation you want to control the strategy step itself. What you will want to anchor for installation purposes, then, is not any particular content, but rather the *act of using* the particular representational system required for the step. You will want to establish your anchors so that they gain access to the use of a particular representational system, or established sequence of representational systems.

As we discuss the various methods of utilizing anchors in installation procedures we will be using the symbol, " $\mathcal{L}$ " to represent an anchor. This symbol means that an anchor has been established for whatever bracketed representational system or sequence follows it. $\mathcal{L}$ [V^i] indicates that an anchor has been established that initiates access to internal activity of the visual representational system. It will be assumed that the anchor indicated by the symbol is unspecified with respect to which representational system it has been established through, unless this is specified by a superscript. $\mathcal{L}$ ^{Ke} would indicate a tactile kinesthetic anchor (such as a touch or squeeze), $\mathcal{L}$ ^{Ad} would indicate a verbal anchor (a word), $\mathcal{L}$ ^{Vc} would indicate an anchor in the form of a constructed visual image and so on.

6.11 Anchoring An Entire Strategy Sequence.

If your strategy design calls for the use of a particular strategy sequence or subroutine already available in some form in the client's existing repertoire of strategies, it is possible to anchor that entire existing sequence with one anchor, so that it may be inserted as an entire unit into the new sequence you are designing. It may also be inserted into some situation where it was not available previously as a resource—so that it becomes wired to the contextual stimuli that make up the situation and allows for another possible choice of behavior within that context. It is installed as a resource into situations where the client desires a choice of outcomes.

In such cases the strategy is generally taken from a context in which it occurs naturally and is installed in a context in which it does not occur or has not previously occurred. In performing this operation it is important to be sure that you separate the strategy sequence itself from the trigger that has formerly initiated the

strategy sequence within the context you are extracting it from.
We can show this process visually in the following way:

STEP 1:   Context A $\downarrow$ $V^e \longrightarrow A_d^i \longrightarrow K^i \longrightarrow V^i \longrightarrow A_t^i \longrightarrow K^e \longrightarrow$ EXIT

$$\oint [A_d^i \longrightarrow K^i \longrightarrow V^i \longrightarrow A_t^i \longrightarrow K^e]$$

STEP 2:   Context B $\downarrow$ $A^e \longrightarrow K^i \longrightarrow V^i$

$A^e \longrightarrow \oint [A_d^i \longrightarrow K^i \longrightarrow V^i \longrightarrow A_t^i \longrightarrow K^e]$

OUTCOME: $\downarrow$ $A^e \longrightarrow A_d^i \longrightarrow K^i \longrightarrow V^i \longrightarrow A_t^i \longrightarrow K^e$

Step 1 shows that some external visual stimulus in Context A
naturally initiates the strategy sequence $A_d^i \ldots K^e$. This sequence
is anchored in its entirety by the anchor.

In *step 2* the strategy unit is anchored into Context B where,
formerly, some external auditory stimulus had initiated a
$K^i \longrightarrow V^i$ loop. This allows the individual the choice of accessing
the strategy from Context A in Context B so that it may serve as
a resource.

In our seminars we often demonstrate this process by anchoring an individual's entire *motivation* strategy. The individual is
asked to think of a time when he motivated himself to do something he did not particularly want to do. The steps in this strategy are then elicited through questioning and observation, and
each step is anchored with the same kinesthetic anchor on one of
the individual's knees. Some behavior is then suggested or proposed that the individual does not particularly care to do (for
example, to walk across the room and lift a chair over his head,
or to pick up a pencil that has been thrown on the floor). The
individual is questioned a number of times to establish that he
really does not want to complete the behavior. The motivation
strategy is then triggered by "firing" off the anchor. When the
strategy has been *well anchored,* the individual will automatically
reaccess the strategy sequence for motivation, applying it to the
ongoing context. In many cases the individual will spontaneously
begin to perform the task that, seconds before, he had not been
motivated to do. If the anchor is released before the individual
has completed the behavior he will often stop in mid-reach, remaining immobile until the anchor is replaced.

Subroutines may be extracted from larger strategies and sequenced in the same fashion:

Context 1: $V^e \longrightarrow A^i_t \longrightarrow V^i \longrightarrow K^i$ Context 2: $A^e_d \longrightarrow V^i \longrightarrow A^i_d \longrightarrow K^e$

STEP 1: $\mathcal{F}_1[V^i \longrightarrow K^i]$ $\mathcal{F}_2[A^i_d \longrightarrow K^e]$

STEP 2: $\mathcal{F}_1[V^i \longrightarrow K^i] \longrightarrow$ $\mathcal{F}_2[A^i_d \longrightarrow K^e]$

OUTCOME: $V^i \longrightarrow K^i \longrightarrow A^i_d \longrightarrow K^e$

In the preceding diagram, two existing synesthesia patterns that occur in different contexts have been anchored together to form a new strategy. One strategy segment has been tacked to the end of another, through anchoring, to form a new sequence. In one synesthesia sequence ($V^i \longrightarrow K^i$) the individual derives visceral feelings from internal images. The other ($A^i_d \longrightarrow K^e$) is one in which the individual initiates physical action through internal dialogue. Since synesthesia patterns tend to automatically carry through their own processes once initiated, the important part of this installation procedure is to tie the person's internal dialogue into his feelings.

This method of anchoring may also be used to streamline an inappropriately long strategy by anchoring the last few steps, or the last operation, to some earlier step in the sequence. In this way a number of middle steps can be bypassed, or potentially crippling loops can be short circuited, as shown in the diagram below.

$V^e \longrightarrow A^i_{t,d} \longrightarrow K^i \longrightarrow A^e \longrightarrow V^c \longrightarrow A^i_d \longrightarrow K^i \longrightarrow V^i \longrightarrow K^e$

STEP 1: $\mathcal{F}_1[V^e \longrightarrow A^i_{td}]$ $\mathcal{F}_2[V^i \longrightarrow K^e]$

STEP 2: $\mathcal{F}_1[V^e \longrightarrow A^i_{t,d}] \longrightarrow$ $\mathcal{F}_2[V^i \longrightarrow K^e]$

OUTCOME: $V^e \longrightarrow A^i_{t,d} \longrightarrow V^i \longrightarrow K^e$

An example of how to employ such a procedure is demonstrated in a case in which one of the authors was working with a man who had a long, cumbersome and inefficient decision making strategy. This individual would spend hours or even days in deliberation, putting off decisions for so long that he would invariably end up passing by key opportunities, which would cause him to feel bad. As a consequence he would become deeply agitated and angry with himself for having wasted so much time. The author redesigned his decision strategy such that the individual would take into consideration the possibilities of missing key opportunities and wasting time (this becomes a representation of the outcome sequitur for the outcome of *not* making a decision on time) at a much earlier point in his strategy. This helped provide a motivation for the individual to speed up the strategy process by considering the possible outcomes of over deliberation, and served as a resource to provide a time check in the decision process. The inclusion of this test for negative feelings served as a decision point in the strategy at an earlier stage.

This strategy was installed by asking the person what it was like at the end of his strategy when he began to realize how much time he had wasted and how he may have possibly missed important opportunities. As the man responded, the sequence of representational systems was anchored kinesthetically ($\mathcal{L}$ ^{Ke}) with a squeeze on his knee. The individual was then asked to tell the author about a decision that he would soon be required to make, or a decision that he was deliberating on at present. The individual responded by telling the author about some decision he had been trying to make without getting anywhere. As he began to relate some of the details, the author reached over and squeezed his knee. The man stopped in mid-sentence. And, by observing his accessing cues, the author could tell he began to go through the anchored subroutine. Within moments the individual had come up with at least five things, that would bear upon the decision, that he needed to do. The author then repeated the process with a number of other current decisions the person needed to make, squeezing the individual's knee during the first few decisions they discussed, and witholding the anchor for the last three, as a test to make sure the new strategy was now installed. The installation of the new strategy was so successful that the individual is now the owner of the company that, at that time, had employed him as a secretary.

6.12 Anchoring Individual And Unrelated Strategy Steps.

Individual representational steps may be pulled out of totally unrelated strategy sequences, anchored and then reanchored together in sequence to form a new strategy. For instance, a certain form of internal dialogue may be taken from one naturally occurring strategy, the ability to see clearly externally from another and some internal kinesthetic check or test from yet another. These three representational functions may then be anchored together in a variety of orders and sequences to generate new outcomes and experiences for the individual. The programmer may, for instance, anchor first the ability to see clearly externally, then the internal dialogue, thirdly the positive kinesthetic feelings, and finally the ability to see clearly is anchored again so that the individual may exit again to external experience to gather feedback as more input.

The anchors used to trigger the appropriate strategy step may be kinesthetic (as with touches on various places on the individual's body) or in another representational system such as internal or external visual cues. Words, of course, are anchors (see discussion of language as secondary experience in *Patterns II*), and have the advantage of being culturally standardized to some degree. The programmer, then, may sequence representations using verbal anchors (this can be more generally recognized as "giving instructions").

The effectiveness of your anchoring can be increased by pairing and combining more than one anchor for the particular strategy step. Anchors in different representational systems may be paired to increase their effect as you install the strategy sequence.

Consider the following transcript of one of the authors installing a learning strategy in a participant at one of his workshops. The strategy he has designed and is installing is the one described in the preceding example: $V^e \longrightarrow A^i_d \longrightarrow K^i \longrightarrow EXIT$.

TRANSCRIPT

AUTHOR: Now to begin the installation process, I want to get some good reference structures for you for the kinds of operations we're going to be putting together. First, I'd like you to think of a time when you could *see very clearly* (author raises his voice slightly to establish a tonal as well as digital auditory anchor— Φ ^{Ae})

what was going on in your immediate environment . . . Can you think of a time?

SUBJECT: Ahh . . . (breathing shallows and moves into his chest, eyes flick up and left) . . . Ahh, yes . . . I have one.

A: (Squeezes S's forearm— ⚓ $_1K^e$) Good . . . Now what I want you to do is look at what is going on now around you . . . and keep looking until you can *see very clearly* (raises tonality— ⚓ $_1A^e_{t,d}$, squeezes S's forearm— ⚓ $_1K^e$) the people, motions, colors and any other details you can notice . . . (Pause while S carries out task—A continues squeezing S's forearm). Fine . . . (releases anchor) . . . Has there ever been a time when you were able to *comment explicitly to yourself* (slows voice tempo— ⚓ $_2A^e$) about something that was going on around you?

S: Umm . . . (looks up and left).

A: (Laughs) You won't find it up there.

S: Huh?

A: Never mind.

S: Oh . . . Okay . . . Ummm . . . a time when I was talking to myself about what was going on around me . . . (eyes move down and left).

A: (Laughs, reaches down and squeezes knee— ⚓ $_2K^e$) You were doing it just now.

S: I was? . . . Oh . . . (Laughs) . . . Well, I thought of another time too.

A: Okay . . . Good . . . What is that like. . . . can you *comment explicitly to yourself* (slows voice tempo— ⚓ $_2A^e_{t,d}$) on what I'm doing right now? (A makes a series of gestures and movements with one hand, squeezes S's knee with the other— ⚓ $_2K^e$) . . . All right . . . (releases anchor) . . . Now . . . has there ever been a time when you were thinking about something and you had to *get in touch with your feelings and check it out* (deepens tonality— ⚓ $_3A^e_{t,d}$) for yourself?

S: Mmmm . . . (eyes move down and right) . . UhHuh . . . Sort of . . .

A: (Beginning to squeeze S's shoulder) . . . Exaggerate it then . . . *get in touch with those feelings* and keep *checking it out* (deepens tonality— ⚓ $_3A^e$, squeezes S's shoulder— ⚓ $_3K^e$) until you are really sure.

S: (Eyes and head down and right) . . Yeh . . . (nods) . . . Okay . . . (breath shifts to stomach.)

A: (Releases anchor) Wonderful. . . . Very good . . . Now I'd like to try something out . . . You've been wanting to learn accessing cues haven't you?

S: (Nods vigorously) Oh yes.

A: All right . . . Do you know the generalizations pretty well? Do you know what the eye movements mean?

S: Sort of . . . (shakes his head "no" unconsciously).

A: (Laughs) Your unconscious mind doesn't seem to think so.

S: What?

A: You were just now shaking your head "no."

S: Oh . . . (smiles) . . . You're right . . . I guess I was shaking it "no."

A: Well let's start there, then . . . (draws an eye movement chart on the blackboard) . . . Now . . . I want you to look at this chart so that you can *see very clearly* (A raises his tonality— $\mathcal{J}_1{}^{Ae}$, and squeezes S's forearm— $\mathcal{J}_1{}^{Ke}$) each of the eye positions and what they indicate . . . and as you look from position to position I want you to *comment explicitly to yourself* (releases S's forearm and squeezes S's knee— $\mathcal{J}_2{}^{Ke}$, slows tempo of voice when giving the instruction— $\mathcal{J}_2{}^{Ae}$) about where each position is and what it means . . . and as you do this I want you to then *get in touch with your feelings and check out* (A releases S's knee and squeezes S's shoulder— $\mathcal{J}_3{}^{Ke}$, deepens voice tonality— $\mathcal{J}_3{}^{Ae}$) how good of a handle you have on identifying each of these positions . . . and keep *looking very clearly* (raises voice tone— $\mathcal{J}_1{}^{Ae}$, releases shoulder and squeezes forearm— $\mathcal{J}_1{}^{Ke}$) at each position . . . *commenting explicitly to yourself* (releases forearm and squeezes knee— $\mathcal{J}_2{}^{Ke}$, slows voice tempo— $\mathcal{J}_2{}^{Ae}$) about what each position means . . . and keep *getting in touch with your feelings and checking it out* (releases knee and squeezes shoulder— $\mathcal{J}_3{}^{Ke}$, deepens tonality— $\mathcal{J}_3{}^{Ae}$) until you feel that you've got a grasp of the meanings of the eye skating patterns . . . and when you do I want you to signal me by lifting this finger (indicates right forefinger) . . . (A sequences the kinesthetic anchors once more without the accompanying visual anchors and then stops all anchoring of S to test to make sure the strategy will continue itself.)

S: (S studies the blackboard for about five minutes and then his forefinger begins to raise.)

A: Okay . . . Good . . . Now here's the next step . . . I want you to look at me . . . and I'm going to move my eyes around to a number of different positions . . . and I want you to watch me so that you can *see very clearly* (raises voice pitch— $\updownarrow_1 A^e$, does not apply kinesthetic anchors) each position that I move my eyes to . . . and as you see them I want you to *comment explicitly to yourself* (slows voice tempo— $\updownarrow_2 A^e$) about which positions I'm accessing . . . and *get in touch with your feeling and check out* (deepens tonality– $\updownarrow_3 A^e$) how good your grasp of them is . . . until you feel that you can not only see each position and know what it means but so you can see a whole sequence . . . and when you feel that you can do that I want you to allow your right hand to raise . . . (Note: A only anchors S through the strategy sequence once to test to make sure the strategy will access and perpetuate itself.)

S: (Watches A's eye movements for a few minutes and then raises his hand) . . . Okay . . .

A: Good . . . How is it working?

S: Fantastic . . . I've never felt so confident about any of this before.

A: Great . . . Now I'd like to test the effectiveness of your new learning strategy by running through a bunch of eye movement sequences and then have you tell me which sequence I just did . . . Okay . . . Begin . . .

S is able to follow each of the sequences the author presents. The strategy is then tested again by having S observe two other people from group interact until he is able to recount to the author the eye movement sequences of both people. He then gives S an anchor to access the strategy that S can initiate himself—that of S reaching over and squeezing his own forearm.

We can diagram the process of extracting and sequencing unrelated strategy steps in the following way:

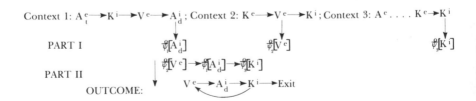

Context 1: $A_t^e \longrightarrow K^i \longrightarrow V^e \longrightarrow A_d^i$; Context 2: $K^e \longrightarrow V^e \longrightarrow K^i$; Context 3: $A^e \ldots K^e \longrightarrow K^i$

PART I $\updownarrow_1 [A_d^i]$ $\updownarrow_2 [V^e]$ $\updownarrow [K^i]$

PART II $\updownarrow_2 [V^e] \rightarrow \updownarrow_1 [A_d^i] \rightarrow \updownarrow_3 [K^i]$

OUTCOME: $V^e \rightarrow A_d^i \rightarrow K^i \longrightarrow$ Exit

6.2 Rehearsal

Rehearsal is a more operant method of conditioning or installing a strategy (as opposed to "anchoring" which more closely
parallels classical or Pavlovian methods of conditioning). In the
rehearsal process the individual practices or rehearses each representational step in the strategy until it becomes available as a
spontaneous intact program. This process essentially involves the
development of self-established anchors for strategy sequences.

6.21 Rehearsing Strategy Steps.

The most basic method of rehearsal would be that in which the
programmer instructs the client in practicing making the transition
through each step in the strategy as the programmer plugs in a
number of different contents. This, of course, was a large part of
what took place in the transcript.

Many times it won't take more than a few minutes of rehearsal
to install a new strategy. Once one of the authors conducting an
out-of-town workshop and was staying at the home of the workshop sponsor. While spending a quiet evening at the sponsor's
home the author observed the sponsor's wife sitting with her second grade daughter and holding up flash cards with words and
sentences on them for the girl to read and then spell. The daughter
was obviously doing very poorly and consistently mixed up the
orders of the words as she read and spelled. Taking an interest, the
author asked the mother how her daughter was doing in school.
Not surprisingly, the mother shook her head and admitted that her
daughter was doing poorly, especially in reading. The daughter
was constantly mixing up and reversing the orders of words, a
condition that a specialist had diagnosed as dyslexic.

Reading, and especially spelling, from flash cards will generally
require that the individual hold an internal visual image in the
mind's eye. The author postulated that if the child had an underdeveloped visual system, it might account for the trouble. Judging
by the child's body type, tonality and accessing cues, she should
have been fully capable of making internal visual images. The
author tested the girl's visual abilities by asking her to make and
describe a series of images, which she could do readily. He then

tested her reading and spelling strategies by flashing a card and asking her to read it and spell it. After looking at the card, the child's eyes immediately moved down and to the left, then, remaining down, over to the right, and back to the left, as she stumbled with the words—unable to achieve the outcome. It was immediately obvious to the author that it was the child's strategy for reading and spelling—an internal auditory and kinesthetic loop $A^i \rightleftharpoons K^i$—that was causing her so much trouble.

The author asked the child if she would like to play a flashcard game with him. This game was to be fun and she would not have to "try" to read or spell anything. She readily agreed. The author proceeded to show the child a flash card. As the author held the card and pointed to each letter in succession from left to right (V^e), the child was to pronounce each letter and sound each word out (A^c_d). Then she was to look back at the entire word and pronounce it ($V^e \rightarrow A^e$) out loud, and, then looking down and right and using her feelings (K^i), tell whether the sounds she made were a real word. If it didn't feel right, she was to look back at the entire string of letters and pronounce them again a different way, and feel that out. She would continue until she felt good about the pronunciation and the word. Every time she pronounced and read the word correctly the author would smile, say "Good" in an encouraging tonality and squeeze her wrist. The fun of the flashcard game came, however, when the author put the flashcard down, for he would then direct her to move her eyes up and left and keep looking up there until she could see the card he had just put down. She could imagine the letters any color she wanted and was especially invited to try her favorite color. When she could see the series of letters clearly she was then to read them off to the author —not "spell" the word, just read the letters off as she saw them. She was even allowed to see the author's finger moving from left to right if she got stuck. (This was her favorite part of the game.) After she had read them off she was to look back at the words in her mind's eye, change the color again if she wanted to, sound out the letters, look back at the whole sequence, pronounce the word and then move her head down and right to feel if she was correct. Again, at each successful completion of the step, she was given positive reinforcement tonally and with a smile; and the kinesthetic anchor on her wrist was reinforced.

A special surprise soon emerged into the game. After a few trials, if the child got stuck, the author could make the internal image or pronunciation appear in her head simply by squeezing her wrist. Eventually, the child herself could make any difficult word-picture or pronunciation appear by squeezing her own wrist.

Another positive aspect of the game was the surprise that was vocally and congruently expressed by the child's mother, who had never heard her read or spell so well. In the half hour spent with the author, playing the somewhat mysterious flashcard game, the child successfully made it through more flashcards than they had previously been able to get through in days—and the child was eager to do more of them, as she had gotten quite good at it. In fact, the little girl at one point exclaimed, "This is a lot easier than what I do with Mommy!" Additionally, even though she would occasionally leave a word or letter out, the child did not once reverse a word or letter during the entire game. (It should be noted that the author stopped pointing to the letters after the first few cards he held up, for the child was soon able to imagine it there as she read.)

Let us review, for a moment, some of the important aspects of this example. (1) The "game" was set up such that the emphasis was on form rather than content, on what to do and when—where to put her head and eyes, when to use feelings and pictures. The processes being rehearsed were framed so that they were more like learning a dance than like spelling. If she began to get stuck she was not corrected for being "wrong" but was simply told where to put her head or eyes. (2) Because the strategy being rehearsed was different from her typical strategy it was truly not "spelling" or "reading" in the sense she knew them. Simply reading the letters from her internal image was very different than "trying" to spell. (3) Her old strategy for reading, which had gone $V^e \longrightarrow A^i_d \longrightarrow K^i$, was not well suited for the task. The new strategy, $V^e \longrightarrow A^e_d \longrightarrow K^i \longrightarrow EXIT$ provided much more efficient tests and operations for the task and outcome of sight reading. (4) Her existing strategy for spelling had been even less appropriate—a simple $A^i \longrightarrow K^i$ loop. Again, the newly designed and installed strategy, $V^i \longrightarrow A_d \longrightarrow K^i \longrightarrow EXIT$, was much more suited to the task.

Emphasizing the "game" aspect of strategy rehearsal can be greatly beneficial to your installation procedures. Playing a game is generally thought of as easier than changing your way of thinking, which is serious business.

We have a used a strategy similar to this one to help people who

want to learn to draw. The outcome of the strategy is that you don't
end up having to "draw" anything, but rather you trace it. The
strategy, simple and easy, begins as the client either looks at the
object he wants to draw or imagines a scene he would like to draw
until he can close his eyes and still see it clearly. He is then to open
his eyes and look at the drawing paper until he can imagine the
picture right on the paper. Then taking his pen, pencil or brush,
he is to simply "trace" the image he sees there.

6.22 Rehearsing Accessing Cues.

Another method of rehearsal (used extensively in the case of the
"dyslexic" child) is the rehearsal of specific accessing cues. Since
accessing cues are the primary method we use for naturally accessing our representational systems, this is an extremely effective
installation method. This particular method also has an advantage
in that accessing cues can be rehearsed and installed as a sequence
without the client having to be conscious of representational content—the person's full conscious attention can be directed to the
details of where to put his head and eyes, where and how fast to
breathe, how to posture his body, etc. For this reason the rehearsing of *only* accessing cues, for strategy installation, can serve as a
very powerful covert tactic. The individual simply rehearses the
appropriate sequence of accessing cues which will lead automatically to the representational systems required for the strategy. The
programmer tunes only the client's body—but still elicits the
desired representational sequence. When the individual has
learned the sequence to the point that it is automatic, the eye
movements, postures, gestures, breathing rates and other behaviors that he has learned will automatically access the designed
sequence of representational systems.

A client who has had no experience with NLP, will have no
conscious understanding of what is occurring but may be very
surprised and pleased when he finds that his behavior begins to
change radically.

One way to keep this process even more covert (or when one is
in situations where it is not appropriate to verbally instruct someone through the various accessing cues) is to lead the eyes of the
subject to the appropriate accessing positions with hand gestures,

or by leading them to the appropriate positions with one's own eye movements.

6.23 Rehearsing Synesthesia Patterns.

Rehearsing synesthesia patterns is another powerful method of installing sequences of representational system activity that is independent of specific content. For many people, certain synesthesia patterns will be unfamiliar and underdeveloped, and they may experience difficulty in making the transition from one certain type of representational system to another. Practicing synesthesia patterns, independent of specific content, will increase the ease of access and the the "representational vocabulary" (the discriminative capabilities) of particular individuals with underdeveloped systems.

If the programmer wanted to install a strategy that followed the sequence $A_d^i \longrightarrow K^e \longrightarrow A_t^i \longrightarrow V^i$, he would instruct the client, starting with any particular portion of an internal dialogue, to generate *seven tactile body sensations* or *movements*. The instructions might go: "As you *listen* carefully to those *words in your head*, pay attention to what *body sensations* come from them. When you have identified one set of *feelings, listen* to the *words* again and allow another *feeling* to emerge from the *words*. Keep doing this until you have come up with *seven different feelings.*" The client is then instructed to pick the feeling that is most appropriate to the words being pronounced internally, and from that feeling he is to generate *seven sounds that are not words.* For example: *"Get in touch* with that *feeling* and allow it to *turn into a sound."* Have him repeat the process until he has generated *seven sounds.* Next, have him choose the sound most appropriate to the feelings it was derived from and instruct him to generate *seven internal visual images* from that sound.

Visually, we can represent this process in the following manner:

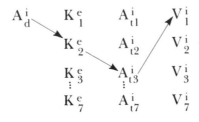

The synesthesia process may be greatly facilitated by teaching the individual to *overlap accessing cues.* For example, taking a deep breath in the abdominal area while looking up and to the left would help to produce a $V{\longrightarrow}K$ overlap (or fuzzy function). Looking down and right, defocusing one's eyes and breathing high and shallow in the chest will facilitate $K{\longrightarrow}V$ overlap. Looking up and right and touching one's face or chin would promote $V^c{\longrightarrow}A^i_d$ synesthesia.

Have the individual repeat the process until the transitions become smooth and easy.

Within the process of installing any particular strategy, of course, the programmer will want to use combinations of both anchoring and rehearsal techniques. Some steps will be more appropriately anchored in, while others should be rehearsed to help make the transitions smoother. For instance, the programmer may want to have the individual rehearse a synesthesia pattern that is difficult for him, but then choose to anchor the next step on to the synesthesia. The programmer will most often want to establish anchors for each step and fire them off as the individual rehearses.

6.3 Interrupting Strategies.

Installing a new strategy requires that you make it as available in context as an existing one. As we said at the beginning of the chapter, this can generally be accomplished with ease through timing—firing of the anchor(s) you have established for the new sequence at the appropriate time in the existing sequence—or by conditioning the new sequence via repeated rehearsal. If the new strategy you have designed is sufficiently adaptive it should reinforce and perpetuate itself naturally.

Sometimes, however, the existing strategy will have a particularly well-beaten path and will be unusually ingrained. If the outcome of the strategy interferes with what you are attempting to accomplish and is producing behaviors that are counterproductive to the achievement of the meta-outcomes of the client (such as the depressive strategies we discussed in the design chapter), it will be to the client's benefit for you to interrupt the existing strategy.

There are three basic ways to interrupt a strategy: (1) through overload, (2) by diversion and (3) by "spinning out" the strategy.

6.31 Interruption By Overload.

Overloading occurs when more information is being poured into a strategy or strategy step than it can handle. Overloading happens naturally in many everyday experiences—for example, when a person in a noisy place "can't hear himself think," or when a person feels so good (or bad) that he doesn't know what to do or say (this is often called "being overcome by emotion"). Other natural interruptions are situations like being *overwhelmed* by beauty or practically *"knocked out"* by some smell or fragrance.

The behavioral result of overloading, as with any of the interruption phenomena, is that person's strategy is stopped from completing its cycle. When a strategy is interrupted completely, the individual is left without a next step in behavior (in a sort of behavioral "limbo," or what is sometimes known as "somnambulistic trance" —see *Patterns II*) and is prone to jump for whatever next step is offered to him by the situation. That is, they display a strong tendency to respond to whatever anchor for response is provided by the situation. This is a phenomenon that you can easily take advantage of to install a strategy, if you time your anchors right.

Occasionally you may want to interrupt an existing strategy simply to stop its ongoing negative outcomes. As one of the authors was preparing to leave his house to board a plane for a week long trip, the phone rang. When the author answered it, an extremely worried and frantic voice came through the receiver, pleading with him to help a deeply depressed relative who was on the verge of suicide. It was impossible for the author to postpone his trip to work with the phone caller's relative, so he quickly told her to bring the suicidal relative to the airport and gate he would be departing from. He would see what he could do. They arrived just as he was preparing to board the plane. Left without time to attempt anything then, the author simply reached out, grabbed the relative's wrist, and squeezing it as hard as he could, made an extremely animated and contorted face and yelled at the top of his lungs, "Everything that you do this week *has to* come through this channel." He then released her wrist and boarded the plane. The rationale was that the simultaneous multi-sensory overload was sure to interrupt any ongoing strategy. Upon returning the following week and working finally with the depressive relative, the author was told how she had remained around the house all week, entertaining no thoughts of suicide. All she could remember experiencing, in fact, was a sustained visual image in her mind's eye of the face the author had made at the airport.

6.32 Interruption by Diversion.

A strategy is diverted when a particular input shifts the representational sequence away from the ongoing strategy. A person who is lost in thought, for instance, will be interrupted when some noise or movement draws his attention to his external environment. The stimulus does not overload the person's strategy; it instead overrides the ongoing sequence, drawing the person's behavior to some other locus. Often, after such an interruption, the person who was formerly lost in thought may have a difficult time reaccessing the strategy he was in and may even forget what he was thinking about. Diverting someone's attention so that it breaks his concentration or stops him from completing some particular behavior, has been employed as an effective interruption technique throughout the ages.

Stopping or blocking a person's accessing cues is an extremely direct and powerful way of interrupting his ongoing strategy. Strategies may be interrupted and diverted by waving or moving your hands in front of someone's face and knocking away their eye position cues. Having a depressed client sit up straight, hold his head up high, take a full breath in the chest, throw his shoulders back, open his eyes wide and smile, is one of the most rapid and effective ways of drawing a depressive out of a negative state. The typical depressive posture probably does more to elicit and perpetuate the depressed state than any other element. The posture is generally slumped and hunched over, eyes and head oriented downward to produce full kinesthetic access—it's no wonder that he isn't able to *see* or *talk* himself out of his problems. As we pointed out earlier, there tends to be an inverse relationship between the internal and external focusing of the same representational system—the more you are talking to yourself in your head, the less you can hear what's going on around you, and so on. For the depressed, then, who spend most of their time focused on internal kinesthetics, tactile awareness, especially through physical exercise and sports, will be an extremely effective diversion. To interrupt someone who is depressed, have him *do* something, no matter how meaningless the activity may seem.

A therapist once told the authors about an emergency call she received from a person who was very depressed and contemplating suicide. At the time of the call, however, the therapist was involved in a critical intervention with another client, one she could not abandon. Out of desperation, the therapist in a firm and congruent voice told the caller that she was to go out immediately, take a bicycle ride for at least 20 minutes and was to call the therapist again when she returned. The therapist's reasoning was that this would keep the person occupied so that she wouldn't harm herself, until the therapist had finished with the other client and could turn her full attention toward helping the caller. Much to the therapist's surprise, when the potential suicide called back, the crisis had passed. The bike ride, the caller said, had been just what she needed to break the depression. Prior to the ride she hadn't been out of her house for days because she'd been feeling bad. She said that she now realized how that had only contributed to her negative state. She still needed to work on a number of problems she faced, but the bike ride had averted a crisis.

6.33 Interruption By "Spinning Out" a Strategy.

A strategy will "spin out" when the end of the strategy becomes anchored to its beginning in such a way that the strategy keeps feeding back into itself (like the proverbial snake swallowing its own tail). Because it can't exit, the strategy is forced to continue looping. Most strategies have a kind of test, a meta-test you might call it, such that if the strategy operations are ineffectual after a certain period of time, the program will exit into a completely new strategy—thus, the "spin out."

The following is an illustration of how a belief strategy may be spun out:

A: How do you know that you can't get X outcome?

B: My experience tells me that I can't.

A: How do you know that your experience tells you that?

B: Because I've tried before and failed.

A: How do you know that you've failed?

B: I remember it.

A: How do you know that you remember it?

B: Because I can see it.

A: How do you know that you can see it?

The pattern here is obvious—whatever output is received from the strategy is fed back through the strategy again. This continues until eventually the strategy essentially runs through itself.

One of the authors was once working with a young man who was having motivational difficulties in his business. He kept finding himself taking on much more than he could possibly handle. Upon eliciting his motivation strategy the author found that it was such that if the young man was asked if he could perform some task or favor by a client, friend or associate he would immediately attempt to construct an image of himself doing what they had asked of him. If he could see himself doing it he would then think that he *should* do it and would begin to carry out the task requested of him, even if it interfered with other things he was currently involved in. The author tested the strategy by asking the young man if he would run up and down some nearby stairs for the rest of the afternoon. The young man replied that he could only see himself running up and down the stairs for a half an hour at the most, but actually began to get out of his chair to begin the task for that half an hour. The author then asked the young man if he could visualize himself *not* doing something that he could visualize himself doing. A rapid and profound trance state ensued as the man's strategy began to spin out. The author took advantage of this state to install some more effective tests and operations into the young man's motivation strategy.

Another way to spin a strategy out is to establish one anchor for the beginning of the strategy and another for the end of the strategy; then, collapse the anchors so the beginning and the end become tied together. A man who came to a workshop put on by one of the authors, claimed he'd been trying to go into a hypnotic trance for over 25 years and had never succeeded. He firmly believed it was impossible for him to enter a trance state even though he had been desperately wanting to for all those years. His belief strategy was spun out as a demonstration by anchoring the beginning to the end through collapsing two anchors established for those steps. The man's initial reaction was confusion and some agitation, but within an hour he had (and most importantly was convinced that he had) the first trance experience of his life.

Each of these techniques for interruption is designed to stop the progress of an ongoing strategy so that an intervention may be made by the programmer. The same techniques can be used to stop someone's strategy if the outcomes of that strategy are annoying to you or are being used to your detriment. The subtle "knocking away" or diversion of a person's accessing cues with hand gestures or head gestures, can be used to interrupt a person's strategy if it is important or necessary for you to get the upper hand in a situation, or to gracefully force a shift in the flow or direction of the communication. (Subtle clicking noises made with your mouth tend to be a very effective covert means of causing a change in someone's internal pictures—eye movements can also be covertly directed by indicating, with your own eye movements, which position should be accessed next.)

6.4 Interference Phenomena.

Interference phenomena, commonly called *"resistance," "blocks:" "sabotage," "dissention," "objections,"* and so on, form probably the most frequently encountered obstacles to anyone dealing with human behavior to achieve outcomes. The businessperson, manager educator, therapist, lawyer, politician, etc., must deal with these phenomena, whether manifest as inefficiency, learning disability, incongruence, hesitation, personal problems or conflict.

In the neurolinguistic programming model such experiences as objections, incongruence, and resistance are utilized as valuable tests for the effectiveness of the installation of a strategy. Rather than rejecting interference phenomena as "sabotage," we use them to check on the strategy in operation (whether it is pre-existing or newly designed and installed). *Interference to the operation of a strategy generally occurs (1) when some other resource (in the form of a representation or a sequence change) is still required for the successful securing of the outcome, or (2) when the strategy is not effective for all contexts in question.*

Objections do not mean the programmer has failed in designing a good strategy, but are rather accepted as *natural feedback,* and utilized to modify the strategy in order to make it more effective. Interference is the result of naturally occurring tests for personal ecology.

If you have elicited or designed and installed a strategy and the strategy *does not secure the intended outcome* when you attempt to utilize it there are a number of things to check: (Each of these checks should be made, of course, *after* you have tested to make sure you have not broken rapport.)

1) *Calibration* of the strategy: Are each of the representational systems involved and are their corresponding accessing cues clearly delineated and at the appropriate order of magnitude?— That is, make sure none of the representations are too weak to work properly. Make sure the designated representational system for each step in the sequence has the highest signal value for the ongoing 4-tuple at that point in time. If, when you anchor, the individual has an internal dialogue that says "This won't work," firing anchor will retrigger this internal dialogue. It is important to maintain the representational integrity of each strategy step (this is the "chain-is-no-stronger-than-its-weakest-link" aspect of strategies). If the representational systems in question are lacking in amplitude, work on fine tuning the strategy steps by having the individual exaggerate or practice the appropriate accessing cues and by consciously focusing on the designated representational systems.

2) Make sure the transitions between the steps in the strategy are smooth enough that they *do not interrupt the flow of the sequence.* If the individual does have difficulty with some of the transitions, have them rehearse the synesthesia patterns until they become more adept.

3) Congruency Check:

a) *Clearing personal history:* Make sure the individual is *congruent* about achieving the desired outcome. Compare the specific outcome against the meta outcomes of the individual, or organization, to make sure that it is compatible and ecological. Many times an individual will, at earlier times in his personal history, develop *negative anchors* for some outcome that later on he desires to attain. Other times, reaching a particular outcome will lead to the possibility of accessing other experiences and outcomes that the individual is not yet prepared to accept or face. In this case the programmer will need to either (1) modify the outcome so that it does not present any threats to the personal ecology of the individual, (2) integrate the negative 4-tuple from the past with the one that desires the

outcome in the present context (by anchoring them sequen-
tially and then collapsing the anchors) so that it no longer
presents any interference, or (3) access and add in other resources from the individual's personal history that will allow
him to handle or avoid any problematic residual effects of the
outcome. (See *Patterns II* and *The Structure of Magic II* for more
material on congruency.)

b) Make sure *none* of the steps anchor *multiple responses.* Are all
of the steps specific enough that they do not generalize and
anchor more than one strategy that is vying for prime control?
If this occurs, check the *context markers* (or design and install
one) at the *decision point,* the operate-or-exit point of the strategy (see design).

4) Make sure all steps are in the appropriate order and that no
representational system important for the task has been left out.
a) If the strategy has been designed, check it against the *well-
formedness conditions,* and/or access additional resources from the
client's personal history. b) If the strategy was elicited, go back
over the elicitation procedure to make sure no steps have been
mistakenly left out or added in.

6.4.1 Reframing

Reframing is one of the most fundamental technique/concepts
of NLP and is the most effective tool for dealing with interference.
The process of reframing changes how some representation, or,
indeed, any part of a system, fits into that system as it functions in
varying contexts. In doing so it transforms what previously have
seemed to be blocks to the operation of the system into resources.
The essential goal of reframing is to *create a framework in which all
parts of the system become aligned toward achieving the same meta-outcomes*
(ie., the survival, protection, growth, etc., of the system) by accepting and acknowledging all aspects of the system (positive or negative) as valuable resources to the system, given the appropriate
context.

The fundamental presupposition of reframing is that *all behavior*
(strategies) *is or was adaptive given the context in which and for which it
was established.* NLP assumes that *all behavior is geared toward adapta-*

THE REFRAMING TOTE

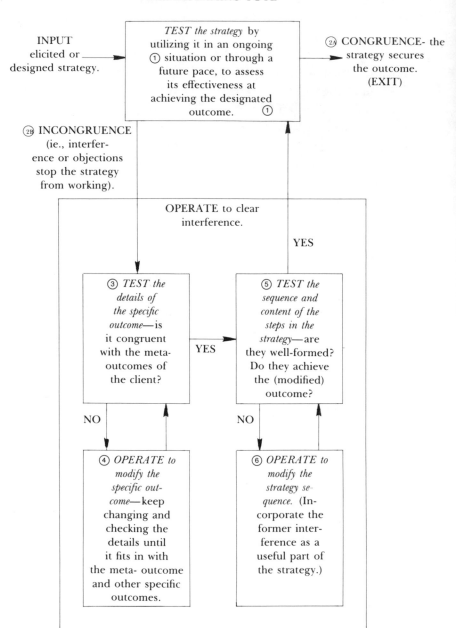

INPUT
elicited or
designed strategy.

TEST the strategy by
utilizing it in an ongoing
① situation or through a
future pace, to assess
its effectiveness at
achieving the designated
outcome.   ①

② CONGRUENCE- the
strategy secures
the outcome.
(EXIT)

② INCONGRUENCE
(ie., interfer-
ence or objections
stop the strategy
from working).

OPERATE to clear
interference.

YES

③ *TEST the
details of
the specific
outcome*—is
it congruent
with the meta-
outcomes of
the client?

⑤ *TEST the
sequence and
content of the
steps in the
strategy*—are
they well-formed?
Do they achieve
the (modified)
outcome?

YES

NO   NO

④ *OPERATE to
modify the
specific out-
come*—keep
changing and
checking the
details until
it fits in with
the meta- outcome
and other specific
outcomes.

⑥ *OPERATE to
modify the
strategy se-
quence.* (In-
corporate the
former inter-
ference as a
useful part of
the strategy.)

tion and only becomes maladaptive when it is generalized to contexts in which it is not appropriate, or when it is stopped from adapting to changes in the individual or in the individual's ongoing contexts. Our contention is that *every human being makes the best choices available to them at any given moment, based on the contents of their personal history and their ability to generalize or to make discriminations about their sensory experience of their ongoing context.* Further, we claim as we pointed out earlier that every individual has available, at any point in time, the resources needed to make the appropriate changes and choices required to adapt to any situation, if these resources can be accessed and ordered in the appropriate sequences. This process is what this book is all about.

Reframing, considered in all its aspects, becomes a very sophisticated process, and we have decided to devote an entire future volume, *Reframing,* to this technique alone. For the purposes of this book we have chosen to present the basic steps of reframing as the following 2-part TOTE (see diagram of previous page):

The diagram describes a series of interactions that would procede in the following order:

1. The preexisting or newly designed strategy is *tested* to *find out if it achieves the appropriate outcome.* This may be done by creating or recreating the specified contextual conditions for the strategy internally by having the individual recall specific experiences or by future pacing. This may also be accomplished by providing the appropriate conditions in the ongoing external context. The individual should be taken through each step of the strategy so the performance and efficiency of the strategy as a whole may be evaluated.

2A. If the strategy sequence *is* appropriate and workable the outcome will be achieved smoothly, and the strategy will *exit* onto some other program of behavior.

2B. If the strategy or outcome *is not* satisfactory or if it violates the personal ecology of the individual, a representation of *incongruence* or interference will emerge at some point in the execution of the strategy—either the individual will complete the steps in the strategy without securing the outcome, or the strategy will be interrupted in mid-sequence. What is important for the programmer here is to *identify how* the interference is represented (i.e., whether it is an internal voice, a feeling or an image). The most direct way to elicit this information is to simply ask, *"What stopped you?"* When you ask a question such as this, be sure to *pay close attention to any following nonverbal responses,* especially accessing cues. Often the individual will be *unconscious* of the actual representation that created the interference, but will show you by responding with the appropriate accessing cue. The programmer should also pay attention to the tonalities the individual employs as he is going through a step involving internal dialogue. Many times, for example, an individual will say to himself the appropriate words (digital portion) for the strategy step but say them in an incongruent tonality.

3. This step begins the "reframing" of the interference. The incongruence or objection is *acknowledged and accepted as a valuable resource* for supplying feedback needed to improve the functioning of the strategy. The interference is put to work for the programmer and the individual by determining the *purpose* or *intent* of the interference. The programmer will first want to *test the client's representation of the outcome:* Are there any negative 4-tuples anchored by the individual's current representation of the outcome? Sometimes the individual will fear losing the choice of some previous outcome. An example of this might be that of an individual who desires to have the ability to be more assertive in social situations, but has experienced a part of himself being "put off" at times by assertive people, and is afraid that by becoming assertive, he might lose the ability to be "nice." The outcome *looks* good but doesn't *feel* right. These kind of objections may be easily discovered by eliciting the outcome sequitur.

Another thing to test for is whether the outcome is directly contradictory to a meta-outcome, or another outcome of priority from another strategy or part of the individual, causing an internal conflict. In other cases the outcome may lead to experiences the individual is not yet ready for.

Each of the phenomena described thus far applies to groups and organizations as well as to individuals. In the case of larger order systems, the representations, strategies and parts of the system are characterized by the people, departments, subsystems, etc., that make up the operating units of the total system in question. The interference or objections will be represented in the behavior of individuals or other subdivisions rather than through representational systems. The kinds of conflicts over outcomes listed previously will be found within an organization in the same way they can be found within an individual.

4. If the outcome is *unsatisfactory* to some part of the individual or organization, the programmer should help the individual/organization *operate to modify the outcome,* or, rather, the representation of the outcome, so that the intent of the interference is satisfied. Depending on the nature of the outcome and of the objection, the programmer may choose one of five possible operations:

(1) *Meta-model the client's representation of the outcome* to make the representational details of the experience more explicit. Meta-modeling ambiguous outcomes, such as "assertiveness," mentioned in the example given previously, will make them more specific and attainable in terms of the client's sensory experience and will *decrease the possibility of multiple responses to ambiguous stimuli.* In some cases this will clearly separate the client's new desired outcome from other experiences in the client's personal history (negative or frustrating instances, for example). In other cases it will make the association between the client's desired outcome, and other more resourceful experiences in the client's personal history, more apparent.

(2) Simply ask the individual if he can *modify his representation of the outcome in such a way that the intent of the interference will be incorporated.* For example, you may ask, *"What would it* (the outcome) *be like if you could* be assertive and still be nice?"

(3) *Integrate any negative 4-tuples* that were accessed as interference by collapsing them together with the positive 4-tuples accessed by the outcome.

(4) *Provide a framework in which all parts or aspects of the system (interference included) are working toward the same goal* by generalizing the outcome and/or the intent of the outcome to a meta-outcome, until it is general enough that all parts can agree on it. This would involve generalized outcomes such as "survival," "protection," "growth," "making sure all parts get their needs met," etc. This provides a context such that objections and interference no longer function destructively or as "sabotage," but, *since* all parts are working toward the *same outcome,* they will be constructive contributions.

(5) Work on *establishing, reestablishing or refining the context markers* (decision points) around the outcome to allow the client to determine more specifically which outcome will be most appropriate, when, where and in which situations. This will dispel conflicts

between outcomes vying for prime control.

5. When the individual/organization has modified the representation of the outcome to incorporate the changes required by the interference, the client and the programmer will need to work together to modify or redesign the strategy to insure that it achieves the new outcome. (Note: Sometimes the outcome will not require modification—the interference will have appeared because the strategy design was incomplete or faulty. In such cases, where the outcome remains the same, the client and programmer will be able to exit through the outcome test phase directly to the strategy test.) In this phase of the reframing, the *strategy sequence* in question is *tested* to find out if it will be satisfactory for the modified outcome. Check the strategy against the well-formedness conditions, and make sure it is calibrated and sequenced appropriately (that is, so the individual is able to congruently access the designated representational system to the appropriate degree and in the appropriate order). Also check to make sure that the appropriate context markers and decision points are included.

6. If the strategy sequence needs more work, the client and the programmer *operate to modify or redesign the strategy* so that the new outcome is achieved. This is done by *accessing resources* for the individual in terms of:

a. Accessing appropriate reference structures and representations from the client's personal history (or imagination) to be sequenced in with the other steps in the strategy.

b. Accessing the individual's creative strategy, so that the client may apply it to come up with new alternatives.

c. The programmer may simply ask the individual something like, "What do you need to do in order to insure that you can be nice and still be assertive?"

d. Have the client model someone else in order to get the choices he wants. For example, ask him "Do you know any one else who can achieve the outcome you want? What does he do in this situation?"

e. Rehearse or reanchor more completely the old steps in the strategy.

The final and most important part of the reframing, is to use the interference itself as an important part of the modified strategy. This is done by having the interfering representation serve as a context marker to assure that the client knows when, where and how to apply the modified strategy. That is, the interference is itself turned into a decision point *within the strategy,* so that it actually becomes an important step in the strategy rather than being interference *to* the strategy.

The following transcript is an example of how this TOTE may be applied step-by-step to an actual installation process. In the transcript, a woman has come to one of the authors to work on a weight problem. The woman, in her mid-thirties at the time, was approximately 30–40 pounds overweight. She had tried a number of weight loss plans without success.

TRANSCRIPT

AUTHOR: Do you find that you overeat regularly? . . . Or does it happen in spurts?

COMMENTARY

The author begins by gathering information about the client's present state—testing to find out if it is a generalized response or one that is contextually based.

CLIENT: Oh, its pretty consistent. I'll finish dinner and know that I've had enough . . . but then I'll see something left over (eyes move up and left, then shift down and right) . . . or see some dessert (eyes move up and left) that looks so good . . . (eyes down and right) and the next thing I know I'll be eating it.

C identifies the response as a general one, and initially indicates that her motivation strategy for over-eating is a rapid synesthesia pattern that cycles from the sight of food directly to the act of eating it: $V^e \longrightarrow K^e$.

A: How do you "know" that you've had enough to eat?

A gathers information about C's test for when she has eaten enough.

C: (Eyes move down and left) I tell myself that I've eaten plenty . . . I shouldn't be eating any more . . . I keep a close watch over what I eat, you know . . . But it just doesn't seem to make any difference.

C indicates an internal auditory cue that derives from external visual sources. $V^e \longrightarrow A^i_d$. Notice that C's strategy for "knowing" when she's had enough does not include a kinesthetic component at all (a component

A: Have you ever tried to stop yourself from overeating?

that plays a major role in her motivation strategy to eat).

A gathers more information about C's present strategies.

C: Oh sure . . . I keep telling myself that I shouldn't be eating any more (eyes down and left) . . . But it doesn't seem to do any good . . . (eyes down and right) the impulse is too strong by then.

C's motivation strategy for not eating appears to consist primarily of internal dialogue. (The other two representational systems are involved in her motivation strategy to eat— since there is no overlap between the strategies, it is no wonder that they may both be in operation at the same time without interfering with one another). Because C's eating strategy is wired directly to her actions (K^e) and her auditory motivation is evidently not, her motivation to eat will always pre-empt her motivation not to. Also, C's motivation strategy not to eat is not triggered until *after* she has already begun the behavior—this essentially means that she actually has to access her motivation strategy for eating and begin the process of eating *before* she can even access her motivation strategy for not eating!

A: Has there ever been a time when you *were* able to control your eating?

A begins to elicit resources.

C: Oh yes . . . (eyes up & left) in fact when I was in high school and college I used to compete

C accesses an appropriate reference structure.

in beauty contests . . . I used to
have quite a figure . . .

A: How were you able to control
your weight then?

A attempts to elicit the former
effective strategy, to be utilized
as a resource in the present context.

C: Well . . . it wasn't me controlling it mostly . . . my mother was
a very controlling sort of
woman . . . (eyes move down left
and then shift over to the right)
. . . She pretty much was in control of what I ate and how much
. . . (eyes shift back and forth
between down left and down
right) . . . She told me what to
do and when . . . (eyes flick up
and left) I didn't have very
much confidence in myself . . .

C relates that her primary motivation for keeping her weight
down had come from exter-
nal sources—specifically, her
mother (who, judging by C's accessing cues, was probably the
source of C's current internal
dialogue about eating).

A: You didn't have to rely much
on your own resources?

C: No . . . I didn't have much
choice in what was going on
with my life (eyes back and forth
between down left and down
right) . . . it really wasn't a very
happy time in my life . . .

In response to the results of his inquiries, the author decides to
abandon his search for applicable resources from C's personal
history (since her relevent reference structures all appear to be
associated with negative 4-tuples) and decides to opt for artificial
design. Given the information he has gathered, it is evident that
some specific conditions the strategy will have to meet will be (1)
that C's motivation strategy for controlling her weight will need to
include all representational systems, and (2) that the weight control strategy will have to be initiated *before* C has hooked into her

motivation strategy for overeating. (3) C's test for knowing when she's had enough to eat operates only from external feedback (V^e) and does not involve any internal check (this, as we mentioned above, is probably a result of the programming done by C's mother). The result is that the test, though probably accurate, initiates no internal intervention (it is missing the operate phase). The author, then, must be sure to design such an operation into the strategy. (4) C has no representation of the desired state in the strategy, and, thus no means for obtaining feedback.

C's problem strategy was basically a polarity loop that cycled between the impulse to eat and an internal dialogue telling her not to:

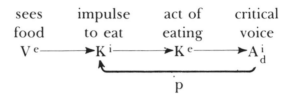

sees food	impulse to eat	act of eating	critical voice

$$V^e \longrightarrow K^i \longrightarrow K^e \longrightarrow A^i_d$$

$$p$$

The new strategy designed by the author, separated into sections to aid the reader in following its structure, was sequenced as follows:

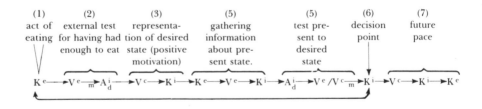

(1) act of eating　(2) external test for having had enough to eat　(3) representation of desired state (positive motivation)　(5) gathering information about present state.　(5) test present to desired state　(6) decision point　(7) future pace

$$K^e \longrightarrow V^e_m \longrightarrow A^i_d \longrightarrow V^c \longrightarrow K^i \longrightarrow K^e \longrightarrow V^e \longrightarrow K^i \longrightarrow A^i_d \longrightarrow V^e / V^c_m \longrightarrow K^i \longrightarrow V^c \longrightarrow K^i \longrightarrow K^e$$

(1) C begins, of course, with the act of eating.

(2) This will trigger her naturally occurring strategy to assess, by watching what she eats, when she's had enough. It is at this point that the author chose to install the new strategy sequence, as it is just before the problem loop starts. In addition to the feedback that she has eaten enough, (an internal step is established later in the strategy) the author added another verbalization to the internal dialogue that went, "I've had plenty to eat *and* if I stop eating now

I'll be able to get skinnier." (This verbalization was rehearsed a number of times in conjunction with C's existing response.)

(3) This verbalization was to anchor a step in which C made a constructed image of herself the way she would like to look (V^c). This image was, in turn, to access the experience of how good it would feel to have accomplished the outcome that she had desired so long (K^i).

(4) As soon as she was able to get this feeling she was to immediately get up from the table (K^e) and go look at herself in a mirror. (She was given special instruction, if she did not have one already, to get a full length mirror and hang it in the kitchen, if possible, or in a room close by.) This step had an added advantage in that it forced an interruption of her external visual contact with food. After she looked at herself closely, she was to close her eyes, take a deep breath and check out her feelings, and test if she had had enough to eat. This was to verify (or contradict) the earlier communication from her internal dialogue. This step was sequenced after she had interrupted her external visual contact with the food on the table to make sure that the feelings were uninfluenced by her $V^e \longrightarrow K^i$ synesthesia pattern.

(5) C was then to comment on those feelings to herself, describing explicitly the feelings she experienced (note how this changes the role of her internal dialogue in her eating strategy—it is now describing the feelings as opposed to having a polarity response to them). After she had described the feelings, she was to ask herself if she wanted to eat more or to put everything away. In making this decision she was to compare the image of her desired state to what she observed of her present state (V^e/V^c) and allow a feeling to emerge to help her decide which it was to be.

(6) If she truly felt that she should have more to eat (which the author guessed would rarely be the case) she was to respect the decision of her feelings and eat, but first she was to construct a specific image of what else, and how much of it, she was to eat. If she didn't feel the need to eat, she was to imagine as if looking through her own eyes, in as much detail as possible, putting each of the items left on the table away, and then leaving the kitchen to do something else. As she imagined these scenes she was also to include the representation of feeling good, as she did the specific actions, about having accomplished her outcome successfully. (The use of the visual constructs was to provide a self initiated

future pace that would help reprogram the problematic synesthesia pattern. The act of putting the food away or of eating only
so much would be initiated by the sight of the food instead of the
eating impulse. If she did go back to eat, the imagery would also
help her "keep watch" over how much she was eating.

Various reference structures were accessed and anchored for
each step in the strategy, and then the strategy was rehearsed. But,
although C could elicit and perform each of the pieces of the
strategy separately, she had an extremely difficult time getting
through the whole strategy. Every time she tried, she would miss
a step or something would go wrong. This, of course, does not
satisfy the test step 1 of the reframing TOTE.

We pick up the transcript again just after C has made another
attempt at completing the strategy. This puts the author and the
client at 2B in the reframing TOTE.

TRANSCRIPT

C: Gee . . . I'm really sorry I
keep bumbling things up . . . I'm
just too stupid or something I
guess . . . (eyes down left, then
down right).

A: Before you start feeling bad
about anything I'd like to ask
you a question.

C: Okay.

A: What would happen if you
were able to incorporate this
strategy?

C: Well . . . I'd stop eating, I
guess.

A: Well I hope you wouldn't
stop eating, . . . that could be
disastrous.

COMMENTARY

Having met with interference,
the author moves to step ③ of
the reframing TOTE, and tests
the specific outcome sequitur of
the strategy.

A also tests his rapport with C
by venturing a playful remark.

C: (Laughing) Well I mean . . . I wouldn't stop eating altogether . . . I'd stop *over*-eating . . .

C responds positively indicating that rapport has not been broken. A continues to test the outcome in more detail. (Still step ③)

C: Ummm . . . I'd be thinner . . . I'd look thinner.

A: You'd look thinner.

C: Yes . . . I'd look the way I want to to be able to . . . the way I did in college . . . I want to look the way I did when I didn't like myself . . .

C's last comment seems to imply a connection between the way C looked at an unhappy time in her life, and the kind of person she was. If she was indeed to not like herself again if she looked thinner, this would be in conflict with a very basic meta-outcome, that of liking oneself. In the least case, looking thinner is probably a bad anchor.

A: Are you aware of what you just said?

C: What I said about what?

A: That you want to look like you did when you didn't like yourself.

C: Well . . . sort of . . .

A: I'm curious . . . How much have you changed since then . . . since you put on weight?

A inquires about possible resources that A gets from her weight, a very important question. We pointed out earlier in the book that body type was a very powerful and important accessing mechanism. Heavier people tend to generally have more awareness of internal kinesthetic experience; thinner people tend to be more visual. People who change their weight at all significantly often undergo a change in their state of consciousness. A person who is losing weight becomes more conscious of the way he *looks* and has to deprive himself of many kinesthetic luxuries in the form of food and drink. Many people who attempt diets are not prepared for the accompanying change in state and are not willing to go along with those outcomes. They resist the change in their state, but want the physical changes. This can be a very frustrating situation if one is unaware of it.

C: Oh I've come a long way since then . . . (eyes move down and right) . . . (voice tone deepens and tempo slows) it hasn't been easy . . . but . . . back then I couldn't even stand on my own two feet . . . I'm a lot more in control of *me* now . . . a lot more grounded . . . I really like myself as a person a lot better . . .

C lists a number of resources that she has gained in connection with her weight, which, judging by her accessing cues and predicates, are primarily kinesthetic.

A: MmHmm . . . Now if you lost weight so that you looked like you did before, do you think you'd be able to still have all of these important resources?

A tests C's representation of her specific outcome to find if it is congruent with the meta-outcomes she has just named. ③

C: Ummmm . . . Well (eyes move from up and right to down and right, then to down and left and back up and right) . . . I guess so (voice hesitates, eyebrows furrow, eyes move to down and left).

C expresses her incongruence.

A: You don't sound very sure about that . . . Would you do something for me . . . would you again describe to me that image you have of yourself being this way?

A begins to test the specific details of the desired outcome.

C: (Looks up and right) Well . . . I look very thin . . . like I did in college . . .

A: What about her face . . . is it smiling? . . . Does she look grounded?

C: Well . . . (looks back and forth between up left and up right.) . . . I can't really see the face . . . It's just sort of an image of a body . . . with no head . . .

A: Oh . . . I see . . . she doesn't have a very good head on her shoulders, huh?

C: (Laughs) . . . I guess not.

A: You know . . . I have this theory about people who are overweight . . . My theory is that the reason they are heavy is because they are "weighting" for some

A states the details of the modified specific outcome of the new strategy that he has been attempting to install. ④. He also has begun the second special resources that they need . . . Do you think that it would be possible for you to get thin *and* remain grounded and like yourself?

sub-TOTE of the reframing process—that of testing the strategy sequence to find out if it will achieve the modified outcome. ⑤

Note also that A takes advantage of the phonological ambiguity between "wait" and "weight" to reframe C's problem with losing weight.

C: That would sure be nice.

A: I'm wondering if you can look up there (indicates up and right) and see an image of what you would look like if you were able to be thin *and* be grounded, standing on your own two feet and liking yourself?

A begins reframing step ⑥, and starts modify the original strategy steps so that they will achieve the outcome as modified in steps ③ & ④.

C: Ahhh . . . (looks from up right to up left and back) . . . I . . . I'm having a hard time . . . (furrows eyebrows) . . . I'm going blank . . .

A: Okay . . . stop for a minute . . . I want you to try something that I think will help you out . . . (moves C's right hand so that it is resting palm up on her right knee) . . . I want you to look down here and see on this hand a picture of what you look like now . . . Can you do that?

A begins to establish an internal visual anchor for C's present state. Note that A has C orient her head to the kinesthetic accessing position by having her look down and right at her hand. This will serve to help anchor the reference structure he is eliciting to the kinesthetic abilities and resources C has achieved through her present state.

C: (Looks down and right at hand) . . . UhHuh.

A: And as you continue looking at it. . . . I want you to be sure that you can clearly see the details of her face, so that you can see the expression, and her posture and gestures . . . Can you see her expression?

C: UhHuh . . . She looks very grounded and comfortable with herself . . .

A: (Interrupting) I don't want any interpretations, now . . . I want you to be able to see the color of her skin and the muscle tensions around her nose and mouth and eyes . . . You can see those can't you?

A calibrates the image to make sure it is completely visual.

C: Sort of . . . (squints her eyes as if she is focusing) . . . It's getting clearer now.

A: Okay . . . good . . . now keep looking at all of those details and as you do I want you to begin to imagine the feelings of having stepped into her body so that you can feel all those feelings of groundedness . . . self-control . . . and self respect . . . all those resources . . . and feel the problems she has too . . . like her difficulties with eating . . . and as you feel those feelings . . . imagine her de-

A elicits a full internal 4-tuple representation for C's present state, to be anchored to the constructed image of herself.

scribing them to you so that you can hear the sound of her voice . . . the speed with which she speaks . . . the tonal qualities . . . and as she speaks, observe her breathing patterns . . . how fast and from where in her body she is breathing . . . and any smells that she may be aware of as she breathes . . . Can you do all that?

C: MnHmmm . . . (eyes remain *transfixed* down and right, pupils defocused).

C's behavior indicates that she has developed a light trance state.

A: Good . . . now come back here . . . and back with me, look at me so that you can see me clearly and hear my voice . . . (waits for C to respond) . . . Now I want you to look down at the other hand (moves C's left hand so that it rests on her left knee palm up) and make a picture of what you used to look like when you were thin . . . in college . . . and I want you to look closely at her face, now, so that you can see her expression, and all the details of her eyes and mouth . . . Do you have that picture?

A interrupts the state to bring C out of the 4-tuple for her present state and begins to have C create a visual anchor for her current representation of the desired thin state. Note that for this reference structure A has C look down and left (the access for internal dialogue). This is to help associate it with the internal dialogue she experiences in connection with her existing eating strategies (that has been postulated to be a residual of her mother's influence). Also note that, because the author has C orient her head to accessing cues other than visual, she has experienced some difficulty in getting the image until she overlaps the visual accessing cue of squinting onto the other accessing cue. The task he is having her do is quite complicated and in both instances she eventually develops a slight trance state (which is a general access to all internal processes —see *Patterns II*) in order to carry out the task.

C: (Squinting) Sort of . . . It's hard to imagine her face.

A: Do you have any photographs of what you looked like then? . . . What do they look like?

Accesses a reference structure to help C with the task.

C: (Eyes move up and left then back down and left) . . . Oh . . . Okay . . . I can see it now . . . She doesn't look very happy.

A: Now I want you to look at her face so that you can *see* what specific indicators let you know that . . . and for a moment *just look* at her . . . (pauses while C responds) . . . And now I would like you to imagine stepping into *her* body so that you can feel her feelings . . . perhaps of imbalance and unhappiness . . . but her good feelings too . . . and remember what it felt like to have a thin body . . . so that you can be aware of the differences . . . and listen to the sound of her voice as she tells you what it is like to be her . . . and as you *listen* be aware of the qualities of her breathing

A again calibrates C's visual experience and then proceeds to elicit a full internal 4-tuple representation of C's present (and problematic) representation of her desired state.

. . . and any smells or tastes that she may be aware of . . .

C: (Eyes defocus, pupils dilate, and face flattens, indicating that she has developed another slight trance.)

A: Okay . . . now come back . . . and look at me again . . . You here?

C: (Blinking her eyes) . . . UhHuh . . . I think so.

A: Now I want you to look back down at each of your hands so that you can see those two parts of you . . . the thin one in your left hand and the fat one in your right hand . . .

C: (Looking back and forth at her hands) Okay.

A: Then what I want you do is ask the thin one what she has to say about the fat one. And listen to what she tells you.

A continues to build on to the reference structures he has created, accessing and anchoring representations of both the positive and negative aspects of her present state from the strategy associated with her reference structure of her desired state. ⑥

C: Well . . . she thinks the other one is much too fat . . . she's appalled at her eating habits . . .

A: What does she think of her resources and abilities?

C: (Voice quieting) Oh, she envies her . . . she wants to be able to have her strength and control . . .

A: Now ask the fat one what she feels about the thin one.

C: (Looks over at her right hand. As she does so she unconsciously turns her left hand over and begins to rub her left knee) . . . Well . . .

A: (Laughing and turning C's left hand back to the palm up position) Don't do that . . . You'll squish her!

A ventures a humorous remark to test rapport and keep a positive frame on the interaction.

C: Huh? . . . Oh . . . (laughs) . . .

A: That's better . . . Now how does that one feel about this thin one?

A recommences the process of building up the reference structures to include representations of both the positive and negative aspects of each state. (Notice that he specifically asks the fat one how she "feels" about her counterpart, while she asked the other one—related to the internal dialogue—what she had to say about her counterpart.) ⑥

C: (Looking at right hand) . . . She thinks the thin one has a lot

of problems . . . she feels sorry
for her in a way . . .

A: What about the thin one's resources?

C: (Looking back and forth between her hands) . . . Well she'd
like to be able to have her body
. . . She likes that . . . and she
admires the thin one's energy
. . . the thin one has quite a bit
more energy to do things than
the heavy one . . .

A: All right . . . fine . . . Now, you
know what I'm aware of? . . . I'm
aware that both of these parts of
you have their own problems
and their own special qualities
and resources . . . *And* that each
could use the resources of the
other to help them with their
problems . . . and something
else . . . and I'd like you to check
this out . . . I think that you may
be surprised to find that both of
them, when you get right down
to it, actually want the same
thing . . . I'll bet that both of
those parts would like to be able
to have an existence in which
they could be comfortable and
balanced and get the full benefit
of your total resources as a person . . . Is that right?

A now puts a meta-frame
around the qualities of the two
representations by framing
their individual properties in relation to the meta-outcome of
the balance and harmony of the
entire person, and begins to
propose an integration of the
individual outcomes of the two
states as a more effective way of
achieving this meta-outcome.

C: (Looking back and forth
from hand to hand) . . . Oh yes
. . .

C responds positively to the
proposed integration.

A: Now I want you to ask each of those parts if it would be willing to share its resources with the other, and help the other out with its problems . . . What do they say?

A continues to set up the integration process, again framing the qualities of the individual states in relation to the meta-outcome.

C: (Nodding) They both say that they'd be willing to try.

C's response is congruent.

A: Wonderful . . . Now what I want you to do is to look back and forth between those two parts and make a series of pictures . . . like separate frames of a movie . . . and see the metamorphosis or transition that takes place as each one changes to the other . . . Make about five pictures . . . so that the one in the middle here (gestures to a point in between her two hands) is a complete integration of the two . . . Okay? . . . And take all the time you need to to that . . . and just nod when you're done . . .

A chooses a method of visual integration, since he has been working with visual anchors, that involves dividing C's transformation into discrete steps of change happening in equal increments from both directions.

C: (Keeps looking back and forth between her two hands for a period of time, and then nods.)

A: Now I want you to bring your hands together slowly . . . so that one palm ends up overlapping the other . . . and as you overlap them together I want you to see all of those images merging together . . . so that when you've brought your hands together thay will have

A begins the process of collapsing the anchors, both visually and kinesthetically (by having C bring her hands together). ⑥

combined to make a sharp clear image of one that's in the middle . . . take all the time you need . . .

C: (As C begins to bring her hands together her face flattens and pupils dilate, and her breathing slows and shallows. Hands begin to show slow and jerky movements common to ideomotor movements exhibited in trance states) . . . (she begins to nod when her hands have overlapped.)

A: You can see that image clearly.

A tests to make sure the integration is taking place.

C: (Nods.)

A: Then your last step is to draw that image into your body . . . and you can put it wherever is the most appropriate place . . . go ahead . . .

A then completes the process of collapsing the anchors with a final kinesthetic gesture.

C: (Draws her hands toward her stomach in the same slow, jerky fashion. As her hands touch her stomach, she begins to cry gently) . . . It feels so good . . . I didn't realize that I'd been in conflict with myself for so long . . .

C's response indicates that the integration has been quite successful.

A: (Waits until C has collected herself) . . . I want to go back over that new strategy we were trying a while ago, in a few minutes . . . and I want you to sub-

A returns to step ⑤ of the reframing TOTE and sequences the integrated representation of C's desired state into the new eating strategy.

stitute the new image and the new feelings that you just got as your goal for what you want to accomplish . . . Okay?

C: (Smiling and nodding) You bet.

A: But before we go back to that . . . I want to take care of one other thing . . . You know what it feels like to be grounded and balanced . . . right?

As an added measure A also redesigns C's kinesthetic test for her present state by including a test for "groundedness" in it, with accompanying operations (that don't involve eating) for achieving that particular outcome. (He cycles again, then, to step ⑥.)

C: (Nodding) Yes . . . (glances down & right).

A: Do you know what it feels like if you're getting ungrounded or unbalanced?

C: (Looks down and right) . . . Ummmm . . . (starts nodding) yes . . .

A: I want to change something else in your new strategy . . . when you're looking at yourself in the mirror and checking out your feelings . . . I want you to make sure you're not getting ungrounded . . . Do you know how to do that?

A sequences the new test and operations for "groundedness" into the decision point in the new eating strategy—⑤.

C: (Eyes down and right) UhHuh . . . I think I can do that.

A: Now I'm aware that your
major way of grounding yourself in the past has been
through eating . . . so I want to
work out a couple of ways in
which you'll be able to ground
yourself without eating if you
begin to find that you're becoming ungrounded as you start to
lose weight . . . like making that
picture of yourself as a balanced
person . . . or closing your eyes
and taking a deep breath . . . or
things like that . . . Okay?

C: Sure . . . let's get started
. . .

The author went on to help C include operations for grounding
herself, which were incorporated into the strategy at the decision
point. The author, having modified the strategy to include the
changes in C's representation of her desired state, and adding in
the grounding operations at the decision point, then returned to
step 1 of the reframing TOTE and tested the new strategy modifications by rehearsing C through the steps and future pacing her
for that evenings meal, C's ability to access and sequence the steps
had dramatically improved, and the installation process was completed rapidly and smoothly. A week later C called up the author
with the happy news that she had already lost eight pounds. To
date the client continues to maintain her weight and her sense of
groundness.

6.5 Installation and Interference in Groups and Organizations.

The installation or start-up of new behavioral sequences in
groups and organizations, as with a single individual, takes place
through rehearsal, schedules, and the establishment of the appropriate cues, or anchors. In working with an organization, however,
the duties of the programmer are somewhat expanded in that, in

conjunction to dealing with the sequencing of organizational functions and operations, the programmer will also be dealing with the internal functions and strategies of the individuals that make up the organization. The behavior of each individual (a system within himself) makes up the elements of the larger system, or meta-system. The operating principles of the larger system will be isomorphic to those involved in the strategies of the single individual. Every organization or family, for instance, will have a present state, desired state, and a sequence of tests and operations which take them from the present state to the desired state. These sequences of tests and operations are performed by people (or machines) that each have their own individual present states, desired states, tests and operations (see Design section 5.32). Each person will serve as a specific resource to the operation of the organization as a whole, and each person will have a specific set of resources that contribute to his own individual operation.

One difference in working with the operations of an organization as opposed to the strategies of an individual, is that "hierarchy" in operations in organizations tends to be more obvious. Since our first discussion of strategies and TOTEs, of course, we have talked about hierarchy in the various subroutines of a particular strategy—where the outputs or results of one part of the whole sequence or system are the inputs to one of higher order. The decision point in a strategy, for instance, is a good example of a hierarchical division of labor. The decision point assesses the output of its subroutine(s) and must then indicate whether the job must be done over again or whether the strategy is ready to proceed to the next stage (it supervises the operation of the strategy). It also dictates the work load of the various strategies within the individual's repertoire of possibilities, choosing which one will be most appropriate for dealing with the specific situation. Hierarchically ordered positions within a group or organization operate off of the same principles as the decision points in a strategy. The programmer will treat them in essentially the same manner as decision points in a person's strategy are treated.

The process for the effective installation and implementation of new strategies, operations and routines in groups or organizations will also follow essentially the same procedures as that of the installation of a strategy in an individual:

1. Establish Meta-Outcomes: Often, when changes are made in

the daily routines of work activity which employees have become habituated to, many employees find such changes upsetting or bewildering. This, in turn, can adversely effect their work performance—although the changes are later appreciated by these same employees. It helps a great deal if installations of new procedures are accompanied by a built-in reframe, in which all changes are framed and justified with respect to meta-outcomes. Modifications in employee outcomes or routines, for instance, would be framed as contributing to the achievement of meta-outcomes that are desired by all members of the work force, meta-outcomes such as: improving job satisfaction and efficiency, increasing production and return, providing variety to job conditions and routines, and so on.

In social groups, the installation of new strategies and interactions may be justified by meta-outcomes like: improved member relations, contributing to the harmony and growth of the family or group, etc.

2. Establish Specific Outcomes and Outcome Sequiturs: Explicit sensory based representations and descriptions are established for the present state and the desired state, and specific indicators should be set up for testing and feedback purposes. (See Design 5.32.)

3. Establish the Needs and Resources of Each Element of the System (each member or department of the group or organization): Find out what you have to work with. Elicit the decision making, motivation, learning, and creativity strategies of the group members. Or, depending upon the level at which you are working with the organization's operations, assess the various capacities of the departments, divisions, bureaus, etc., that make the organization function.

4. Install the new routines and operations of the members and /or departments of the organization by scheduling the activities of each member or department according to their particular capabilities.

A. *Redundancy and Feedback.*

When giving instructions or establishing new schedules or routines it is a good idea to make sure that the instructions and directions (or anchors) that are to organize the behavior of the members of the organization are made available in forms that will appeal to all representational systems. In other words, in order to insure that the behavior will be anchored, make sure that, to whatever extent possible, the directions for the behavioral sequences are translated and coded into each representational system; that is, the instructions will be redundent in each representational system. For example, kinesthetically, the individual can be walked through operations and given a feel for them; visually, the individual can be shown written schedules, flow charts and diagrams, or personally observe others; auditorily explicit verbal descriptions may be given of their operation, and verbal feedback and supervision may be provided as they are learning their routine. By establishing anchors for the steps and sequence of the operations in all representational systems, you will insure the maximal transmission and coding of the information.

It will also be extremely helpful to establish a feedback network between relevant personnel, group members, and any other people or elements involved in the operation, so that they can get feedback on the outcomes of their operations and so you can get feedback on the effectiveness of the operations you have installed. (How close to completion is the project? Was the product ordered? Delivered? Received? What changes or operations still need to be made to accomplish the desired state? Who will be taking on what task?) Redundancy in feedback and the type of feedback will also be very important. Operations may be slowed down and information may be lost if the appropriate feedback is not employed. Often, installing the procedure so that direct auditory and visual contact is available between members participating in the operation can streamline the feedback and operation processes.

One of the authors was once consulting for a corporation that had just installed a computer system into their operation, with which to record, store and send orders for their product. Shortly after the installation of the new system, however, the company's number of "lost orders" increased dramatically. The "lost orders" were a great mystery to everyone. The author then observed the operation of the new computer system. The computer performed three basic operations: (1) storing the name, address and order of the person or company requesting the product, (2) sending this information to the terminal of the distributor of the product, and (3) informing the computer operator of the receipt of the order at the terminal of the distributor. In order to first get the computer to take in and store the information about the purchaser, however, a specific format had to be employed to enter the information. When the format was followed and the computer took in the information it would print out the feedback: "accepted/done." Different feedback would be given for the successful completion of the other operations. What the author realized, was that, because of the ambiguity of the word "done," many of the employees who were naive about the operation of computers would enter orders and assume the computer feedback "accepted/done" meant that the order was sent and received and that the job was completed. When the situation was remedied by changing the feedback to read: "stored," "sent," and "received by _____," the number of "lost orders" declined dramatically.

Another common task facing business is the selection or training of personnel to occupy vacated positions within their organizations. The decision to recruit or train is an important one which we discussed earlier. One input which an effective manager will require in order to make that decision intelligently is a job description. The higher the quality of information regarding the actual behavior required to be effective in a job position, the higher the quality of decision that manager will be able to make regarding the recuitment/training issue. (This is isomorphic to getting a full 4-tuple representation of the desired state in individual strategy installation.) One technique designed by one of the authors to elicit high quality information about actual job requirements is given below. Provide first line supervisors with forms (see example form A on the next page) to be distributed to personnel who they supervise. These forms are to be filled out in context (i.e. the employee is to fill out the form while working in position). To insure this, the supervisor will keep as privileged information the specific times the employees are to fill in the forms. The supervisor is responsible for:

1. Providing their employees with the form and its accompanying reframe, 3 days in a row. (See procedure 1)

2. Informing employees to fill forms in at the times designated (known only to the supervisor—these times will be randomized throughout the working day) during a three day period.

3. Collecting forms and checking them for intelligibility/legibility.

The point of having employees fill out forms in context is, of course, to minimize the slippage between their actual behavior and the words they use in attempting to report it on the form. After this initial information is gathered (assuming a move refined description is appropriate), the following steps would be appropriate:

1. Have first line supervisors compile a list of the six most frequently occurring activities/tasks as reported by their employees (spot check to keep them honest).

2. Design a form whereby the activity/task is placed in context by having each employee select a specific example of each one of the six most frequent activities/tasks and describe what they had to do to get ready to do that task efficiently (typically not more than 5 minutes before starting the task) and what they had to do to insure the task was completed, followed up on (e.g., File information with whom?, Positive receipt procedures to be used?, Information routed to whom?)

FORM A (Sample)

Division	Job Title/Position	Date

Each of you when you first came to work at your present job experienced both a sense of excitement as you faced something new and a sense of uncertainty about what was expected of you— what exactly you were supposed to do. These are a normal part of fitting yourself into a new job. We, here at company X, are interested in promoting that sense of excitement while reducing the frustration which sometimes accompanies the uncertainty. We are doing this by asking you experienced employees to take a minute breather several times a day for the next few days, and jot down where you are and what specifically you are doing. By doing this, you can help us help your future co-workers and help us help you when you move into any new position. Please indicate with as few words as possible where you are and what specific activity/task you are involved in at the times when your supervisor indicates. For example:

TIME	LOCATION	ACTIVITY
9:05	at desk or phone	giving new standing orders to shippers
10:15	at computer terminal	entering information on trail orders

- -

TIME	LOCATION	ACTIVITY
_____		
_____		
_____		
_____		
_____		
_____		

6.51 Interference.

Interference to the installation or start-up of an operation in an organization can be treated essentially the same way as it is with an individual strategy.

If the operation does not achieve the outcome, the first thing to check is the calibration of the operation—that is, are they all doing what they are supposed to be doing? If they are not, change their behavior so that they are, making use of the meta-outcomes to reframe your intervention (as described earlier). If they are, and you are still not getting your outcome, then you can essentially follow the same TOTE sequence diagramed earlier in this chapter to test and modify the specific procedures and the outcomes of those procedures.

Another important check to make is on the rapport between the members of the organization that are interacting with one another to carry out the installed operation. How do the employees react to one another? If you find that you have rapport problems, one very effective way to resolve them is to teach the employees, managers and executives about representational systems, strategies, pacing, anchoring, and so on, and help them to develop the tools of rapport building.

If there are specific conflicts, breaks in rapport to the point of precipitating crises, you may wish to use the arbitration and negotiation strategy described below.

6.511 Arbitration and Negotiation.

The processes of arbitration and negotiation provide a good example of the application of NLP principles to the handling of interference in organizations. The steps of the procedure are a slight modification of the reframing TOTE (they are very similar, in fact, to the procedure used with the two conflicting parts of the overweight client in the transcript presented earlier in this chapter).

1. Establish the specific outcome of each individual involved in the conflict in relation to a meta-outcome that all parties agree upon.

For example, have each person make the following statement, filling in the blanks. "I specifically want the outcome of_____, for the purpose of_____.

Their purpose will be a meta-outcome. If their meta-outcomes do not at this point match one another in some way, have each of them repeat the process again, this time substituting the meta-outcome each has come up with in the last statement as the specific outcome of this statement. Keep repeating this process with the newly generated meta-outcomes until you arrive at a general goal that everyone agrees upon. Then anchor their agreement.

Establishing that all of the parties actually have the same goal immediately puts a frame around the rest of the interaction. When all parties agree that they are attempting to achieve the same outcome, their conflicts become reframed as a matter of detail to be worked out, and the rest of your task is essentially team-building.

A. It also helps to establish from the very beginning that the *conflict* between the negotiating parties is counter-productive

to the achievement of their meta-outcomes and specific outcomes, and to have all parties agree that it should be resolved
as quickly as possible.

2. Get all parties to agree again on what a successful outcome
of the negotiation would be. For instance, find out what would
constitute an acceptable decision. And if a successful settlement
is not made, find out what further information is needed, who
will get it and how the information will be gathered. (See Design
5.32.)

3. As the parties are considering the issues and making decisions
about what is to be an appropriate outcome to the negotiation,
observe their strategies for decision making.

4. Access reference structures for possible resources—such as,
"Have you ever been able to settle a negotiation before in a way
that you were satisfied with?" or "Has there ever been a time when
you were able to communicate with someone really effectively and
suprised yourself by setting something right that you had previously thought would never get straightened out?" Covertly anchor
these experiences so that you can put them into play at the appropriate time.

5. Control the analogue communications of the parties so
that they produce no adverse effects on the negotiation proceedings. We believe that most of what actually gets communicated
in our verbal interactions is the result of the accompanying
nonverbal or analogue cues. When we arbitrate for organizations (or work with groups—as in family therapy) we pay attention to and control the nonverbal portions of the interactions
more than we do the verbal portions. In our experience, this
has made a tremendous difference in the parties' responses to
one another. If an individual, for example, were to raise his
voice and point his finger at someone while making a point or
statement, and if we noticed that the person to whom he directed his nonverbal gestures began to tense up and stop
breathing (indicating a negative response), we would have the
person who made the statement stop, change their analogue
and repeat the exact same statement. In practically every instance this will change the other individual's response to, or
understanding of, the statement.

6. Utilize the decision making and motivation strategies of each
party to influence their decision making processes (especially if

you are a negotiator) when you think it is appropriate or necessary, making use of any anchors that you have established.

7. Act as a translator (especially if you are an arbitrator) reinterpreting and recording what has been said into the vocabulary of the different representational systems when you find that differences in the strategies of the individual parties are getting in the way. Establishing some rapport with each party via overt or covert pacing, will also be a very effective tool.

8. As you carry out the negotiation process, start with the meta-outcome that everyone is in agreement with and move on to specifics from there, gathering information and altering each party's position until you can find the middle ground. Any time that you run into problematic disagreements return to the meta-outcome to reestablish the positive framework.

VII. CONCLUSION

The Denver Zoo, so the tale goes, was very interested in acquiring a polar bear. The director of the zoo at that time, a grey haired old gent with a long white beard, had quite a penchant for polar bears. He had always been awed by their large and muscular bodies, and respected the primordial intelligence that he felt they demonstrated in their slow but elegant movements and that he saw so clearly in their keen eyes. Most of all, however, he liked their long, thick, pure white fur that reminded him of the hair that adorned his own face. Because of this special affinity that he felt toward the bears the director decided that the polar bears of the Denver Zoo should have the largest and most naturalistically built cage of all the animals in the zoo. So he set his designers, engineers and construction crew to work to build an enclosure that was so big and naturalistic in its representation of the splendor of the arctic terrain that it would rival in craftsmanship and expense the cages of even the largest and most famous zoos of the world.

The construction of the polar bear's enclosure was only about half completed, however, when the director was offered a good deal on one of the most beautiful polar bears he had ever laid eyes upon. In fact, when he was inspecting the animal the director almost had the experience that he was looking in the mirror when he looked into the eyes of the beast who swayed slowly back and forth as he returned the directors stare.

Since good deals on polar bears don't come along very often (and such a magnificent polar bear at that) the director decided to go ahead and purchase the bear even though its enclosure was only partially completed. The bear was sedated and when it awoke it found itself in a small cage made of thick metal bars that had been placed directly in the middle of the giant naturalistic enclosure that was still under construction. It was to remain in the smaller cage until the larger structure was finished.

The small enclosure was just large enough that the polar bear could take about four good sized steps before being halted by the cold metal bars. Having nothing else in particular to do while inhabiting the small cage the bear soon developed a habit of pacing its tiny environment. It would take four steps in one direction, rear up on its hind legs as it made a 180 degree turn slowly and with a conviction that only polar bears are capable of, and take four steps in the opposite direction before rearing up by slowly thrusting its front paws high into the air as it made its turn. All day long the bear would slowly pace back and forth in its cage carefully observing the work crew as they labored away on the huge enclosure that surrounded it.

Finally, after months of painstaking craftsmanship and steady labor, the zoo's construction crew completed the polar bear's new home. The bear was against sedated and small cage of metal bars that had been the bear's world for so many months was removed. A large crowd of zoo visitors along with the entire zoo staff and construction crew and, of course, the proud director, gathered around the enclosure and anxiously waited to see how the bear would take to its beautiful new environment. The polar bear awoke, cautiously got to its feet and shook the remains of the drug induced sleep from its head. The director could almost feel the excitement that must have surely been building in bear's own breast as it made ready to explore its beautiful lifelike environment. He eagerly watched as the bear took four slow but steady steps before rearing up, paws high in the air, and turned around to take four steps in the opposite direction, rearing again as it turned and retraced its first steps and reared. . . .

*　　*　　*　　*　　*

The examples and description we have offered you in this book represent only a few of an infinite number of possible applications that may be made using the Neuro-Linguistic Programming model we have presented within these pages. You now have the unprecedented opportunity to go into the world in which you have chosen to involve yourself and explore, discover, rediscover and generate experience that you might not even believe possible. NLP, as we have said over and over, is a user oriented model. The information we have imparted to you here will be useless to you unless you go out and begin to APPLY IT to your lives. We strongly urge you to take the patterns you have learned about here and try them out for yourself. Our guess is you will find that they work, uncannily. If you do find discrepancies in the model, grey areas, or counter-examples we congratulate you and remind you that discrepancies, grey areas and counter-examples are not necessarily indications that a model should be tossed out or ignored but rather point out the directions in which the model may be clarified, expanded and evolved. Whenever you do something that doesn't work fate has provided you with an opportunity to learn something more about yourself and the world around you. The map is not the territory.

Limiting yourself to a particular model of the world (including the one we have presented here), no matter how "real" it may appear to you, can stop you from expanding and enriching your experience of the world. If, as you attempt to apply these patterns and techniques or as you read over portions of this text, you have the experience that many people label "confusion" we invite you to try to try something new and stay with it for once rather than try to avoid or dispel it. Confusion is the gateway to new realities. Confusion simply means things do not make sense (and we like to think of "sense" in its literal meaning here) given your current model of the world.

In reading over this book ourselves we are well aware that it is not an "easy" book to read in many ways - that was not our intent writing this text. We have written and published other books (such as *Frogs to Princes*) where we have put the patterns presented here into simpler and more entertaining language. Our purpose in writing this book the way we have has been to push to create a new vocabulary, a new syntax, a new way of thinking about the world rather than trying to make the Neuro-Linguistic Programming model fit existing ways of thinking. The rigor and syntax of this book are themselves an attempt at programming. If you have read this entire book your perceptions and ways of thinking about human behavior will be dramatically altered. This book has been an invitation and a challange to the reader to think and process as we do.

If you have found the content of this book exciting and wish to learn more, or if you are unconvinced that this material is valid or useful, we again extend our invitation to you to join us at one of our seminars or workshops where we will make these patterns easily available to all of your senses. We also invite you to read any of our other books including the next book in this series, *Neuro-Linguistic Programming, Volume II,* in which we will apply the model that has been developed here to present and analyze the strategies that we have found to the most effective and well-formed for achieving the outcomes for which they were created. In Volume II we will present the strategies that have been proven to be most efficient and elegant for achieving successful results in areas and disciplines ranging from learning physics, to playing chess, to making decisions, to learning to play a musical instrument, to creating entirely new models of the world for yourself. In the second volume we will also explore more specifically how to apply Neuro-Linguistic Programming to your work and everyday life.

If you are planning to have future contact with us, we look forward to meeting you. Until then, enjoy your explorations.

NOTA BENE

It is a common experience with many people, when they are introduced to Neurolinguistic Programming and first begin to learn the techniques, to be cautious and concerned with the possible uses and misuses of the technology. We fully recognize the great power of the information presented in this book and whole-heartedly recommend that you exercise caution as you learn and apply these techniques, of a practitioner of NLP, as a protection for you and those around you. It is for this reason that we also urge you to attend only those seminars, workshops and training programs that have been officially designed and certified by *THE SOCIETY OF NEURO-LINGUISTIC PROGRAMMING*. Any training programs that have been approved and endorsed by *THE SOCIETY OF NEURO-LINGUISTIC PROGRAMMING* will display on the cover of the brochure (or on the front page of the literature) a copy of the registered certification mark of *THE SOCIETY OF NEURO-LINGUISTIC PROGRAMMING* shown below:

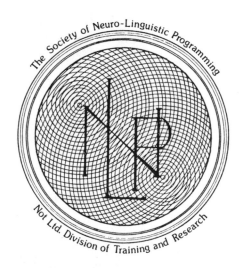

THE SOCIETY OF NEURO-LINGUISTIC PROGRAMMING is a partnership made up of Not Ltd., a corporation, and Unlimited Ltd., a corporation, set up for the purpose of exerting quality control over those training programs, services and materials claiming to represent the model of neurolinguistic programming. Not Ltd.'s Division of Training and Research is the international headquarters and coordinator for all approved training programs in neurolinguistic programming.

There are three levels of certification granted by *THE SOCIETY OF NEURO-LINGUISTIC PROGRAMMING*:*Practitioner, Master Practitioner* and *Trainer*. The certificates are granted with respect to the skill level of the trainee.–*Trainer* representing the highest level of ability.

If you are considering seeking the services of a person who is skilled in neurolinguistic programming we recommend that you find someone that has been appropriately certified. A directory of all certified individuals is maintained and distributed by Not Ltd. D.O.T.A.R.

If you would like further information on training programs, certification, research or publications on topics relating to neurolinguistic programming please feel free to contact:

Meta Publications
P.O. Box 565
Cupertino, CA. 95015

RECOMMENDED READINGS

Ashby, William Ross; *Design For A Brain: The Origin of Adaptive Behavior,* Science Paperbacks, 1965.

Ashby, William Ross; *Introduction to Cybernetics,* London University Paperbacks, 1964.

Bandler, R and Grinder, J.; *Frogs Into Princes,* Real People Press, 1979.

Bandler, R., and Grinder, J.; *The Structure of Magic I,* Palo Alto, Calif. Science and Behavior Books, 1975.

Bandler, R. and Grinder, J,; *Patterns of the Hypnotic Techniques of Milton H. Erickson, M.D.,* Cupertino, Calif,: Meta Publications, 1975.

Bateson, G.; *Steps to an Ecology of Mind,* Ballantine Books, 1972.

Bateson, G.; *Mind And Nature,* E. P. Dutton, 1979.

Dilts, R.; "Neuro-Linguistic Programming: A New Psychotherapy", unpublished manuscript, 1977.

Farrelly, F. and Brandsma, J.; *Provocative Therapy,* Meta Publications, 1975.

Goleman, D.; "People Who Read People", *Psychology Today* July, 1979.

Gordon, David; *Therapeutic Metaphors*, Meta Publications, 1978.

Grinder, J., and Bandler, R.; *The Structure of Magic II,* Palo Alto, Calif. Science and Behavior Books, 1976.

Grinder, J., and Bandler, R., and DeLozier, J.; *Patterns of the Hypnotic Techniques of Milton H. Erickson Vol. II,* Cupertino, Ca.: Meta Publications, 1977.

Grinder, J., Bandler, R., and Satir, V.; *Changing with Families,* Palo Alto, Calif., Science and Behavior Books, 1976.

Haley, J. (ed.); *Advanced Techniques of Hypnosis and Therapy: Selected Papers of Milton H. Erickson, M.D.,* New York, Grune and Stratton, 1967.

Haley, J.; *Uncommon Therapy: The Psychiatric Techniques of Milton H. Erickson, M.D.,* New York: W. W, Norton & Co., Inc., 1973.

Kuhn, T.S.; *The Structure of Scientific Revolutions,* University of Chicago Press, 1970.

Miller, G.; "The Magical Number Seven, Plus or Minus Two", *Psych. Review,* Volume 83, 1957.

Miller, Galanter and Pribram; *Plans And The Structure of Behavior,* Henry Holt & Co., Inc., 1960.

Pribram, K.; *The Language of the Brain,* Prentice-Hall, 1971.